Paddling Maryland and Washington, DC

Paddling Maryland and Washington, DC

A Guide to the Area's Greatest Paddling Adventures

Jeff Lowman

FALCONGUIDES

GUILFORD, CONNECTICUT
HELENA, MONTANA

FALCONGUIDES®

An imprint of Rowman & Littlefield.
Falcon, FalconGuides, and Outfit Your Mind are registered trademarks of Rowman & Littlefield.

Distributed by NATIONAL BOOK NETWORK

Photos by Jeff Lowman unless otherwise noted.
Maps by Melissa Baker © Rowman & Littlefield

British Library Cataloguing-in-Publication Information available
Library of Congress Cataloging-in-Publication Data

Lowman, Jeff, 1954-
 Paddling Maryland and Washington, DC : a guide to the area's greatest paddling adventures / Jeff Lowman.
– First Edition.
    pages cm
 "Distributed by NATIONAL BOOK NETWORK"–T.p. verso.
 ISBN 978-1-4930-0593-2 (paperback : alk. paper) – ISBN 978-1-4930-1492-7 (e-book) 1. Stand-up paddle surfing–Maryland–Guidebooks. 2.   Stand-up paddle surfing–Washington–District of Columbia–Guidebooks. 3. Sea kayaking–Maryland–Guidebooks. 4. Sea kayaking–Washington–District of Columbia–Guidebooks. I. Title.
 GV840.S68L68 2015
 797.122'409752–dc23
                                    2015020936

The author and Rowman & Littlefield assume no liability for accidents happening to, or injuries sustained by, readers who engage in the activities described in this book.

Contents

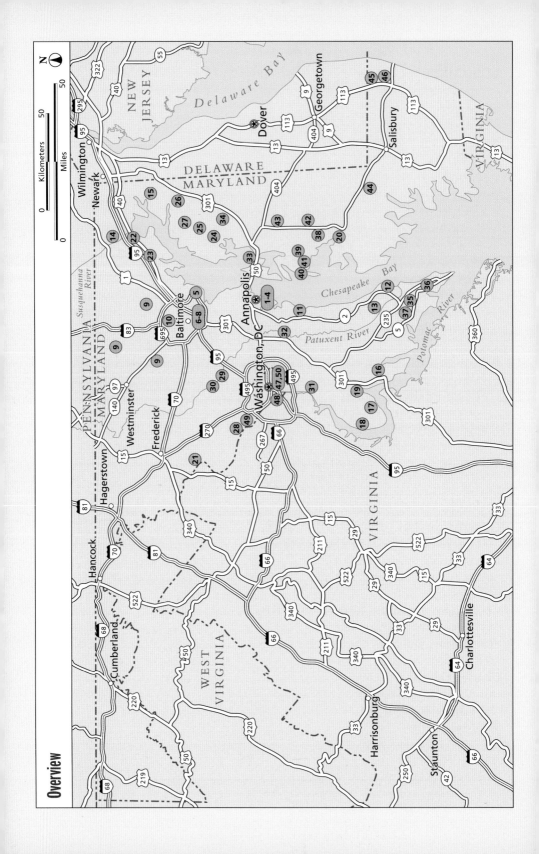

Overview

Introduction

Every adventure I have written about, I have double-checked the research by walking the walk or paddling the paddle. I've talked to park rangers, harbormasters, county, state and federal administrators, and folks from all walks of life on the water. The pictures are from my camera, so they aren't perfect, but they are real. Whether you are a slowpoke sun-worshiping paddler like my wife, a paddleboarder in search of a quiet cove, a canoeist looking for the perfect creek headwaters, or a sea kayaker able to cover a lot of miles in a single route, I've tried to cover you all in each adventure.

We have met several paddling clubs in our travels and found that these are folks you can truly call interesting companions. We heartily recommend saying hello. Paddling is always better and safer with friends and a partner. Maryland has a lot of shoreline and creeks. I'll take you to safe and different places—real adventures where you determine how long to paddle and where to jump in and pull out.

About Maryland

Maryland is sometimes called "Little America" due to the wide range of environmental differences from north to south and east to west; variety and choice are a way of life. Marylanders embrace their history and proudly show it off as part of their culture. It is one of the smallest states in the United States, but has an astoundingly long shoreline. Maryland is said to be the most affluent state in the nation due to the high income per capita. But those figures must be old—it does not feel like money; it feels like county and city mixed with crab and beer. We welcome you all to our world.

In 1607 and 1608 Captain John Smith traveled Virginia and Maryland, and his maps are recognized as one of the first detailed descriptions of Maryland's shores and Native American tribe locations. He traveled up the Potomac River to the Anacostia River and up and down the Chesapeake Bay exploring the eastern shore and up into the Susquehanna River.

The original Maryland colony was located on St. Clements Island, but the seat of the colonial government later moved to the location of St. Mary's City. In 1695 the capital was moved to Annapolis where it still resides. St Mary's is now a walking museum adjacent to St. Mary's College of Maryland.

Maryland was one of the nation's original thirteen colonies and was proud to be the seventh state to ratify the US Constitution. For a brief time Annapolis was the nation's capital city and the place where on December 23, 1783, George Washington set an important precedent by resigning as commander-in-chief to run for election as a civilian for the president of the United States.

In 1791 both Maryland and Virginia gave up territorial land to create a separate area for a national capital, the District of Columbia. Virginia's portion was returned to the state. Like siblings, the two states have been fighting ever since about anything

A Washington, DC weekend, paddling the Potomac (paddle 48)

that provokes a disagreement—politics, boundaries, fishing rights, and baseball teams. Though generally they do both support Washington, DC's NFL team.

In 1814 Francis Scott Key wrote the words to "The Star-Spangled Banner" during the British bombardment of Fort McHenry. The British invasion of Maryland is still the largest US invasion by a foreign country. The British officers were picked off by sniper shooters, and the whole army retreated to their ships and tried attacking New Orleans instead.

Maryland Today

The state of Maryland is divided into twenty-four sections: twenty-three counties and Baltimore city. Each county has its own local government and ideas on how to run its own shoreline. In the last few years we have seen counties cooperate with the Maryland Department of Natural Resources and the National Park Service to share costs and responsibilities for boating access.

The state can also be subdivided into geographical regions. The counties farthest to the west along the Mason-Dixon Line with Pennsylvania and Virginia compose our Northern region. The Central region includes the most populous counties. The final two are the Southern and Eastern Shore regions.

Some of the best Maryland kayaking is done in our major reservoirs. We have five that are noteworthy. We have tried to show off some of the well-known waterway sites but tried to concentrate on areas other adventure books have not covered. Our Chesapeake Bay has always been a magnet for writers but for weekend recreational boaters the open water is sometimes just a bit too rough. Due to the Chesapeake Bay and the many estuaries and rivers along our western and eastern shores, Maryland has one of the longest waterfronts of any state. The Bay, as an estuary, produces more seafood—oysters, crabs, clams, finfish—than any comparable body of water in the United States. In 2009 President Barack Obama signed the Chesapeake Bay Restoration and Protection Executive Order that called on the federal government "to restore and protect the nation's largest estuary and its watershed."

Leave No Trace

If floaters are careful, rivers can be floated again and again without showing signs of use. Your attentiveness to caring for the river could prevent the need for permit systems that limit use. Floaters on overnight trips should be especially mindful of their activities. Here are a few suggestions.

Plan Ahead and Prepare

- Know and respect the regulations for the river you plan to visit.
- Prepare for extreme weather conditions and emergencies.
- Float in small groups to reduce social conflicts and impacts.
- Plan river trips that are compatible with the skill level of everyone in the group.

Camp on Durable Surfaces

- Durable surfaces include designated campsites, rock, gravel, and dry grasses.
- Concentrate use on existing campsites; avoid places where impacts are just beginning.
- Water-saturated soil and wet vegetation are particularly vulnerable to impact from recreational users.

Dispose of Waste Properly

- Littering degrades Maryland's rivers. Police your campsite before leaving, and pack out all litter.
- Deposit solid human waste in a "cat hole" 6 to 8 inches deep at least 200 feet from water sources, campsites, and trails. Fill in and disguise the cat hole when finished.
- Strain and scatter dish washing and cooking water.

Leave What You Find

- Preserve the past: Examine but do not touch or remove archaeological, historical, or paleontological resources.
- Leave rocks and plants and other natural objects as you find them.
- Avoid introducing or transporting nonnative species.
- Do not build structures or furniture or dig trenches around campsites.

Minimize Campfire Impacts

- Campfires cause long-lasting impacts on our rivers. Consider using a portable stove for cooking and a lantern for light.
- If you must have a campfire, contain all fires in established rock fire rings, metal fire grates, or your own portable fire pan.
- Do not construct new rock fire rings—they blacken rocks, sterilize the soil, and leave lasting impacts.
- Collect only down and dead firewood that can be broken by hand, or pack in your own firewood.
- Keep fires small, and burn all wood down to white ash. Ensure that fires are completely extinguished before leaving.

Respect Wildlife

- Observe wildlife from a distance. Do not follow or intentionally approach them.
- Feeding wildlife is harmful to their health, alters natural behavior, and exposes them to predators and other dangers. It is also unsafe and unlawful.
- Protect wildlife and your food by securing rations and trash properly.
  For more information visit the Leave No Trace website at LNT.org.

What to Bring

Remember the key word is "adventure." I plan to take you where you haven't been before, so bear with me if this list sounds like it would fill two suitcases for an overnighter at a friend's house. And also, guys and girls have different ideas as to what is important to pack. After thirty years of marriage, you can call me on that; till then check with the lady in the group to see what you need to pack, if she is going. Women are usually right about these things. These are suggestions we use all the time:

- **Sunglasses:** The reflection off the water can make your eyes sting even on cloudy days.
- **Chapstick and sunscreen:** There's a lot of wind on the water, and your lips will get dry. All day on the boat, even with clouds, will burn your face, arms, legs, and feet. Please, "take care of you" as the Southern saying goes.
- **Hat or bandanna:** On cloudy or sunny days, the sun's rays can give you a headache. Sports caps are only second best, as a good gust of wind might make it fly. Your hat should have a chinstrap.
- **Whistle (or better yet, a *loud* child's bike horn):** In crowded harbors full of big-ego boy toys, kayaks are almost invisible. Play it safe by using a horn or whistle, plus folks will wave back at the bike horn and smile. Sound travels on open water, and in an emergency folks will help if you can get their attention.

A fall paddle on College Creek near the Annapolis capitol (paddle 3)

- **Sponge:** Even the best paddlers get a bit of water inside the boat now and again when the wind stirs and blows it off the paddle. Also, launching off muddy shorelines does not mean sitting in dirt the whole day.
- **Water shoes:** If you get out of the boat along an unknown shoreline, you might encounter mudflats, broken glass, prickly pine nuts, sea barnacles, slippery-slimy cement ramps, and other hazards. Need more reasons?
- **Rope:** A 6-foot pier tie-up and a 25-foot tug line with clamps (to pull you off boulders or mudflats) is recommended for some Eastern Shore adventures. When the tide starts running low, paddle faster and stay to the middle.
- **Cable and padlock:** When life is good, and the situation says let's walk around town, play it safe and *lock it up*. When life is an emergency, and you need the first restroom you can paddle to on the shoreline, *lock it up*.
- **Map:** Photocopy a page out of an ADC book, or blow up a folding map section in the area you are going. Have something written down and put it in a ziplock baggie. A GPS is a wonderful gadget, but it works off a battery and shuts itself down just when you need it.
- **Camera:** Take even a cheap one for the fun of it. Most of my adventures are *camera time*! It could be cute ducks or geese, monuments to brag about, that shot of a view that makes you smile forever, or just your friend that you made a little happier.

MARYLAND FISHING

The Maryland Department of Natural Resources (DNR) is justifiably proud of its website that's fully stocked with current, accurate, and instructive information.

The website includes information on fish found in Maryland waters, where they grow, what they eat, and what season you will be most likely to catch them!

Check out the Chesapeake and Coastal Bay Life interactive encyclopedia (www.dnr.mary land.gov/bay/cblife/) and the Maryland Department of Fisheries' Fish Facts interactive format (http://dnr2.maryland.gov/Fisheries/Pages/fishfacts-index.aspx), which presents a file for each fish image touched and reads like an uncle or old fishing pal, patiently explaining each fish as though it were a personal friend.

- **Waterproof bag:** They come in different sizes, but all fold over and snap shut. This is a highly recommended tool for clothes and valuables. It floats even if you do not. (For boaters not ready to buy an excellent waterproof bag, at least bring small and large food baggies that seal tight.)

- **Multiuse tool:** Bikers have one, anglers have one, the Swiss Army had one, so too should kayakers. I have a tool with pliers, a knife, a pick, and a mini saw. Never thought I'd ever use it—till a support rope on my kayak chair broke.

- **Spring float:** This ingenious swimming gadget has a spring coil inside that shoots out when unfolded into a blow-up that is a flat or sitting upright flotation device. The blow up is a skinny ring that supports a cool mesh. What makes this great for kayaking is in the summer when you'd like to take a dip but are unsure of the water's bottom and swimming is not planned, this device will allow you to float in water of only a few inches deep and cool your whole backside. Lots of models and shapes. Folds flat again for storage. (Holds fully grown men and women if you follow my drift.)

- **Rain poncho:** Buy a cheap full-length plastic poncho for late afternoon rain showers. In this area if the weatherman says cloudy with chance of rain—it might not actually rain till nightfall, or it might downpour for 10 to 15 minutes right after lunch and then the sun will come out. Weekends are precious—how much fun can you afford to lose?

- **Rubber boots and fleece socks:** In the summer you go barefooting; in the spring and fall you wear sandals that can get wet or boat shoes that can be dipped in the water to wash off the mud. But in the colder months, we suggest wearing heavy rubber boots while launching in freezing water, then removing the boots and putting on thick fleece socks once you're in the boat. Fleece will keep you warm the entire day and are water resistant, unlike wool or cotton.

- **Personal Flotation Device:** The Coast Guard does not just recommend it—they require one per person in all boats. The penalty may not just be a warning, but an expensive ticket. However, there are approved PFDs other than the bulky life jackets. Look at angler catalogs and see the skinny over the neck to the waist type, or get real lucky and find the belt type that uses a CO_2 cartridge that blows up with a tug of a tiny handle. These cost a bit more, but you will feel cool and forget it's there most of the time.

- **Napkins or toilet paper:** Most women are smarter than men in knowing not to drink coffee and tea (or especially beer) before getting into a tiny boat for the day. But just in case Mother Nature calls, having a baggie of dinner napkins or a handful of toilet paper is always a great idea. Port-a-potties are random and not always well serviced, but trees are everywhere.

- **Spare paddles and cords:** In the last couple of years, we have noticed more boaters carrying two sets of paddles. Sometimes the extra is strapped in the front or rear with bungee cords, or tucked away under the bow. The excuse is always the same—it's just a good precaution, especially if you go paddling alone. We bought a cord that Velcro's midway around the paddle handle and attaches to the inside of the boat. It drives you crazy the first day, and then you forget it. You will be glad it's there if you "almost" lose your paddle in the mud or it's being dropped in the water while fidgeting around.

- **Wind/rain jacket:** The day is sunny, there is a slight breeze, and the water is calm. By two to three o'clock in the afternoon, the wind picks up and the water becomes choppy. That cotton shirt you're wearing that says "Paddle faster I hear banjos" becomes a little thin. The afternoon breeze is always there year-round. Roll out the jacket and smile. A rain jacket is waterproof and is a better year-round piece of standard equipment.

- **Pants:** It's hard to imagine wearing anything but a swimsuit while paddling in the heat, especially if you are out for just a couple of hours. But long-distance boaters most likely will be paddling back home in the evening. When the sun sets, it can get cool. Convertible pants that zip at the knee are an excellent idea. In the cooler months try pant shells—waterproof or water-resistant pants that shed the drips of water from paddling. Look at rain gear pants or snow ski shells and order a size smaller.

- **Gloves:** In the cooler months, by the second hour of paddling your fingers might get a little blue. We found Fagan type gloves (cutting the top fingers off the gloves at the knuckles) will give you a much better grip while holding the paddle.

- **Towels:** My beautiful wife and kayak companion is only 5 feet tall. I tease her about needing to sit on phone books at the dinner table and receive well-earned shin kicks. But with sit-in kayaks, her height did cause a paddling problem—she didn't get good deep strokes and got wet with paddle drippings. So we bought beach towels that match her kayak to use as comfort cushions

Francis Scott Key Bridge over Baltimore's Patapsco River (paddle 6)

on the molded plastic chair. I liked them also for the comfort till I bought an upgraded fishing kayak with an overstuffed pullout chair. Towels don't work so well on these. We also recommend hand towels for sweat and wiping off suntan lotion from the hands, for a better paddle grip.

- **Baking Powder:** Most books advocate taking a first-aid kit. Got a broken nail or a popped blister? You know enough to bring a spare bandage. The first aid I want you to bring is a homemade remedy for summertime jellyfish stings. We call them sea nettles, and their long tentacles have chemicals that when brushed on skin leaves bright red welts and hurts like the dickens. Baking powder relieves the pain slowly but surely. The welts go away, but the lash marks on your pride last for a few hours. It's ok to scream and bite your tongue and kick something hard—the pain is more inside your head than your arm or leg. Yes, you can keep on paddling.

Food to Bring

- **Lunch:** Kayaking should be a fun and enjoyable experience. We have often brought sandwiches, fresh fruit, a thermos of hot soup, salads, applesauce, and what not, just to break up the day with a rest stop. A 15-minute break will give you mucho grande energy later on!
- **Water bottles:** During the winter months one bottle per person is just right, but during Maryland's warmer months and on longer paddles, we go through

The Tilghman Island country Store is called the "heartbeat" of Tilghman Island; visit (paddle 40) and you'll see why!

several bottles each. Plain water can get to be a bore after a while. If you pack ice cubes in smaller bags, the cool melted water tastes even better! Try the water flavoring that comes in small squirt bottles; they're usually sugar free and just a squirt is concentrated enough to do the trick. We highly recommend plastic cups instead of the bottle on the dashboard. Most recreational kayaks have molded plastic holes for drinks that are usually too large for bottles but just right for plastic coffee containers or foam rubber zipups.

- **Electrolytes:** Highly recommended. This natural energy-producing powder or candy chew is used by athletes worldwide and will give your muscles the energy you need for that last hour of paddling.

- **Munchies:** The days we actually get on the water, we throw our normal meal schedules out the window. On really disorganized days we grab whatever left-overs are easy to warm up and go to a fast-food stop for burgers or sandwiches to put in the lunch cooler for later. As a fully grown adult, my internal clock says that I am still hungry. Now is the time for trail mix or cut veggies/fruit for healthy pre-lunch snacking.

- **Tea time:** Late in the afternoon we love to see the sunset glow on the water. Whether on the water or after the boats are put away, hot tea and peanut butter or cheese crackers are mighty welcome. Atkins for diabetics makes low-sugar snack bars, and granola bars are always good pick-me-ups.

- **Frozen fruit baggies:** For long paddles in the warm summer months, pack mixed frozen fruit in baggies and use them for ice packs in the cooler. This is a wonderful healthy-ish hit of natural sugar that is a cool treat.
- **Duck food:** We began with old cereal, then added bread pieces—just scraps but what a lot of fun to throw handfuls of food onto the water where birds swim almost right up to the boats.

How to Customize Your Kayak

- **Pull-up straps:** Being a full-grown adult, I found getting up and down in my seat in the kayak not a graceful exercise. I found two 24-inch straps that were each glued in a circle and then I drilled two holes on both sides of my kayak dashboard area. I merely slid the strap through the hole and into itself on each side. I was able to pull myself up easily. When I did it at a beach full of folks, I felt like a commercial for EF Hutton. Everyone got real quiet, then they all gathered round and asked to try it out. Easy peasy.
- **Front pouch:** Now that the holes were drilled, I installed a front pouch for knickknack storage. The best pouch has been a cheap trash bag meant for cars. The straps can get tied in the back and the Velcro holds it firmly. The vinyl only lasts for a couple of years with heavy wear and tear, but for ten bucks it's a great idea.
- **Doormats:** In the summer one of the best feel-good things is bare feet against the dry plastic floor of a kayak cooled by creek water. But during the cooler months, a rubber doormat is more comfortable and gives good insulation. Doormats come in many sizes and I found a slightly larger size for my fishing kayak.
- **Old-fashioned GPS:** Photocopy part of a map and fold it into a square or rectangle. Find a clear, stiff plastic envelope to put the map in. At a hardware store I found a "tile pick-up tool," a $5 plastic suction cup device that is perfect for the next step. The handles move back and forth to create the suction. Unfortunately the suction does not work well on kayak plastic, but the handles can be held together with rubber bands, creating an upright stand to hold the map envelope. The whole contraption can be duct taped in front of you on the dashboard or forward area. This homemade gadget will allow you to paddle and read the map at the same time.
- **Back padding for kayak seats:** Most kayak seats are molded plastic with just a hint of foam rubber. Some seats have strings that push seats forward for better support, but sore butts and stiff backs are the norm for long-distance paddlers. The solution is to buy a Granny Back Supporter made for cars. These are usually black, about 24 inches high, with stiff metal supports and mesh inside. Then look for a simple inch-thick stadium foam rubber mat. Lastly look for a stadium foam cushion mat to sit on. The Granny mesh fits upside down with

The Hyatt Regency Hotel in Cambridge, Maryland, has a water view (paddle 20)

the new inch-thick form rubber mat inserted inside. I found a few 18-inch plastic tie-ups poked through holes made by a screwdriver could be matched up with the original molded plastic chair. Fasten the tie-ups tightly and balance the brace. You'll enjoy a firm comfort level that will give your back muscles surprising energy. You are welcome.

How to Use This Guide

Every paddling trip begins with a brief summary of the river, creek, or reservoir and its unique features. Basic information for each waterway can then be found in the at-a-glance section. The information includes these headings, as appropriate.

County
Suggested launch sites: including options
Suggested takeout sites: including options
Length and float time
Difficulty: The difficulty of the paddle from a beginner's point of view.
Current
Fishing
Season
Fees or permits
Nearest city/town
Boats used: suggested car-top boats
Organizations
Contacts
Rest areas
Restaurant pullouts

Remember, this guide contains only the minimum information needed for a safe trip. Rivers, creeks, and reservoirs are living, dynamic systems that change constantly. A channel free of barriers one year may contain a dangerous logjam the next, or there may be a diversion dam or a new barbed-wire fence. Thoroughly check out the stretch of waterway you plan to paddle before launching your craft.

Carefully check water conditions before starting any trip. US Geological Survey (USGS) offices are usually good sources of information. Sporting goods stores can often provide information as well.

While the river adventurer won't face the perils of Odysseus—Sirens, Cyclops, or giant whirlpools—floaters should be aware of the hazards that await them. These include diversion dams, fallen trees, and logs, weirs, and fast water studded with rocks. Know in advance how to deal with each hazard, and know what to do in the event of an upset. Consult a kayaking and canoeing manual for recommended rescue techniques, and practice them in a safe setting—perhaps a pool or pond where the water is warmer and slower than what you'll find on many streams.

About the Maps

The maps that accompany the text provide a general picture of the waterway, the location of access points, and points of interest along the way. I suggest you use them in combination with either electronic or paper maps to plan trips.

Legend

95	Interstate Highway	⏝	Bridge
50	US Highway	■	Building/Point of Interest
97	State Highway	▲	Campground
	Local Road	⊛	Capital
=======	Unpaved Road	—	Dam
⊢—⊢—⊢—⊢	Railroad	⑤	Kayak/Canoe Rental
------------	Paddle Route	⚲	Lighthouse
- - -- - -- ...	State Line	▬	Lodging
∼	Small River/Creek	①	Paddle
⬭	Body of Water	P	Parking
▭	National/State Forest/Park	🏠	Ranger Station/Headquarters
▭ ▲	State/County Park	🍴	Restaurant
▭	Miscellaneous Park	🚻	Restrooms
⌐ _ _ ¬	Miscellaneous Area	o	Town/City
⤤	Access	❓	Visitor/Information Center
⪢	Boat Ramp		

Annapolis

A T-shirt in a tourist novelty store on Main Street captured the true feeling that underlies the city of Annapolis for those who live in and near the Maryland state capital:

"Annapolis—a little drinking town that has a sailboat problem."

The nickname "Naptown" is still trying to find a permanent footing, but it does not always fit because Annapolis is not a sleepy little town and things are always in motion year-round. Besides the hustle and bustle of lively tourism shops and scores of first-class restaurants, there are year-round museums that show off the inside of colonial homes and walking tours that tell of our country's birth and how this city played more than its part. There are festivals on the downtown docks for art shows, the world-famous powerboat and sailboat shows, and lots of community events. The Maryland State Capital is downtown, and there are numerous taverns and bars with live entertainment year-round. Two colleges: St Johns and the US Naval Academy both have proud and extensive campuses downtown, and both have waterfront boating access for students. Apart from its colonial history and day-to-day politics of running the state, Annapolis is defined by its wholehearted embrace of pleasure boating of every type and boat size. Due to the constant breeze the Chesapeake Bay produces, sailboating seems to claim the main attention, with sailing schools for children of all ages as part of their educational curriculum. Annapolis also has four creeks where boats from all over the world come to dock and moor.

Annapolis is a kayak friendly town. Visitors are always welcome (paddle 1).

1 Spa Creek

For speed demons it is a 2-hour round-trip from Truxtun Heights Park to the harbor at the mouth of the creek. Instead, leisurely explore the coves and paddle the shoreline watching folks and waving, paddle up Ego Alley where the big-boy toys show off to tourists (a good place to have a whistle or a bike horn to help warn the yachts who are not looking down), and paddle the harbor.

County: Anne Arundel County
Suggested launch sites: Truxtun Heights Park
Suggested takeout sites: Prince George Street, and Ego Alley in Inner Harbor for visiting tie-ups
Length and float time: 2 miles round-trip; 2 hours (1 mile per hour slow paddle), or all day if you get out to visit
Difficulty: Easy
Current: Mild to none
Season: Year-round
Fishing: Spa Creek anglers might find bullhead, brown trout, brook trout, largemouth bass, bluegill, smallmouth bass

Fees or permits: Usually none; recent signs at Truxtun Park ramp ask for honor use fee for "all boats using ramp"; use Truxtun Park beach if the minor fee is a problem
Nearest city/town: Annapolis
Boats used: Recreational boats and paddleboards
Organizations: None
Contacts: Annapolis City Parks and Recreation—Annapolis Harbormaster
Rest areas: Multiple up and down the creek at low-floating piers.
Restaurant pullouts: Bring a wire and lock for harbor visiting

Put-In/Takeout Information

Truxtun Heights Public Ramp (Kayak Annapolis, at ramp, rents kayaks, canoes, paddleboards, and does tours), Primrose Road, Annapolis; (443) 949-0773 or (800) 979-3370; GPS N38 58.109' / W076 29.912'

Annapolis Canoe and Kayak (dinghy dock launch) rents and sells kayaks, canoes, and paddleboards and supplies, 311 Third St., Annapolis; (410) 263-2303

Amos Garrett Park, Amos Garrett Blvd. & Spa View Ave., Annapolis, MD; GPS N38 58.223' /W076 30.0580'

1st Street, Annapolis MD; GPS N38 58.503' / W076 28.8360'

3rd Street, 311 3rd Street, Annapolis MD; GPS N38 58.384' / W076 28.927'

5th Street, Annapolis MD; GPS N38 58.300' / W076 29.060'

Charles Street Park, Charles Street, Annapolis MD; GPS N38 58.511' / W076 29.612'

Lafayette Park, 199 Lafayette Ave., Annapolis MD; GPS N38 58.380' /W076 29.9790'

Prince George Street Park, Prince George Street, Annapolis MD; GPS N38 58.621' / W076 29.056'

Truxton Kayak Rentals is a fun place to start, bring your own or rent. Let the smiles begin!

Overview

Spa Creek is the largest and perhaps the most colorful of the local waterways, not just because of the variety of old and new homes, or the types of boats moored, or the band music from the Naval Academy stadium during football games, or the tourists waving from water taxis and touring boats, but because of the number of kayaks stored along the creek banks like multicolored fall leaves on display year-round. The city even has a colonial law that states that any public street ending at the waterfront must be accessible for public use. That translates into an awful lot of public bulkheads with ladders and more than enough public shoreline launch areas, as well as a couple of public parks with boat ramps. This is in addition to all the private clubs and marinas that service the yachting crowd. Little Zodiacs are the busiest boat tenders and tend to hog the best places to tie up while tourists are visiting, but that is part of waterway life too.

The Paddle

The Truxtun Heights Park at the head of the creek has multilane public cement boat ramps and a small beach to put-in and takeout car-top boats when the ramps are packed. A boat rental company that takes folks on tours up and down the creek recently put up a shack and now offers kayaks and paddleboards year-round in the ramp area. Sights to look for along the way:

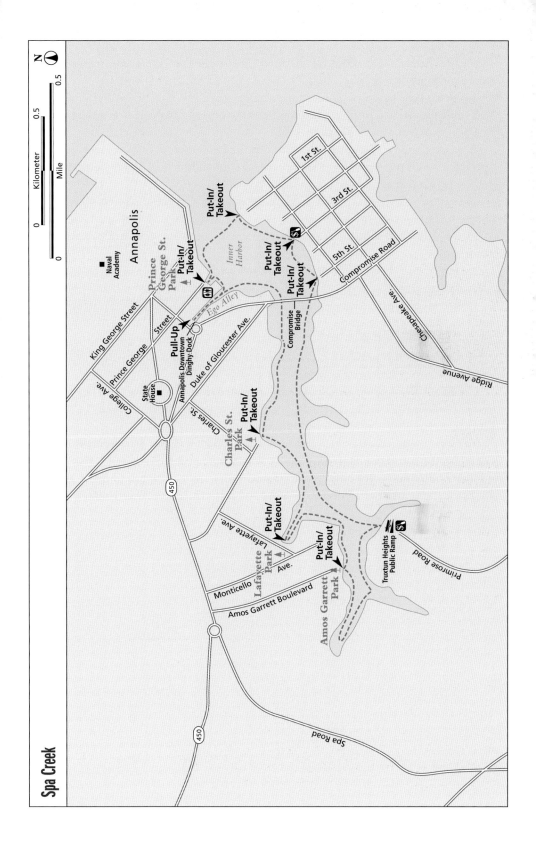

Spa Creek

N

Kilometer
0   0.5
Mile
0   0.5

Annapolis

Naval Academy ■

Prince George St. Park

Put-In/Takeout

King George Street

Prince George Street

College Ave.

State House ■

Charles St.

Pull-Up

Annapolis Downtown Dinghy Dock

Ego Alley

Inner Harbor

Duke of Gloucester Ave.

Put-In/Takeout

Charles St. Park

Put-In/Takeout

Put-In/Takeout

Compromise Bridge

Compromise Road

1st St.

3rd St.

5th St.

Chesapeake Ave.

Ridge Avenue

450

Lafayette Ave.

Put-In/Takeout

Lafayette Park

Monticello Ave.

Amos Garrett Boulevard

Put-In/Takeout

Amos Garrett Park

Truxtun Heights Public Ramp

Primrose Road

450

Spa Road

Charles Street Park—Pose for pictures with larger than life goose statues. This quiet residential area is close enough to walk to and from downtown.

Lafayette Park has steps to and from a grassy knoll and benches to the shoreline. The small pier is nice to hold onto for a rest. At times of high tide or flooding the little pier can disappear under the water!

5th Street ends at the waterfront with only inches between the pavement and the water. This is a great place for a temporary takeout and lockup while picnicking at the nearby elementary school playground.

3rd Street, where Annapolis Canoe and Kayak stores and launches its boats. The store is half a block up the street. Also look for the pirate ship docked here! Kids and adults can sail out for birthday tours of the creek complete with eye patches and pirate songs.

1st Street, directly across from the downtown harbor. A quiet shoreline pull-up for a rest and great vistas of the harbor and the Naval Academy.

Prince George Street Park—situated at the back door to the Naval Academy and within walking distance of the Harbor Masters office (with 24-hour year-round toilets) and downtown stores.

A dinghy dock is provided but Zodiacs are pushy. Recommend wire and a padlock for tie-up.

Annapolis Downtown Dinghy Dock—the head of Ego Alley can also be used to tie up. Look at Alex Haley Statue (a popular tourist attraction) and head to Storm Brothers for one-of-a-kind ice cream flavors.

In fact it might take the weekend recreational paddler almost four hours or more just to paddle and if you lock the boat up with a wire and padlock and take a shore stroll around town or stop for a picnic, it might turn into a delightful holiday. Watch the clock and remember to figure for wind and tide changes on your paddle back.

2 Back Creek

A quiet and short afternoon paddle that is colorful and safe for all types of car-top boating.

County: Anne Arundel County
Suggested launch site: Ellen O. Moyer Park
Suggested takeout site: Same
Length and float time: 2 miles (add 2 miles to complete loop to Annapolis Harbor); 2 hours (4 if you do the loop)
Difficulty: Easy
Current: Mild to none
Fishing: Anglers might find striped bass, white perch, black sea bass

Season: Year-round
Fees or permits: None
Nearest city/town: Annapolis-Eastport
Boats used: Recreational boats and paddleboards
Organizations: None
Contact: Annapolis City Parks and Recreation
Rest areas: Multiple
Restaurant pullouts: Multiple

Put-In/Takeout Information

Ellen O. Moyer Park, 7322 Edgewood Rd., Annapolis MD 21403; GPS N38 57.632' / W076 28.821'

Davis Park, 4th Street and 403 Chester Ave., Annapolis MD; GPS N38 58.137' / W076 28.795'

Annapolis Maritime Museum, 723 2nd Street, Annapolis MD; GPS N38 58.141' / W076 28.574'

Horn Point Dog/Kayak Park, 1 Chesapeake Landing, Annapolis MD; GPS N38 58.382' / W076 28.611'

Severn Ave., Annapolis MD; GPS N38 58.455' W076 28.689'

Overview

Back Creek is the second-largest creek, in Annapolis. With large marinas located cheek to jowl up and down the waterway. Here and there are private homes and condo buildings that have their own dockage. Some owners have as much money invested in their yachts as they do in their homesteads.

Ellen O. Moyer Park has a plastic public ramp for car-top boat launching. The park and pier are a favorite with the Zodiac crowd, as the local shopping center is only a 30-minute walk away. There are a handful of parking spaces, and boat portage is about 15 yards. Use a length of cord to assist with launching. The plastic ramp is slippery, and your boat will get away from you. The brainiest idea we heard recently was to rappel the ramp—don't tie the cord to the front of the boat but loop it around a pier piling and slowly let the cord out while sitting in the boat, letting the boat slide down in a coordinated manner. Sounds crazy on paper but wait till you find the

Parking at the Maritime Museum is tight, but paddling is great. Bring the camera!

loaded boat in the water waiting for you while you are still at the top. A slick plastic ramp—what a goof!

The Paddle

From top to bottom and back again, the slow paddle circumference of the creek takes about 2 hours.

The Mears Marina has a dinghy dock and an outside bar available during the summer season (open for nonmembers too). This marina caters to members like a fancy social country club, and their reputation is well deserved.

Davis Park is at 4th Street and offers benches, a small utility pier, and sometimes a little beach at low tide. Directly across from the park is a neighborhood bar and grill open year-round.

The Annapolis Maritime Museum is at the creek's mouth. This is a city park with a sandy shoreline launch area. It also has an interesting hands-on museum for kids and adults alike, with information about oysters. The building also rents out for catering events on a regular basis. Local boys like to crab from the docks but catching anything is a different story—so a bored girlfriend told us. It's a great place to have lunch, and public bathrooms are available. This is a put-in and takeout location.

Option

For speed demons wanting more paddling, we offer a ***caution*** that Chesapeake Bay open waters are rough and choppy during the prime summer season. Hug the

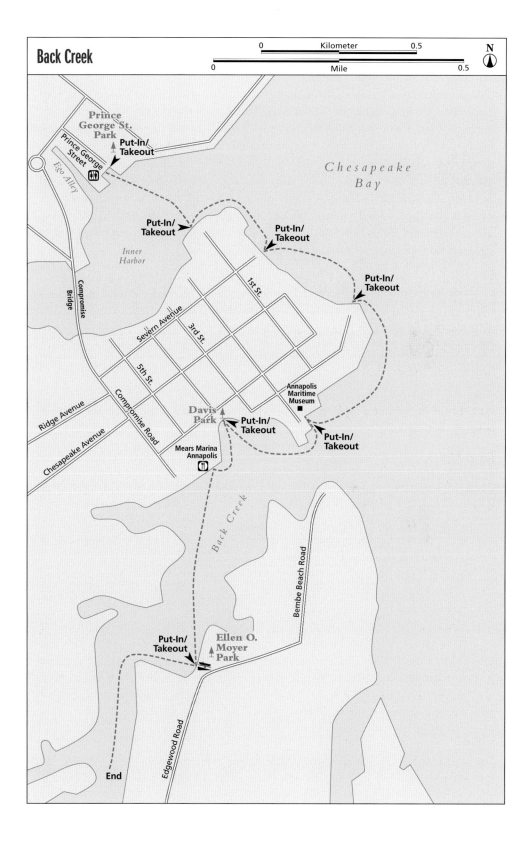

Back Creek

Kilometer
0   0.5

Mile
0   0.5

N

Prince George St. Park

Prince George Street

Ego Alley

Put-In/ Takeout

Chesapeake Bay

Put-In/ Takeout

Put-In/ Takeout

Put-In/ Takeout

Inner Harbor

Compromise Bridge

1st St.

Severn Avenue

3rd St.

5th St.

Ridge Avenue

Compromise Road

Chesapeake Avenue

Davis Park

Put-In/ Takeout

Mears Marina Annapolis

Annapolis Maritime Museum

Put-In/ Takeout

Back Creek

Bembe Beach Road

Put-In/ Takeout

Ellen O. Moyer Park

Edgewood Road

End

coastline and paddle north around the Eastport Peninsula, heading to the Annapolis Harbor. Look for the Severn Avenue end of the road access; the Severn Sailing Association marina has a long dinghy dock in the rear for non-sailboat folks. As you enter the harbor and Spa Creek, on the left is 1st Street, a good place to pull up and enjoy the harbor vistas without being in the main channel. Eastport is a fine place to walk around and to enjoy Annapolis. Lots of first-rate restaurants are only a few blocks away along Severn Avenue. Want to see the downtown? Paddle across Spa Creek and harbor (use a whistle or bike horn) and make for the back door area of the Naval Academy. There is a long and easy tie-up dinghy dock off Prince George Street if the Zodiacs don't hog it all. It's an easy walk to the harbormaster's office with public restrooms and to the stores along Main Street. Watch the clock and remember to figure for wind and tide changes on your paddle back.

3 College Creek

The mouth of the creek is at the confluence with the Severn River. Sometimes the river at this location is as calm and flat as a mirror, with only a minor ripple from a breeze. But those moments are rare. During prime-time use, motorboats and yachts churn up the water with wakes that range from a constant chop to 2-foot swells with little whitecaps when the big-boy toys go zooming by at full speed.

County: Anne Arundel County

Suggested launch sites:
Annapolis Harbor at Prince George Street
Jonas Green Park or Severn Inn (shoreline launches)
Weems Creek at Tucker Street launch
Naval Academy (with DOD car permit)
College Creek Park (with caution due to low tides)

Suggested takeout sites: Same

Length and float time:
Annapolis Harbor to College Creek mouth—20 to 30 minutes
Jonas Creek to College Creek mouth—20 to 30 minutes
Weems Creek to College Creek mouth—45 minutes

Naval Academy car-top boat beach along cement banks—10 minutes
College Creek mouth to College Creek Park—60 minutes one-way

Difficulty: Easy, as creek is protected, but the river can be choppy with traffic swells.

Current: Mild to none in the creek

Season: Spring flooding is best, but year-round is fine

Fees or permits: None

Nearest city/town: Annapolis

Boats used: Recreational boats and paddleboards

Organizations: None

Contact: Annapolis City Parks and Recreation

Rest areas: Multiple, with pier and ramp at St. Johns College as prime

Restaurant pullouts: Severn River Inn

Put-In/Takeout Information

College Creek Park, 2 Rideout St., Annapolis MD; GPS N38 58.815' / W076 30.092'

Jonas Green Park, 1990 Governor Ritchie Highway, Annapolis MD; GPS N38 59.718' / W076 29.103' (Paddle or Peddle rents kayaks, canoes, and paddleboards, 410-222-6141.)

Severn River Inn, 1993 Baltimore Annapolis Blvd., Annapolis MD; (410) 349-4000; GPS N38 59.678' / W076 28.922'

Tucker Street Public Ramp, 498 Tucker St., Annapolis MD; GPS N38 59.572' / W076 30.294'

US Naval Academy (shoreline launch with DOD car permit), Ramsey Road, Annapolis MD; GPS N38 59.460' / W076 29.436'

St. Johns College's visitor access from College Creek

Overview

The creek can be accessed with a 20- to 30- minute paddle from the Annapolis Harbor, around the Naval Academy campus's waterfront banks and toward the south. The creek entrance goes through the Academy grounds for a bit. ***Caution:*** The cement banks along the shoreline of the Naval Academy act as a backwash and throw the waves and wakes back at boats traveling its length. On the bright side, the creek waterway is always protected inside and well worth the time and effort to travel across the Severn River—just do it with care.

The creek's mouth is also a 20- to 30-minute paddle across the river from Jonas Green Park. A bit longer and more exposed is the 45-minute paddle from Weems Creek and the Tucker Street public launch ramp.

The easiest access to the creek's mouth is if you have a military Department of Defense (DOD) sticker on your car, then you can drive onto the campus through the south gate, unload at a small area on the creek at the edge of the soccer field, and park nearby; or drive near the satellite dish on the shoreline area, unload directly onto the sandy beach, and paddle for 10 minutes along the cement banks.

There is public access to the creek without all the work of paddling the Severn River, at the headwaters, but here is the biggest caution: The regular tidal waters leave the College Creek Park launch in mudflats during low tide. Much of the creek has a white sandy bottom with clear water viewing to about 2 feet deep. The mud at the

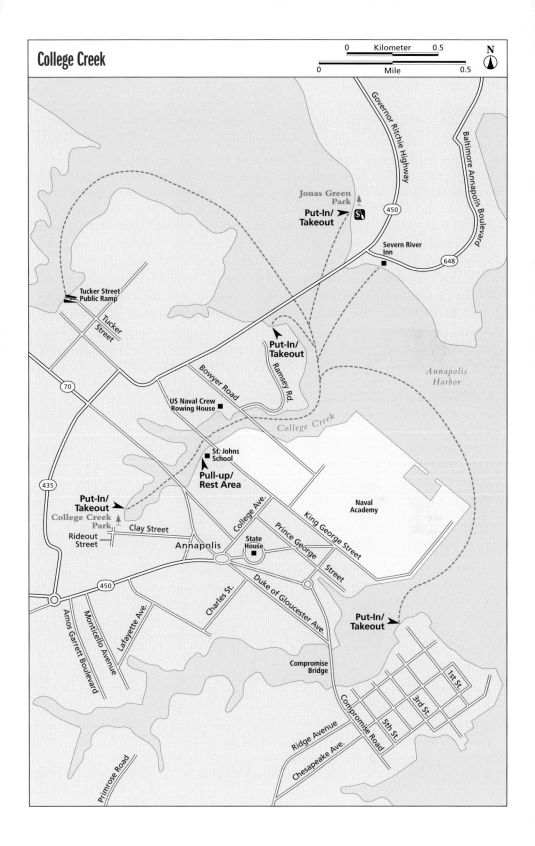

College Creek

0 Kilometer 0.5
0 Mile 0.5

N

Governor Ritchie Highway

Baltimore Annapolis Boulevard

Jonas Green Park
Put-In/Takeout
450

Severn River Inn
648

Tucker Street Public Ramp

Tucker Street

Put-In/Takeout

70

Bowyer Road

Ramsey Rd.

Annapolis Harbor

US Naval Crew Rowing House

College Creek

St. Johns School

Pull-up/Rest Area

435

Put-In/Takeout

College Creek Park

Clay Street

Rideout Street

Annapolis

College Ave.

State House

Prince George Street

King George Street

Naval Academy

450

Amos Garrett Boulevard

Monticello Avenue

Lafayette Ave.

Charles St.

Duke of Gloucester Ave.

Put-In/Takeout

Compromise Bridge

Compromise Road

1st St.

3rd St.

5th St.

Ridge Avenue

Chesapeake Ave.

Primrose Road

public launch is black (your foot will sink a foot or two when stepping into it). What is needed is a 20-foot-long pier extension over the mudflats to the deeper waterway.

The Paddle

The creek is aptly named since it passes by two famous colleges in Annapolis—the US Naval Academy and St. Johns College. Both have rowing teams with boat shells stored in their own private campus boathouse areas. Although from top to bottom and back again, the paddle is only 2 hours long, the scenic vistas, especially in the fall, can be breathtaking. When we paddled this, we heard a Navy football game being cheered with a band playing in a nearby stadium, and beautiful bells chiming from a waterfront church on the creek. If you are lucky, you can catch the rowing teams practicing up and down the creek and into calmer Severn River waters.

St. Johns College has a small boat ramp next to a utility pier and a few park benches to eat lunch on. Secure your boat, then explore the immaculate grassy campus and view the few historical monuments as a pleasant diversion. The waterfront Severn River Inn restaurant adjacent to Jonas Green Park is good for an upscale lunch, dinner, or evening glass of wine. The restaurant's view of the Naval Academy, the water traffic, and the fact they have their own sandy shoreline make this a great rest stop. The creek itself as a paddling adventure may not be long enough for a full day, but it would be a great part of any paddling loop of the area. Watch the clock and remember to figure for wind and tide changes on your paddle back.

4 Weems Creek–Severn River

This adventure takes boaters from a small Annapolis creek to the Severn River. A kayak-friendly marina is the turnaround waypoint, and a longer one-way adventure to the end of the river is offered.

County: Anne Arundel County
Suggested launch sites:
    Tucker Street Public Ramp
    Smith's Marina
    Severna Park Yacht Basin
    Indian Landing Marina
Suggested takeout sites: Same
Length and float time: 1.5 miles per hour (medium paddle)
    Weems Creek—2.5-mile loop
    Weems Creek to Smith's Marina—5 miles
    Smith's Marina to Severna Park Yacht Basin—3 miles
    Severna Park Yacht Basin to Sandy Island—1.5 miles
    Sandy Island to Indian Landing Marina—0.5 mile

Difficulty: Creek is protected; Severn River can be calm to rough and choppy
Current: Mild to medium pull in the river
Fishing: Anglers might find spot and white perch
Season: Accessible year-round; off-season water can be calmer
Fees or permits: Smith's Marina charges a fee for ramp use as put-in or takeout
Nearest city/town: Annapolis
Boats used: Sea kayaks and recreational boats; paddleboards not recommended
Organizations: None
Contact: Annapolis City Parks and Recreation
Rest areas: Multiple beach areas throughout loop
Restaurant pullouts: None

Put-In/Takeout Information

Tucker Street Public Ramp, Weems Creek, 498 Tucker St., Annapolis, MD; GPS: N38 59.572' / W076 30.294'

Smith's Marina (Severn River/Round Bay), 529 Ridgely Rd., Crownsville, MD; (410) 923-3444; GPS: N39 02.565' / W076 34.539'

Severna Park Yacht Basin (Severn River/The Narrows), Absolute Marine Services, 454 Severn Rd., Severna Park MD; (410) 647-4450; GPS N39 04.450' / W076 34.567'

Indian Landing Marina (Severn River/headwaters), 942 Indian Landing Rd., Millersville MD; (410) 923-6565; GPS: N39 04.629' / W076 36.764'

Overview

Weems Creek is a nice little protected creek that harbors lots of anchored sailboats on the outskirts of Annapolis City. The ramp off Tucker Street is made of rubber mat with holes into which gravel has been poured. This is just fine for small boats on small trailers, but there are always motorboat fans that push the capacity and end

Scenic view of Severn River Bridge

up tearing and scraping the ramp as their trucks try to find footing and leverage to pull the heavy boats out. (A few contrite faces, but not enough for them to not try it again another day.) The city tries to soothe the few homeowners who live on the tiny cul-de-sac by saying the ramp can only be used by "Annapolis city residents" and fines are issued for boat trailers parked on any residential road without proper parking stickers. The majority of consistent ramp users are visitors who park their Zodiacs from their anchored sailboats on the beach during their stay. Lots of kayakers find the launch site, and there are always fishing boats that can't imagine why anyone would think the ramp wasn't built for them. This is a drop and launch location. Parking is found at the top of the hill next to a public school. This is a safe and secure location, but the neighbors are sometimes cranky due to the overwhelming use by boaters who are not polite and observant of their needs. Smith's Marina has a professional dock and cement ramp. They are firm about collecting the per-boat fee. This marina is kayak-friendly.

The Paddle

It takes about 90 minutes to slow paddle the circumference of Weems Creek. The headwater takes boats a breath away from Route 50 just before it crosses the Severn River Bridge. The creek is pleasant year-round, and during low tide the paddle is still doable; the mud banks just make the circumference a bit shorter. The mouth of the creek comes out to the Severn River and the bridge looming over the waterway.

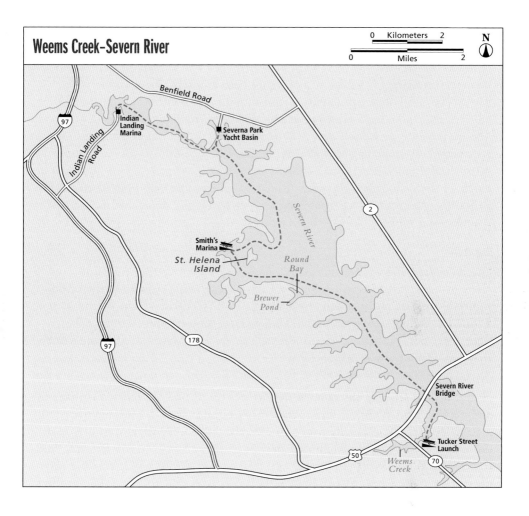

Indian Landing Marina
Severna Park Yacht Basin
Smith's Marina
St. Helena Island
Round Bay
Brewer Pond
Severn River
Severn River Bridge
Tucker Street Launch
Weems Creek
Benfield Road
Indian Landing Road

Caution: During the prime season the water is heavily traveled and wakes pose a problem, as do the afternoon breezes that turn the waterway into a wind tunnel. But on calm days this is a great place to be! Paddle north and keep to the left shore. You can explore several protected coves or make great time going the length.

There are four islands on the river. The largest and most predominant, St. Helena Island, is found in Round Bay. This private island, with multiple homes built on it, has its own marina on the shore next to Smith's Marina, which has a well-kept boatyard and a fee for boat ramp use. During the summer motorboats and water skiers own the waterway, and everyone else gets a good splash of water either from the skiers' fancy spray or the churn of the boat wakes. All good fun—unless your boat is only 12 inches above the water.

The return should only be a minor challenge, with possible afternoon wind in the off-peak seasons. Going back, hug the right side of the river, as most motorboats go straight and on the left side. Notice the high cliffs and soil erosion. That area is a federally designated nature preserve called Brewer Pond. About halfway to the bridge, you will see a long line of riprap a few feet from the shoreline that also has erosion problems. We are told that 50 yards of protective rock cost $3 million and was funded by the Severn River Association, a powerful citizens group that is a river watchdog. The Sherwood Forest community is also proud of its contribution of land to the preserve and winning federal protection for the surrounding cliffs and waterway. The cozy nature preserve is only a 20-minute slow paddle round-trip; at its mouth is a community launching area with about thirty-plus colorful kayaks and canoes on storage racks, a nice bench, and a small cement ramp—just perfect for a quick rest or lunch for the polite guest. It is an estimated 10-mile paddle loop from Weems Creek to Smith's Marina and back again. Check your watch and remember the afternoon wind kicks in strongly on wide-open water.

Option

Speed demons who want more river to paddle will want to keep going north, but we recommend this as a one-way paddle with a two-car system if possible. Another 2 hours or so will take you midriver and to the Severna Park Yacht Basin. There is a small beach to pull out on, but no restrooms. The shallow boat ramp is gone, filled in, and reconfigured for more pier space. The management at Absolute Marine Services are friendly folks who remind you of a bachelor who can't seem to keep his apartment picked up. Access to the beach always seems to be a second thought, and dodging wooden poles and trucks parked haphazardly is the norm. They are genuinely surprised at kayakers wanting to launch from their marina and are not set up to accommodate car-top guests, but if you smile a lot and shake a hand or two they usually say yes.

The river gets skinny here and is known as the "Narrows." Another half hour north takes you to Sandy Island. Back in the day, this was a social place for teenagers and water-ski bums. Kids would dig deep to pay for boat gas and everyone hung out. Today the beach is a shadow of its former self, with most of the foundation sand washed away; instead of being a picnic spot, it is now more of a dog park for motorboaters with more dogs than children, but still a good resting stop for paddleboarders. Farther north the river becomes a nature preserve area and shrinks to become Severn Creek. One last boatyard is down at the river's head—Indian Landing Marina, a medium-size facility with no boat ramp. We found a beach area behind a long, low dock and a wide, wooden staircase that could be used to service car-top boats. We spoke to a family member who shrugged her shoulders. The marina is also not accustomed to small boaters and not set up to accommodate them. The parking lot has a steep incline, so if you get permission to launch, try going to the "steps area." (Squeeze between the office and soda machine for a short portage from a temp parking spot for dropping boats only.) At low tide the nature preserve becomes nothing but mudflats as far as the eye can see. Watch the clock and remember to figure for wind and tide changes on your paddle back if you are not pulling out at Indian Landing Marina. The entire paddle from Tucker Street is about 10 miles one-way.

Baltimore

The signature road sign coming into Baltimore from Washington, DC, on a major highway reads, "Welcome to Baltimore . . . Hon." Embarrassed officials have tried to cover up the graffiti for years, but the bright white lettering keeps coming back. The "Hon" is a Baltimore expression of self-appreciation in a friendly land of beer and crabs. Here, the colors to wear in fall are a mix of purple and black, the colors of the Ravens football team, and in the summer orange and black, the colors of the Orioles baseball team. Old Bay seasoning is the spice needed for eating any and all seafood, and the bright yellow can is usually found on tabletops in the condiment tray along with the ketchup, salt, and pepper.

These are folks who will automatically return your smile and wave. In the city they sit on their front steps; in the surrounding county they play baseball or fish in waterfront parks. A small boy with a rod and a fishing tackle box in his school backpack knew more about the fish in "his" creek than the brochure I found from the Maryland Department of Natural Resources.

Baltimore County uses the "anchor" symbol on road signs to designate the location of private marinas with and without boat ramps as well as the location of county public boat ramps.

Baltimore's welcoming blue crab statue (paddle 6)

5 Bear Creek

This quiet paddle takes you through quiet neighborhoods with small scenic surprises at every turn.

County: Baltimore City and County

Suggested launch sites:
  Fort Armistead
  Turner Station
  Inverness Park or Anchor Bay East Marina

Suggested takeout sites: Same

Length and float time: 1 mile per hour (4 hours extending to 8 for long paddle)
  Fort Armistead—8 miles one-way
  Turner Station—6-mile loop
  Inverness Park or Anchor Bay East Marina—4-mile loop

Difficulty: Smooth to choppy on Patapsco River

Current: Strong in the Patapsco River; mild in Bear Creek

Fishing: Anglers might find in Patapsco River largemouth bass, striped bass, pickerel, crappie, catfish, yellow perch, white perch, bluegill, carp

Season: Best in off-season when not competing with fishing and motorboats

Fees or permits: None

Nearest city/town: Baltimore area—Dundalk City

Boats used: Sea kayaks and recreational boats; paddleboards ok in upper Bear Creek

Organization: Canton's Kayak Club

Contacts: None

Rest areas: Multiple throughout loop

Restaurant pullouts: Yes

Put-In/Takeout Information

Anchor Bay East Marina and Hard Yacht Café, 8500 Cove Rd., Dundalk, MD; GPS N39 15.035' / W076 29.372'; Anchor Bay East Marina, (410) 284-1044; Hard Yacht Cafe, (443) 407-0038

Charlesmont Park, 7801 Charlesmont Rd., Dundalk, MD; GPS N39 16.356' / W076 28.915'

Fort Armistead Park, Fort Armistead Road, Baltimore, MD; GPS N39 12.528' / W076 31.964'

Inverness Park, 2025 Inverness Rd., Dundalk, MD; GPS N39 15.410' / W076 29.538'

Turner Station, 23 Rayme Rd., Baltimore, MD; GPS N39 14.644' / W076 29.737'

Long Paddle Put-In: A good place to begin getting a feel for Baltimore County is to take the Route 695 Beltway northeast. Just before you cross the Francis Scott Key Memorial Bridge is a public park with a boat ramp launch site. Fort Armistead Park is named after the colonel who was in charge of Fort McHenry while the British shot their cannons at the extra-large flag Betsy Ross sewed at Armistead's request. Francis Scott Key, of course, wrote our national anthem during this 1812 engagement while "confined" on a British frigate in the harbor. The park is at the confluence where Bear

Bear Creek white swans in flight

Creek meets the Patapsco River. This is wide, deep water, but on a good day without strong winds and big ship wakes, the water would be a good river paddle, even for weekend recreational paddlers, to cross to the other shoreline. The bridge is approximately 1.5 miles long. Crossing the bridge, the territory becomes Dundalk, home of the once world-famous Bethlehem Steel foundry at Sparrows Point. Though a shadow of its former self, this factory shaped the residential areas and the local waterways for decades. It resides on the east side of Bear Creek for half its length. Thousands of people worked here, and inexpensive homes were built to accommodate the workforce.

On the southwest side of Bear Creek starting at its mouth are Clement Cove with Fleming Park and its shoreline launch area, Peach Orchard Creek with the Turner Station boat ramps, Bullneck Creek with Chesterwood Park and shoreline launch, Concrete Homes Park and shoreline launch, Starr Marina with boat ramp, Merritt Point Park with boat ramps, and Watersedge Park with shoreline launch. The Middle of Bear Creek is defined by the Peninsula Expressway Bridge, which also defines the end of Bethlehem Steel's property and starts the adjoining Sparrows Point County Club on the eastern shoreline.

Marina/Restaurant Put-In/Takeout
On the west shore above the bridge is the Anchor Bay East Marina, protected from motorboat wakes by its long jetty piers, with a gas dock and a standout bar and grill called the Hard Yacht Café. This is a sports bar/Ravens Roost hangout with seven

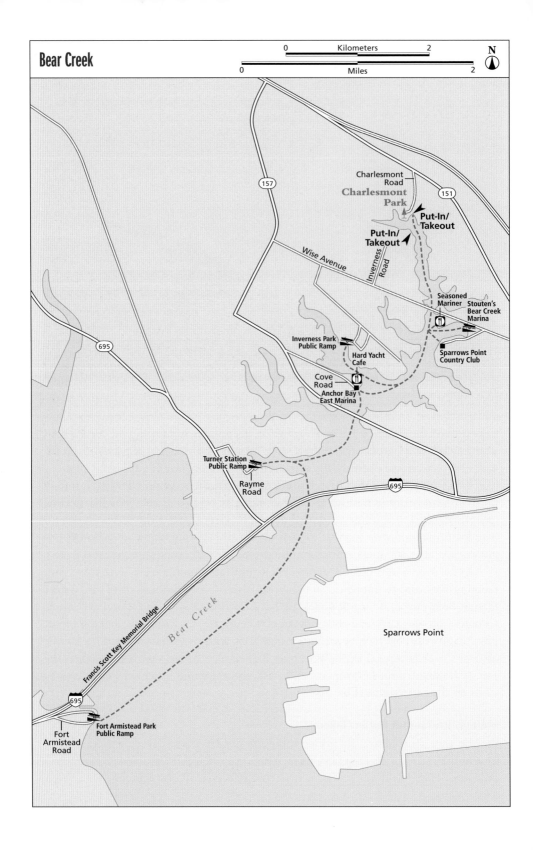

Bear Creek

0 Kilometers 2
0 Miles 2

N

157
151

Charlesmont Road
Charlesmont Park

Put-In/Takeout

Put-In/Takeout

Wise Avenue

Inverness Road

Seasoned Mariner
Stouten's Bear Creek Marina

Inverness Park Public Ramp

Hard Yacht Cafe

Sparrows Point Country Club

Cove Road

Anchor Bay East Marina

695

Turner Station Public Ramp

Rayme Road

695

Francis Scott Key Memorial Bridge

Bear Creek

Sparrows Point

695

Fort Armistead Road

Fort Armistead Park Public Ramp

massive TV screens and warm colorful decorations, large portions of well-cooked food, and live entertainment in the summer (not a family restaurant). Kayaks can pull up on a sandbar and crawl up a cement bulkhead wall or paddle over to a low-floating pier and walkway. Canton's Kayak Club stores kayaks there for members to use. The marina has several kayak-style floating launch ramps.

Public Put-In/Takeout

Lynch Cove is a comfortable sheltered area; Inverness Park has cement boat ramps and a shoreline boat launch area, and a beach where kids swim in the summertime.

Overview

Baltimore County folks are more into aluminum skiffs with small motors and fishing rods than kayak paddling. In Baltimore, access to the water is everywhere and fairly redundant, with parks and launch sites in most neighborhoods. We saw a kayak strapped onto a plumber's truck and a kayak on the side of one yacht, but none on the hundreds of waterfront yards we passed. We saw one rusty canoe but no paddleboards.

The waterways are shoulder-to-shoulder with houses except where there are schools or large and small parklands. Every townhouse neighborhood has a strip of parkland. Waterfront land is valuable and always desirable, but if your whole world is filled with endless possibilities of enjoying the water, then the need to live "on" the water is less of a priority. Bear Creek and its finger coves in Dundalk are excellent examples of local Baltimore waterways. Having a good map showing the local neighborhood roadways is essential, as the launch sites are always found off itty-bitty streets with lots of twists and turns. Even my poor GPS unit got confused.

The parking lots at major launch sites have room for cars with or without boat trailers. In the city/county, port-a-potties are available year-round. Summer weekends find the sites jammed with motorboats and folks always in a hurry to get out and on their way to the larger rivers where the big fish live. It's nice to know that most launch sites also have beaches for slower car-top boating people who don't need to use the ramp.

Baltimore waterways have barnacles, which make for some sharp pilings and protruding riprap rocks. When we paddled here, the water was crystal clear for about 2 feet down with sandy bottoms, and no sea grass was seen on any shoreline. In the summer we saw kids swimming off the shallow water banks at the parks, and most private docks had ladders; even a few waterslides dotted the waterways. Our favorite discovery were the statues of a little boy and girl sitting on the bulkheads of private home shorelines. Weather worn, they exuded a quiet charm of Tom Sawyer and a girlfriend. We saw maybe twenty or so similar statues up and down Bear Creek.

The Paddle

Chink Creek is a small diversion, but does a have a small private neighborhood park with ramp. Ask nicely and you can take a seat at a bench or picnic table. There are

SPARROWS POINT—A BALTIMORE ICON

On Bear Creek, in the conveyance of the Patapsco River, lies 4 miles of a Baltimore icon. Cecillius Calvert (the second baron of Baltimore) granted the land to Thomas Sparrows in 1652. He and his son called it the Sparrows Nest. Originally Native American land, the marshy lands were developed for farming.

STEEL

In 1889 the area was developed into a steel-producing plant due to its deep waters for ship docking. It has been estimated that by the mid-twentieth century the steel plant was the world's largest steel mill, employing 10,000 workers. In 1916 the facility was purchased by Bethlehem Steel of Pennsylvania. Baltimore steel production played a vital part during World Wars I and II.

SHIPBUILDING

Long known for its shipbuilding and ship repair facilities, marine production has always been the community's long-term saving grace. Maryland Steel Company established a shipyard in 1889, and the Bethlehem Steel Shipbuilding division (BethShip) turned out 116 ships between 1939 and 1946. Bethlehem Steel Corporation has been recorded as America's second-largest steel manufacturer, and was at one time the largest shipbuilder.

As part of the BethShip corporation, Sparrows Point was the only remaining location out of seventeen shipyards in the United States by 1990. In 2004 Barletta Industries purchased the site as a business and technology park with an emphasis on reestablishing shipbuilding on part of the site. The new name is Sparrows Point Shipyard and Industrial Complex.

lots of white swans in this area, and we found two that loved human companionship. Just before the drawbridge on the east side following the coastline is Sparrows Point Country Club's private marina with boat ramp and Stouten's Marina with boat ramp, which proclaims to have the "Finest Snowballs in Baltimore." (Snowballs—finely shaved ice in a paper funnel with flavored syrups—are strictly a regional summer delight, but this is a fisherman's community after all!) At the drawbridge at Wise Avenue is the Seasoned Mariner, a seafood establishment for families. It has a long floating pier with one side dipped down for taking out low-riding boats such as kayaks and storing them while eating. The northern side of the drawbridge has homes considerably larger than the one- and two-level homes built in the 1950s during Bethlehem Steel's heyday.

Bear Creek Elementary School runs parallel with Bear Creek Park and together offer four or five good established shoreline launch areas off steep banks with wooden steps and gaps in the riprap rock coastline. At the head of the creek is the Charlesmont Townhouse community. Charlesmont Park is just a small, grassy waterfront patch with parking mixed in with a narrow residential back lane, but there are kayakers who live here. Folks saw us taking pictures of the coastline and pointed to a cleared area where their neighbors wheel their kayaks. Sure enough, a small beach area with a few ducks and swans feeding on the water grass provided the perfect place for launching a kayak. (This is not on the maps or on the Baltimore County Park and Recreation list.)

6 Baltimore Inner Harbor

Baltimore has a first-rate cement public launch ramp at Canton Waterfront Park. The paddle adventure, as a round-trip to the downtown and back, is a long day and well worth the effort. But to paddle your kayak downtown, pull it out on a dock, walk around and buy lunch—is just not going to happen. According to the harbormaster, they are just not set up to accommodate car-top pullouts, and they do not have any future plans to do so. They will ticket and take it.

County: Baltimore City
Suggested launch sites: Canton Waterfront Park (public ramp)
Suggested takeout site: Same
Length and float time: 4-mile loop; 1 mile per hour (slow paddle)
Difficulty: Smooth to choppy with wind
Current: Mild
Fishing: Anglers might find in Patapsco River largemouth bass, striped bass, pickerel, crappie, catfish, yellow perch, white perch, bluegill, carp

Season: Year-round (ice in harbor during winter)
Fees or permits: None
Nearest city/town: Baltimore City
Boats used: Sea kayaks and recreational boats; paddleboards not recommended
Organization: Canton Kayak Club
Contact: Baltimore City Dockmaster's Office, (410) 396-3174
Rest areas: Multiple throughout loop
Restaurant pullouts: Yes

Put-In/Takeout Information

Canton Waterfront Park, 3001 Boston St., Baltimore, MD; GPS N39 16.612' / W076 34.358'

Overview

Baltimore City is lucky enough to have a first-rate boating club—the Canton Kayak Club, which keeps stored kayaks in two "private" waterfront harbor areas: Bond Street Wharf and Inner Harbor East Marina. At the harbormaster's office I was given a map showing where yachts and big motorboats could legally tie up for specific dockage for day and night yacht mooring. The city had planned to have a floating dinghy dock area for local residents to leave their licensed small craft for the season, but the harbormaster patrol told me they no longer put the floating pier out. I saw a floating restaurant in that spot now. It is important to know and understand that the entire riparian right-of-way belongs to the city, which has built a 12-foot-wide boardwalk that surrounds the Baltimore Inner Harbor where folks jog and walk around the residential and commercial areas, from Canton Park to Rash Field where the harbormaster keeps his office in the Rusty Scupper Restaurant building. Baltimore wants you to walk, not paddle. If your goal is to get as close to the tourist area before finding

The "locals" check out the tourists on a Baltimore walkway.

a secure place to pull out your boat for a few hours without getting a ticket or losing your boat to the patrolling harbor police, then good luck. I have not yet found a book or a veteran paddler with that secret. So we highly recommend getting in a good paddle, taking pictures of the museum ships and getting the flavor of the harbor, and then paddling back to your original launch site.

Baltimore is home of the big-boy yachts. We stopped in the West Marine boat store a few blocks from the city public ramp and met the owner. Almost all of his employees live on local yachts and know how to talk and sell parts. The store manager is a kayaker himself, and we swapped some stories and favorite launch sites, but he shook his head about kayaking in Baltimore City. The store has a few general items of interest, but even this downtown store near the boat ramp does not sell kayaks—he takes care of yachts for his bread and butter.

The Paddle

The first place to visit is Bo Brooks Restaurant, 1 block down from Canton Waterfront Park, an upscale restaurant with a low-floating dock and walk-up pier to the parking lot. It's always handy to know a good outside bar and seasonal outdoor crab house! Picnic at the top of the ramp or sit on the rocks. The next site is the Boston Street Pier Park about 3 blocks down. This lonely little pier is sponsored by the Department of Natural Resources and has long steps for pullout of car-tops—definitely not a put-in as there is no temporary parking on the roadway near the park.

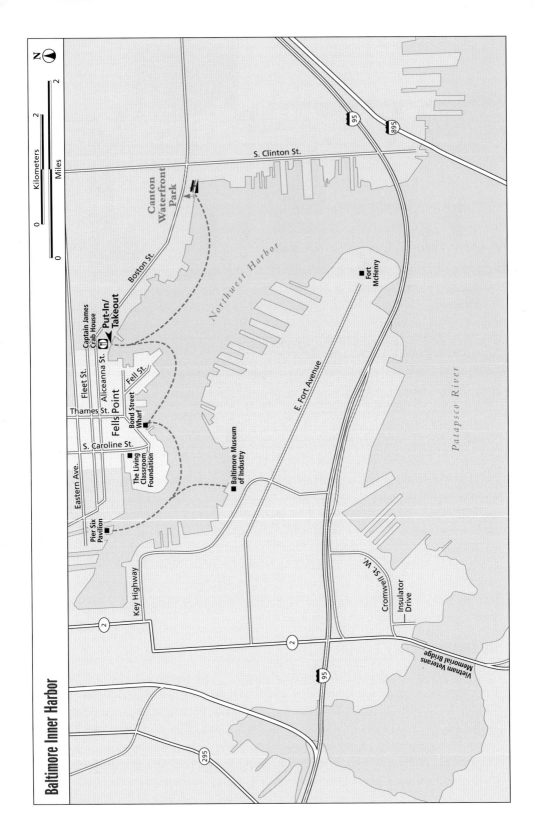

Baltimore Inner Harbor

N

Kilometers
0   2

Miles
0   2

S. Clinton St.

Canton Waterfront Park

Boston St.

Captain James Crab House

Put-In/ Takeout

Aliceanna St.

Fleet St.

Fell St.

Thames St.

Fells Point

Bond Street Wharf

Northwest Harbor

Fort McHenry

E. Fort Avenue

S. Caroline St.

The Living Classroom Foundation

Baltimore Museum of Industry

Eastern Ave.

Pier Six Pavilion

Key Highway

Patapsco River

Cromwell St. W.

Insulator Drive

Vietnam Veterans Memorial Bridge

95

895

2

2

95

295

But across the street is a Safeway grocery store, and nearby to the right is the West Marine Store. Forget to pack a lunch? You are not going to get any food downtown, so this is your last chance at "brown bagging it." Something missing or broken on the boat? Don't go home—the guys at West Marine are funny and knowledgeable. They will do their best to get you going again. Next up is the Captain James Crabhouse. This restaurant actually has a rough takeout area for car-top boats. On our last visit we noticed the owner had put a rough cement layer over the mini ramp. Look at the other side of the road and see Captain James Landing Restaurant, a traditional restaurant in the shape of a huge ship-of-the line, or passenger steamship. One-of-a-kind architecture for sure. This is still a long walk to downtown.

Next is Fells Point and Broadway. There is a party pirate ship that takes folks out for a ride or to purchase a few souvenirs. Come back again without your boat and explore this area; it is famous for its European ethnic group stores and clubhouses. Fells Point is also the central hub for water taxis. Other than a small private pier, which had a few kayaks turned over and no blocking fences, we did not see a secure public location for temporary pullouts.

Following the shoreline, boaters come to Lancaster Street and a long water passage to the right. There is a unique school here that was established by the Living Classroom Foundation. Young men and woman use their hands and minds to create and build things in a classroom atmosphere. The day I visited, the class was engaged in a wood workshop, and the students were in the midst of building a second passenger rescue boat for one of the museum ships in the harbor. The shipyard master said that kayakers could use the low-floating docks for temporary docking and that a cement ramp on the property could also be used for special occasions with the school's permission. It's not in downtown but in the Little Italy section, which is a 2-mile walk to downtown.

Next look for the bright white permanent tents of the Pier Six Concert Stage. We like to picnic on the sidewalks of the Hilton Hotel during concert nights. You can't really see the bands play, but the music is great and the price is right. On summer nights, Baltimore's Inner Harbor waterways glitter with bright neon lights. But none shine or are as entertaining as those from Baltimore's famous waterfront concert hall. The outdoor rock-and-roll concerts get their share of kayaks, sometimes seen bobbing up and down in clusters because they cannot reach the bulkhead cleats even if the bigger boats made room. (**Caution:** Remember, *all* boats at night need running lights, even kayaks.)

Pier Four is where one of the museum ships is parked. Go up and feel how small your boat is next to a real ship. Down a bit farther in the harbor is the National Aquarium and more museum ships. There are brightly colored paddleboats for rent at a floating dock next to Baltimore's Trade Center Building. The famous Baltimore Harbor stores are here, but there is no access. There is even a set of easy steps up to the Science Center that just beg for kayakers to tie up to, but it's 2 little blocks from the harbormaster's office and they are definitely *not* kayak friendly. It may be just a quirk of fate, but directly behind the harbormaster's office in the Rusty Scupper Restaurant building is Federal Hill Park. It's nothing to see today, but in President Lincoln's time, federal cannons were placed there and trained on the Inner Harbor. Historians will tell you the cannons were placed there not to "protect" the good folks of Baltimore but to keep them under control, as the southern side of Mason-Dixon empathy was very strong here.

Want to get out and see Baltimore? Take a taxi. The Baltimore Water Taxi is a well-run operation, and their shoreline metal walking ramps are wide and stable. One of the senior ship captains told me their ships could not carry kayaks to and fro even in an emergency. But should you meet with an emergency, the taxi ramps look very wide and stable enough to support a kayak or two as a pullout. Should the harbor police drive up, just remember that Baltimore folk are usually understanding.

Want to save the Inner Harbor for a later two-part journey? Across the harbor to the south is Locust Point and the Baltimore Museum of Industry. This is a great landing area with an outside pavilion for picnics or getting out of the rain. The museum is a well-stocked and brightly lit history of Baltimore from a commercial and business point of view, oriented for families, entertaining for adults, and a memory lane for folks a little bit older. Paddle east back to the Canton Waterfront Park.

7 Fort McHenry–Locust Point

Baltimore is a port city with history. One of the most famous icons on Maryland's waterfront is Fort McHenry. This is a federal parkland that is controlled and patrolled by park rangers. Locals know of a "sweet spot" for a rest stop pull-up, adjoining the fort on the Baltimore peninsula named Locust Point.

County: Baltimore City
Suggested launch sites:
   Nick's Fish House
   Canton Waterfront Park
Suggested takeout sites: Same
Length and float time: 1.5 miles per hour (medium paddle); 4-hour strong paddle one-way
Difficulty: Deep open water the whole way—expect choppy and smile when it's calm
Current: Medium natural flows, but watch out for ship wakes with big swells
Fishing: Anglers might find in Patapsco River largemouth bass, striped bass, pickerel, crappie, catfish, yellow perch, white perch, bluegill, carp
Season: Year-round
Fees or permits: None
Nearest city/town: Baltimore City
Boats used: Sea kayaks and recreational boats; paddleboards not recommended
Organization: Canton Kayak Club
Contact: Baltimore City Recreation and Parks
Rest areas: Only at Fort McHenry's adjoining property
Restaurant pullouts: None along trail except at Nick's Fish House

Put-In/Takeout Information

Canton Waterfront Park, 3001 Boston St., Canton Waterfront Park, Baltimore, MD 21224; GPS N39 16.612' / W076 34
Nick's Fish House, 2600 Insulator Dr., South Baltimore, MD 21230; (410) 347-4123; GPS N39 15.651' / W076 36.866'

Overview

Nick's Fish House is a waterfront family restaurant that is car-top boat friendly. They store Canton Kayak Club's kayaks near their low-floating docks. Broening Park at Harbor Hospital Center has a public cement ramp area run by the Baltimore City Recreation and Parks, but caution is advised: Trash, wood branches, and sometimes medical waste including used needles are washed up on the banks. The surrounding neighborhood also has more than its share of crime. This is not a secure area.

Canton Waterfront Park is a public cement ramp launch area also run by Baltimore City Recreation and Parks, and it is safe and secure. Whether you make this a 4-hour one-way paddle using the two-car method, or a long loop paddle, weather and season will be major travel factors.

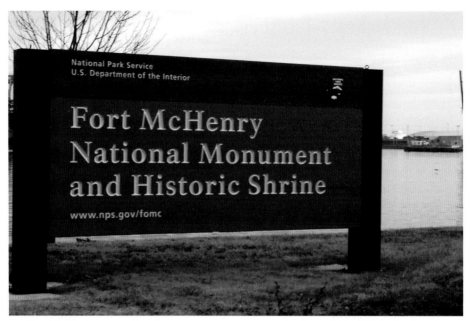

This parcel is not park land, but a Nature Preserve. Bold paddlers can lock up the boats and walk to the visitor center for a tour.

The Paddle

Locust Point combines residential townhomes and industrial companies with docks and shipping. The Patapsco River is deep and wide and covers the southern portion of the peninsula; the downtown designated area becomes the Inner Harbor waterway, although still labeled by some maps as the Patapsco River. Nick's Fish House, located next to the Route 2 Hanover Street Bridge, is in Locust. The bay area to the west of Locust Point is semi-protected and may be acceptable for paddleboards, but is a small area. The bay area is also home to the Baltimore Crew Rowing Team, which stores its boats in a building provided by Baltimore Recreation and Parks. Broening's Middle Park has excellent facilities with low-level launching piers, but resistance to sharing with the general kayaking community is strong.

Go east from Nick's Fish House and aim for the Fort McHenry National Memorial. Just before reaching the thick cement bulkhead that surrounds the entire park, paddlers will find an adjoining, undeveloped parcel of land that is being monitored and restored to its natural habitat by the neighboring community. This parcel is not "park" land. The park has an easy, low wall to climb, which leads to a grassy area with picnic tables and restrooms. The actual park entrance is only a short walk away, and the National Park Service visitor center is where you want to start your exploration. Look for the mounds of dirt marking the fort's cannon placements. This is a laid-back location until holidays, when the fort is peopled with folks in period attire. Look on the fort's website for the best visiting days. As you travel around the bulkhead, notice

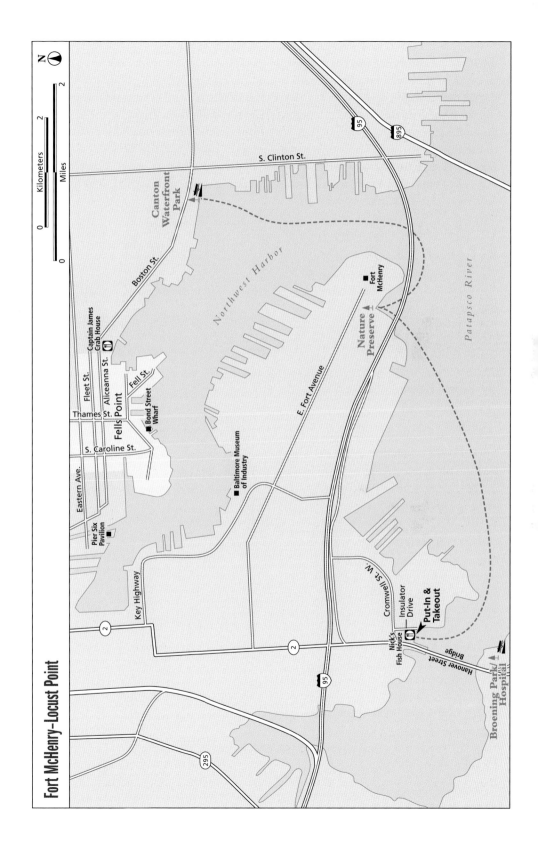

Fort McHenry-Locust Point

N

Kilometers
0   2

Miles
0   2

S. Clinton St.

Canton Waterfront Park

Boston St.

Northwest Harbor

Captain James Crab House

Fleet St.

Aliceanna St.

Fell St.

Thames St.

Fells Point

Bond Street Wharf

S. Caroline St.

Eastern Ave.

Pier Six Pavilion

Key Highway

Baltimore Museum of Industry

E. Fort Avenue

Nature Preserve

Fort McHenry

Patapsco River

Cromwell St. W.

Insulator Drive

Put-In & Takeout

Nick's Fish House

Hanover Street Bridge

Broening Park/ Hospital

95

895

2

2

95

295

the dock on the Inner Harbor side of the park for the waterfront taxi service that takes guests to several locations in and around the harbor, including downtown, during the summer. No tie-ups for any other type of boats are allowed from this pier.

From the fort the paddle is straight to Canton Waterfront Park. This is a secure location for people and their boats. A waterfront walkway leads from this point clear to the downtown area. The city owns the riparian rights, and this walkway and the waterfront taxi are the only ways to "walk around" the harbor stores. The Canton and Fells Point communities have lots of interesting shops and restaurants along the walkway for tourists and residents alike.

8 The Highlands

Baltimore County seems to surround Baltimore City like a protective cocoon. Both city and county speak with the same Baltimore "accent" and are in political harmony. What happens in the city directly affects the immediate suburbs. Baltimore Highlands is a community just outside the city limits. The park is a little hard to find as there are no signs, but your GPS will get you to the ramp.

County: Baltimore City and County
Suggested launch sites:
Nick's Fish House
Southwest Area Park
Suggested takeout sites: Same
Length and float time: 1 mile per hour (slow paddle)
Round-trip from Nick's Fish House—5 miles
Round-trip from Southwest Area Park—3 miles
Difficulty: Easy
Current: Mild
Fishing: Anglers might find in Patapsco River largemouth bass, striped bass, pickerel, crappie, catfish, yellow perch, white perch, bluegill, carp
Season: Best during spring and high flooding tides
Fees or permits: None
Nearest city/town: Baltimore City and Baltimore Highlands
Boats used: Recreational boats; paddleboards from Southwest Area Park
Organizations: None
Contact: Baltimore County Recreation and Parks
Rest areas: Several shoreline areas along waterway
Restaurant pullout: Nick's Fish House

Put-In/Takeout Information

Nick's Fish House, 2600 Insulator Dr., South Baltimore, MD 21230; (410) 347-4123; GPS N39 15.651' / W076 36.866'
Southwest Area Park, 3939 Park Dr. / Georgia Avenue, Baltimore, MD 21225; GPS N39 14.089' / W076 37.348'

Overview

For a long paddle we recommend Nick's Fish House at the northern side of Route 2 Hanover Street Bridge as a safe and secure location for people and boats. For a shorter paddle, go to the public launch site at Southwest Area Park in Baltimore County, another good, safe location. The Patapsco River is a wide and deep river running from the Chesapeake Bay into the Baltimore Harbor. This is a small branch, or creek, off the main river.

The Paddle

One of the most memorable characteristics of this adventure is going under six bridges one-way, with the unreachable goal of the seventh so close yet so far away!

Southwest Area Park public boat ramp

One place to start is from Nick's Fish House and paddle south parallel to Veterans Memorial Bridge, also known as the Hanover Street Bridge. Paddle around the waterfront hospital and under the first two highway bridges. Both sides of the mouth of this waterway are parklands but offer no "safe" resting areas. Continue under the next set of roadway and railway bridges. On your left, if you are a local, you will remember passing this point in a car headed north on I-895 toward the Baltimore tunnel or south toward Annapolis for a surprising half-mile viewing of the river's waterway and shorelines.

On the right side of the shoreline is a small, almost hidden waterway entrance to Southwest Area Park. The water here is usually deep year-round, sometimes enough for motorboats but always enough for car-top boats. A dual cement boat ramp and lots of parking are provided for cars and trailers. This is a Baltimore county park with year-round port-a-potties. This long, quiet stretch is protected from choppy water but not from the wind-tunnel effect, a small challenge to paddle against coming back.

The water trail passes under a major highway bridge, and a bird island mudflat presents itself. We counted ten different species, all happy and singing loudly. There is a fine gravel beach across the water for bird watching and lunch. We noticed lots of local anglers trying their luck on the shoreline, friendly folk who pulled up their lines to make room when we passed by. On the left branch are a few coves worth peeking in, and one with lots of trees for an "emergency call of nature" pullout if needed. Back

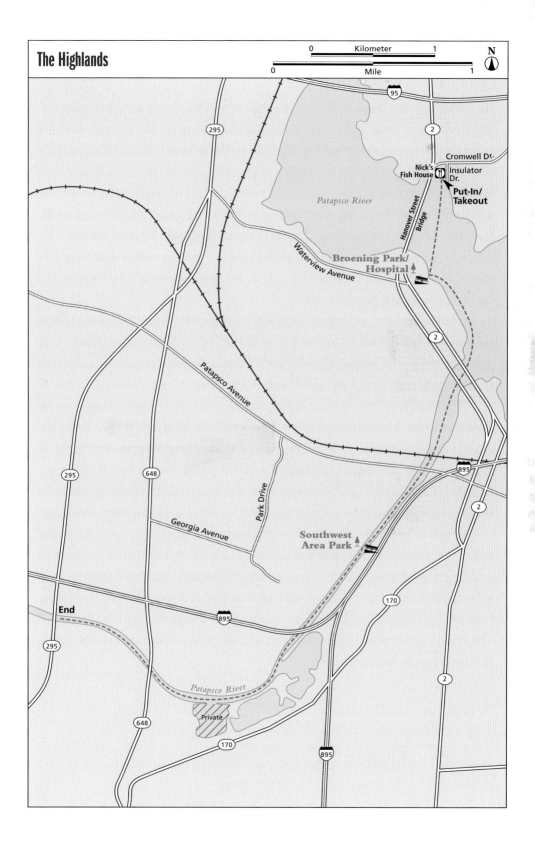

The Highlands

0   Kilometer   1

0   Mile   1

N

95

2

295

Cromwell Dr.

Nick's
Fish House

Insulator
Dr.

Put-In/
Takeout

Patapsco River

Hanover Street Bridge

Waterview Avenue

Broening Park/
Hospital

2

Patapsco Avenue

295

648

895

2

Park Drive

Georgia Avenue

Southwest
Area Park

170

End

895

295

2

Patapsco River

648

Private

170

895

CRABBING IN MARYLAND

Marylanders have crab house restaurants like other parts of the country have steak house restaurants. It is part of our culture. How we go about catching crabs tells as much about our backgrounds as how we were brought up. The usual method is to use a measure of string with a fresh chicken neck firmly tied on. The string is tied to a pier piling, and the bait is dropped down into the water. The crabber allows the crab to try and steal the chicken; in doing so the crab pulls the string taut. The crabber pulls the string back with a fishing net in hand, scoops up the little thief, and plunks him into a bushel basket or a water-filled cooler. Hopefully, the crab is big enough to be a keeper; otherwise it's tossed back into the water for another attempt by both parties. Most crabbers put out several baited lines. Sometimes you win and dine on fresh crab and sometimes you just get a good suntan.

Professional crabbers use crab pot cages with funnel doors that sit on the bottom of creeks and rivers with a colored floating buoy on top. The crabs are harvested on a regular schedule from their boats. Crabbers are licensed to harvest in selected areas. The baited cage method is also used by pier folk, with a cage that has four fold-out walls that clamp together when the string is pulled up.

As a youngster my family and I would go wading for crabs in hand-to-hand combat along the Maryland coastline. Dressed in baggy pants and tennis shoes, we would comb the clear waters and walk through seaweed looking for a fair fight. Once a crab was sighted, the chase would begin; we would scoop up the little rascals into a fishing net made of chicken wire, and the crabs would land in a bushel basket floating inside a blown-up tire tube. Nighttime flashlight crabbing—patrolling the waters and scooping up crabs—was considered ok also, but not as manly as I remember the sport.

Recently we've seen the clever idea of anchoring down a drift line in two spots with chicken necks tied on every few feet. The boat then slowly goes back and forth, and the line is lifted up by a plastic arm attached to the boat; a second person nets the crabs as the line is pulled up. Folks out on the West Coast could not imagine how kayakers manage to fish out of such small boats, I was told. I in turn could not comprehend crabbing out of a kayak till I saw a family doing so with strings and chicken necks. They caught half a bushel basket and their boats smelled strong. Such is the appetite for Maryland crabs.

at the bird flats, the right branch takes you a little farther up the waterway. When the water starts getting shallow, look for the deepest side and zigzag.

At the next railroad bridge we met a young man with about fifteen baited crab cages. Many bridge crabbers use fold-up cages, as the string can be as long as needed so long as the cage sits on the ground. The young fisherman shrugged at the day's catch and explained that the day of and after storms, the waterway shakes up lots of fish and crabs, and one afternoon he caught ten bushels of crabs (well, he was a fisherman with a license to stretch the truth a bit).

The last bridge had lots of trees and branches wrapped around the foundation legs. The bottom gets too shallow here at low tide to go on, but at high tide, boats can paddle almost to the Route 295 bridge going into Baltimore. The day I took pictures, I chatted with a man who told me he started the Patapsco River water trail miles farther up from the Route 295 bridge, with only minor portaging around trees and sandbars coming back. It should be noted he had a very lightweight boat and paddled at an extremely high tide.

Baltimore
Reservoirs

Baltimore City and Baltimore County are culturally the same, and many times their local administration and governments blend hand in hand. The Baltimore reservoirs are a good reflection of that working relationship. Most general information about Baltimore's sister reservoirs concern their history, and the various recreational activities allowed onshore and around the bodies of water. I spoke to an administrator about the limited number of passes sold each year, the invasive species, and how the city/county enforced their rules. The folks who deal with such questions are particularly touchy about complaints, and regard those who are "outside the system" as troublemakers. "Outside the system" are folks who did not get a season pass for their boats in the Baltimore waters.

Here are Baltimore's answers to general questions:

- We only have so many permits; folks who already have one get to renew theirs first.

- Every year people must sign a promissory note saying they will not use their boats with approved permit stickers on any other bodies of water.

- Enforcement of these rules is done with daily patrols of DNR police checking for permits at ramp sites, with fines and impoundment of offending boats no matter the size.

- They get a lot of calls from folks who report others who disregard the rules and whose permits are revoked and not renewed again.

- Invasive aquatic species damage the shoreline vegetation, kill the good fish that are being promoted, and destroy the delicate ecosystem under the water.

- Permits issued are for all three reservoirs, but Loch Raven has its own permit for its waterways and a permit for the Liberty and Pretty Boy Reservoirs is separate and extra!

- For outsiders (presumably like myself), I was reminded that Loch Raven did have permits issued for their fishing rental boats that could be checked out seasonally. There were a few canoes to rent also.

It takes a dam to create a reservoir—in this case, Lake Roland at Robert E. Lee Park (paddle 10).

Baltimore City's simple rules of use while on or near the water:

- No swimming allowed (the water is safe and clean—but you are not).

- No motorized engines that use gasoline (battery power is ok).

- No boats under 12 feet long allowed on the waterways (for stability and safety).
- Without exception, boats allowed on the three sister reservoirs with permits must never be used on other waterways (aquatic parasites called invasive species can cling to a boat's hull and might affect the water supply).

The four Baltimore reservoirs are:

1. Liberty Reservoir, with 3,100 acres of water and two launch areas with cement ramps.

2. Loch Raven Reservoir, with 2,400 acres of water; launch area is the Fishing Center.

3. Pretty Boy Reservoir in upper Maryland, with 1,500 acres of water that is deep and cold.

4. Roland Lake at Robert E. Lee Park, the odd man is with 90 acres and no permits needed.

9 Loch Raven, Liberty, and Pretty Boy

Loch Raven has open basins as well as some long stretches of narrow waterways. Some of Maryland's largest fish species on record have been caught from this reservoir. It's well worth renting a rowboat or a canoe for a nominal fee for a day of paddling without competition from the high-powered motorboat crowd and their wakes. Beg or borrow a canoe or kayak to paddle Liberty and Pretty Boy.

County: Baltimore City and County

Suggested launch sites:
Loch Raven
Liberty
Pretty Boy Reservoir
Lake Roland

Suggested takeout sites: Same

Length and float time: Unknown/ 1.5 miles per hour (medium paddle)

Difficulty: Easy

Current: Mild

Fishing: Loch Raven anglers might find largemouth and smallmouth bass, bluegill, yellow and white perch, crappie, pickerel, walleye, catfish, northern pike

Liberty: largemouth, smallmouth, striped bass, walleye, crappie, catfish, yellow and white perch, sunfish, carp, trout

Pretty Boy: largemouth and smallmouth bass, crappie, catfish, yellow perch, bluegill, sunfish

Season: Closed in winter months

Fees or permits: Special permit for Loch Raven and another for Liberty and Pretty Boy

Nearest city/town: Baltimore City

Boats used: Car-top boats 12 feet and larger

Organizations: None

Contacts: None

Rest areas: None

Restaurant pullouts: None

Put-In/Takeout Information

Liberty Reservoir Ramp, Oakland Mills Road, Eldersburg, MD; GPS N39 23.887' / W076 53.455'

Loch Raven Fishing Center, 12101 Dulaney Valley Rd., Baltimore, MD; (410) 887-7692; GPS N39 27.755' / W076 34.027'

Pretty Boy Reservoir, Spooks Hill Road, Parkton, MD; GPS N39 39.116' / W076 44.501'

Robert E. Lee Park and Lake Roland, 1100 Cooper Hill Rd., Baltimore, MD; GPS N39 22.743' / W076 38.515'

Overview

The city's government administers these bodies of water, restricts and polices their use, gives a grudging shrug for community activity around the water, and watches the quality and content like a mindful parent with no sense of humor. The highest pressure for community use is Loch Raven Reservoir, followed by Liberty and then Pretty Boy. So two permits are issued: one just for Loch Raven and the other

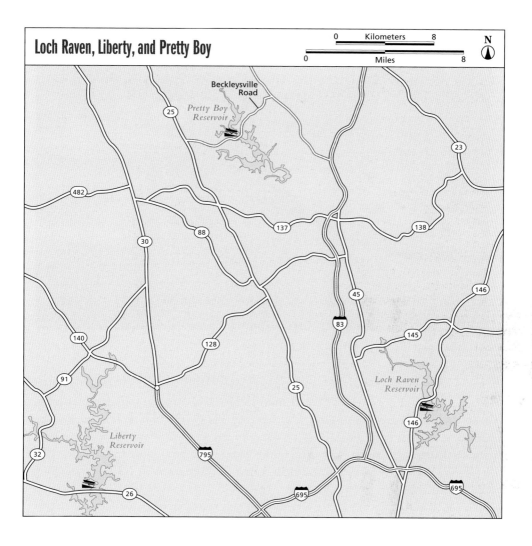

for Liberty with Pretty Boy as an added bonus. Since the current holders of boating permits get to renew first, the scramble to get the few vacant permits can be intense. I was told that men would sleep outside the permit office the night before just to get a single shot at the coming year's permit. I heard something about "gone by 2 a.m. in the morning," but the fisherman stomped away angry at the memory. Loch Raven is the only reservoir with rental boats with current seasonal permits.

The Paddle

Loch Raven

Note the GPS coordinates and address and take your GPS unit as there are no signs

Baltimore's Loch Raven Reservoir public rental boats

posted pointing to the fishing center along Dulaney Valley Road and nothing at the actual small road onto which boaters need to turn to get to the fishing center (even the CIA headquarters in Virginia now has road signs!). The fishing is good, but the facility is not that fancy. Loch Raven is the only reservoir with rental canoes that have a seasonal permit. The shape and size of the waterway is pronounced, and wide-open basins are the basic characteristics. Anglers have said the reservoir has sea grass along the entire shoreline.

I called and tried to reserve a canoe, but the manager was unimpressed: "Don't worry, we got lots of canoes." When I arrived, I noticed his office was decorated with a wall of small photographs of customers and their fish. On a plaque was a string of mounted shellacked fish. The reservoir rule at Loch Raven, according to the website, is that live bait must be purchased from an authorized dealer, and the Loch Raven office sells a variety of types for their clientele. And who frequents places like this? I've since met anglers from all over Baltimore City and Baltimore County, and they've all had stories about this body of water.

For me, a weekend recreational kayaker not really into fishing, the wide basins and windswept waterways were not enticing, but as I looked around and took pictures, I noticed that a good 50 percent of the boats stored year-round, including the rentals, were colorful kayaks chained up with thick cables and massive locks. Many reservoirs offer local residents this additional service of canoes and kayaks for a fee. The all-day rental fee for a canoe is extremely reasonable, especially when the day starts at 6 a.m. and ends at 6 p.m., with gates locked at 6:30 p.m. Rows of rental rowboats, metal

Liberty Reservoir is the area's largest with sweeping basins.

skiffs for little battery-operated propeller motors, and bass fishing boats with a twin battery for larger motors is the real business here.

Many of the stories I heard were about the Canada geese and their droppings. The droppings not only foul the surrounding grassy shoreline for land-based anglers but also for families who just want to walk around. I visited the reservoir two days after a heavy rainfall (4 inches in one day). The first day the flooding was scary, the second day the water receded 2 feet to be an extremely high tide. Lots of folks were visiting just to check out the damage. The fisherman I spoke to said the geese seem to stay year-round, and their (droppings) create the unwanted algae blooms. I am told the entire reservoir has thick sea grass on its shores. I didn't see any, but I was seeing the waterway maxed out with rainwater leftovers. The algae is not good for water purity, but apparently great for fish, as many of Maryland's freshwater catch records were made in this reservoir. I've heard of other smaller lakes taking Christmas trees and dumping them in one end of the water to promote better fishing growth. The branches help stimulate more natural food for the fish, so I guess the algae would too.

Interestingly, I found a golf course off the reservoir (talk about your water hazard!) and a gun range with skeet shooting, and part of the major roadway around the reservoir was blocked off on weekends to accommodate recreational access for joggers. The road winds around to the actual dam that has a natural overflow and a secondary shore-to-shore 8-foot spillover. The Gunpowder River kicks in here and goes quite a distance to its mouth at the Chesapeake Bay. The shorelines for the water from the dam are now part of Gunpowder Falls State Park and go for miles on each

Pretty Boy is smaller and has colder water, but a more secluded route.

side. About a mile south of the dam-released water is a small family restaurant called the Iron Horse overlooking the winding river. To follow the river in a kayak curled my toes, but that's for the next book on paddling Maryland State Parks!

Liberty

Liberty Reservoir in Baltimore County also overlaps by 50 percent into Carol County, but somehow the "whole" reservoir belongs to Baltimore City. Liberty is the largest of the Baltimore reservoirs and is unusual in that it has two cement boat ramps that are barely half a mile apart! This makes for rough and tough access to the water during prime season and prime time. The police who monitor the activity are from the Maryland Department of Natural Resources (DNR). These folks seem to be everywhere with sub-station offices key boating locations, and they mean business. The DNR checks fishing licenses and actual fish caught. There are signs everywhere about permits needed and boat impoundment. The Liberty waterways looked very inviting. I decided to drive around the reservoir on back roads and found a few approved overlooks. It would not be impossible to portage a boat down some of the hillsides, but I believe those spots were for shoreline anglers. I found some photos on the Internet of kids swimming in the forbidden reservoir waters (with and without bathing suits). Amazing what's on the Web these days!

Pretty Boy

The Pretty Boy Reservoir up in northern Maryland is also owned by Baltimore City. Both Liberty and Pretty Boy Reservoirs open their gates on May 1. Finding Liberty was easy. Finding Pretty Boy was almost scary. Please use the GPS coordinates and copy down the driving directions. Pretty Boy is 15 miles north of Hunt Valley on Route 83. The final road is called Spooks Drive and is narrow, long, and full of twists. I was sure I was lost several times. Three miles off the Route 83 exit is Wally's Country Store and BP gas station. Ask for the house specialty—a chicken biscuit—or any of the other fresh-made salads and sandwiches. It's a good last stop before turning onto a developed neighborhood road that quickly becomes a trip into wilderness and ends at a secluded but well-maintained little boat ramp and kayak storage area. Pretty Boy is not a huge reservoir, but has deep, cold depths and narrow, long branches of waterways. The anglers I met while exploring were disappointed in the fish not biting, but they thought I was from outer space when I asked about sea grass growth. It appeared quiet and clean.

10 Lake Roland at Robert E. Lee Park

What is the difference between a pond, a lake, a reservoir and a water impoundment? Is it the size, length and width? Is it the depth of the water or how much water is being measured? Is it the use of the waterway? Is it where the water originated from, or is there a difference in fresh- and saltwater classifications? Is it the amount of fish, wildlife, and other ecosystems involved? Whatever this body of water is, it's now available for short, recreational paddles without any permits or fees, and is perfect for paddleboarders who want calm water.

County: Baltimore City and County
Suggested launch site: Lake Roland
Suggested takeout site: Same
Length and float time: 1 mile/ 1 hour
Difficulty: Easy
Current: Mild
Season: Closed in winter months
Fees or permits: None

Nearest city/town: Baltimore City
Boats used: Recreational boats and paddleboards
Organizations: None
Contacts: None
Rest areas: None
Restaurant pullouts: None

Put-In/Takeout Information

Robert E. Lee Park and Lake Roland, 1100 Cooper Hill Rd., Baltimore, MD 21209; GPS N39 22.743' / W076 38.515'

Overview

Located in the upper area of Baltimore City proper, this park and lake were transferred to Baltimore County in 2013 for general administration. I talked with an engineer who was going for a paddle to take water samples and survey the sea grass growing in the far end of the "lake." The reservoir was originally conceived for drinking water use, but contamination in the soil leached into the water, making it unfit for potable (drinkable) water use. Baltimore County is shoring up the dam and trying to kill off the expanding sea grass, which currently occupies almost 20 percent of the water area. My research said 90 acres—the engineer said "more like 70 acres." I asked if any restrictions or permits were needed? "No, just tell your readers to wear a life preserver and to be safe."

The Paddle

The launch area—a smooth-graveled area for put-in and takeout—is a short portage from the parking lot, and is excellent for beginners and families who need calm waters. The water looks clean but the county is still working to lower the harmful

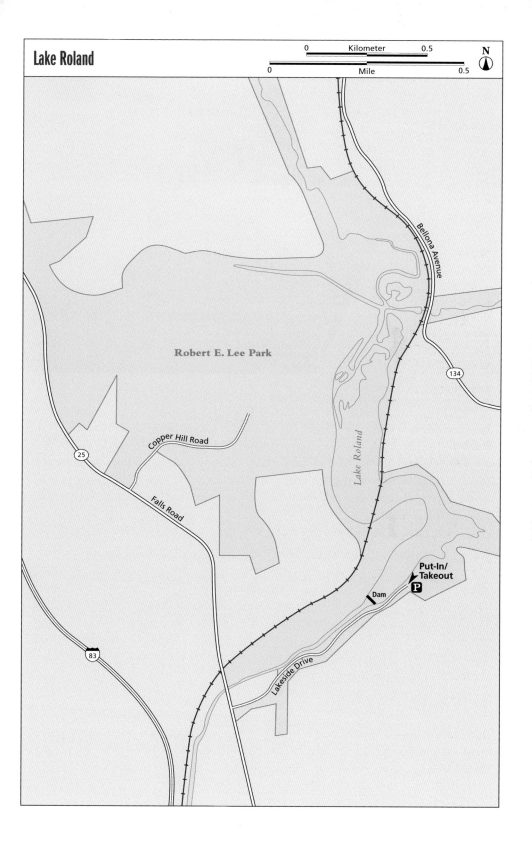

Lake Roland

Robert E. Lee Park

Bellona Avenue

134

Copper Hill Road

25

Falls Road

Lake Roland

Put-In/
Takeout

P

Dam

Lakeside Drive

83

N

0   Kilometer   0.5

0   Mile   0.5

Lake Roland gravel launch area

bacteria. The size of the lake makes for an enjoyable, hour-long circumference kayak paddle.

The reservoir is easy to find, in northern Baltimore City within the beltway. I found a good mom-and-pop ice cream/snack shop at the turn just before the road to the park. Did I mention it is about half and half land and water? I felt very safe in a good neighborhood.

Simple rules of use while on or near the water:

- No swimming allowed (the water has bacteria and is being treated).
- No motorized engines that use gasoline but battery power is allowed.

Calvert County

Calvert County is a 215-square-mile peninsula sandwiched between the Chesapeake Bay and the Patuxent River. This makes Calvert Maryland's smallest county. As a tourist destination there are many opportunities for fishing, crabbing, and enjoying the sandy beaches. The county is proud of its many parks, preserves, and harbors. Numerous museums and historical beach sites like Calvert Cliffs offer visitors many options for learning about the natural and human history of the area.

Solomon's Island is a major yachting center at the mouth of the Patuxent River. On the tip of the island is the Chesapeake Biological Laboratory and its visitor center. The lab is within walking distance of the Williams Street shoreline launch for car-top boaters. The old public ramp was next to the

All boaters large and small owe the Coast Guard a thanks (paddle 12).

commercial Isaac Solomon's oyster packing facility, which had its heyday in the 1800s. As the cement ramp decayed, it was symbolically covered in piles of oyster shells!

11 Chesapeake Beach and Fishing Creek

Fishing Creek is safe year-round at high tide and low tide. The Chesapeake Bay can be calm and tempting, but keep to the shoreline just in case of rough water.

County: Calvert County
Suggested launch site: Rod and Reel Marina West is the only launch site
Suggested takeout sites: None
Length and float time: 1.5 miles per hour (medium paddle)
    Fishing Creek—4.5 miles round-trip (high tide)
    North Beach public beach—2 miles round-trip
    North Beach environmental area—3 miles round-trip
Difficulty: Easy in creek, medium to rough on bay
Current: None

Fishing: Chesapeake Bay anglers might find close to shore spot, croaker, flounder, trout, other saltwater species.
Season: Year-round (creek may freeze to ice in winter)
Fees or permits: Launching fee for North Beach; fee for beach entrance
Nearest city/town: Chesapeake Beach and North Beach
Boats used: Recreational kayaks and canoes; paddleboards good on Fishing Creek
Organization: Calvert County Parks and Recreation
Contacts: None
Rest areas: Private piers to tie up to only
Restaurant pullouts: None

Put-In/Takeout Information

Rod and Reel Marina West (Paddle or Peddle rents kayaks, canoes, and paddleboards), 4055 Gordon Stinnett Ave., Chesapeake Beach, MD 20732; (410) 991-4268; GPS N38 41.470' / W076 32.218'

North Beach Bay Ave., North Beach, MD 20714; (410) 286-37799; GPS N38 42.392' / W076 31.894'

Overview

Chesapeake Beach is the biggest little town in Calvert County. It's the only place on an ADC map with enough residents to rate a yellow shading; even then, half the town calls itself North Beach and is more residential, with 2 blocks of cute downtown stores and a fixed-up swimming beach with 2 blocks of boardwalk. Chesapeake Beach has more condos on the waterfront and is tourist oriented with a big hotel, a water park, large deep-water marinas, and a new 0.5-mile wooden bridge/walkway paralleling the creek for a bit. It's still a small town, though, with speakers blaring the play-by-play of the local school's baseball team, which echoes throughout the wilderness for miles.

A short trail, perfect for families, crosses the creek here and follows the watertrail for about 0.5 mile.

The Paddle

The Community Center shares the parking lot with Rod and Reel Marina West, but when the fishing is hot, the Community Center loses and boat trailers crowd out everything else. Even the recreation park is filled and baseball is put on hold. The marina has multiple cement ramps on two sides of a large parking lot and a small kayak pier for the boat rental company. The cement ramps fill up fast during the summer, so car-top boaters might seriously think about using the kayak rental pier launch to get out of the way. A small launch fee is charged everywhere, but no queuing is needed in the off-season. The Water Amusement Park adjoins the marina, so the place is hopping all summer long.

The first block or two of traveling south on Fishing Creek has motorboat slips in various stages of decay. The commercial fishermen dock here and the slips have crab cages lined up on every finger pier. Boaters have a fine view of the rear of several seafood restaurants. The town's new environmental viewing wooden walkway is several feet higher than water level, and families love to stare and point at the silly little boats with no fishing poles sticking out of them. The odd thing is we have seen lots of crabbers working out of their kayaks but never seen more than a rare fisherman scratching his head wondering where the fish were on a creek named "Fishing Creek"! There are a few private piers decorated with plants and chairs—even one with a pirate flag and an outside tiki bar! **Caution:** Watch the water levels, when the

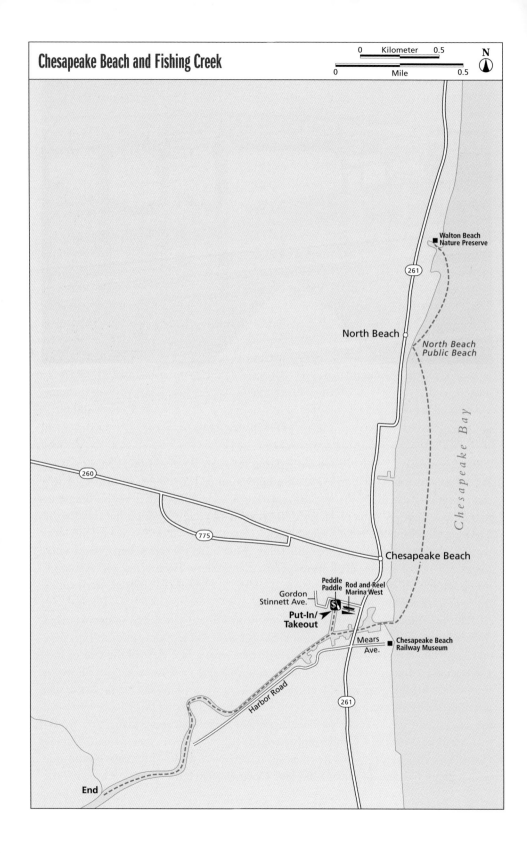

Chesapeake Beach and Fishing Creek

0   Kilometer   0.5

0   Mile   0.5

N

Walton Beach
Nature Preserve

261

North Beach

North Beach
Public Beach

Chesapeake Bay

260

775

Chesapeake Beach

Peddle
Paddle

Rod and Reel
Marina West

Gordon
Stinnett Ave.

S

**Put-In/
Takeout**

Mears
Ave.

Chesapeake Beach
Railway Museum

Harbor Road

261

End

tide goes out, it seems to go in a rush and could leave you in a mudflat area where minutes before you were exploring in the tall weeds. At high tide, boaters are treated to a headwater area with wildlife and fauna a bit different than the rest of the creek. It's a very relaxing paddle.

After you return you might want to just go back and walk the pier, as it is very pleasant, or go see the Chesapeake train depot and hear about Chesapeake Beach's history and the train that brought folks to this biggest little town in Calvert.

Another option is to head north into the Chesapeake Bay. The town of Chesapeake has a small, seasonal railroad museum that is worth visiting; park at the town's hotel—Rod and Reel Marina East—or paddle to the waterfront side of the hotel and temporarily pull up on the sandbar. (There used to be a friendly sharing of the adjacent neighborhood's beach with a kayak rental company but now there is a firm chain-link fence and private property signs—no launching from here anymore.)

Now head north hugging the coastline. Sometimes the Chesapeake Bay can be as smooth as a mirror, and sometimes the water is choppy and rough from the weather as well as swelling wakes from yacht and motorboats that feel the need for speed. The town of North Beach is a delight to walk around, with little shops and a friendly atmosphere. Their public beach and town boardwalk have been frequently damaged by storms, and the latest version was expensive to build. Everyone pays for parking and for the privilege to swim on the beach. Apparently, launching kayaks from the beach area is not a frequent request, and they charge the same as a beach swim fee. Coming from lower Chesapeake Beach and parking the boats at the far northern end of North Beach's beach was ok, and we were not asked for a beach pull-up fee as we walked the town for lunch and ice cream. (At the far end of the beach, the boardwalk wooden fence has a latch and opens like a gate; we found this out later—good luck to you too.)

Now, still in the town of North Beach, at the very northern tip of its authority before it becomes another county, lies a gated environmental beach area. It was not always gated and locked, but it's a good way to steer the tourist and local folk to the fee-for-use beach. Kayakers who know how to strap on a beach chair and picnic basket to their boats will have a great day on the clean, white sand beach, with a rich assortment of waterfowl that will pose for pictures. It's a good swimming hole for sure. Please remember that it is an environmental area and take home your trash and anything else not belonging there.

12 Solomon's Island

The Solomon's Island adventure starts outside the harbor then explores three protected interlocking creeks. There are lots of expensive yachts, numerous places for evening entertainment, and a dozen coves to explore—all in a 6-mile-per-hour speed zone.

County: Calvert County
Suggested launch sites:
   Solomon's Island Causeway (kayak beach launch area)
   Solomon's Island Bridge (public ramp)
   Williams Street Shoreline Launch
   KB Derr & Son Marina
Suggested takeout sites: Same
Length and float time: 1.5 miles per hour (medium paddle)
   Causeway along the narrows and into Solomon's Inner Harbor—1 mile
   Williams Street to end of Back Creek—1.5 miles
   Headwaters of Back Creek to Turkey Bar—1 mile
   Turkey Bar to headwaters of St. John Creek—1.5 miles

Headwaters of St. Johns Creek to Mill Creek—1 mile
Mouth of Mill Creek to KB Derr & Son Marina—1.5 miles
Difficulty: Easy
Current: None or little wakes, as the speed limit is 6 miles in all creek areas
Fishing: Anglers might find croaker, spot, and white perch
Season: Year-round
Fees or permits: None
Nearest city/town: Solomon's Island
Boats used: Recreational boats and paddleboards
Organizations: None
Contact: Calvert County Parks and Recreation
Rest areas: Multiple throughout paddle
Restaurant pullouts: Multiple

Put-In/Takeout Information

Solomon's Island Causeway (kayak beach launch area); GPS N38 19.495' / W076 27.710'

Solomon's Island Bridge (public ramp), 14195 S. Solomon's Island Rd., Solomon's Island, MD; GPS N38 19.728' / W076 28.077'

Williams Street Shoreline Launch, Williams Street, Solomon's Island MD; GPS N38 19.218' / W076 27.205'

Holiday Inn Solomon's (Patuxent Adventure Center with kayak rentals 410-394-2770), 155 Holiday Dr., Solomon's, MD; GPS N38 20.226' / W076 27.747'

KB Derr & Son Marina, 12565 Rousby Hall Rd., Lusby, MD; (410) 326-7089; GPS N38 20.700' / W076 25.530'

Overview

Calvert County is situated on one enormous peninsula with the Patuxent River running its length on the west side and the Chesapeake Bay running its length on the east

Public boat ramp at Solomon's Island Bridge on the Patuxent River

side. Solomon's Island is a small city on the tip of the peninsula, just inside the Patuxent's mouth as it conjoins with the Chesapeake. The three creeks that flow through the town total about 5.5 miles of protected paddling at its best. There's lots to see and do, and boat wakes are minimal because the speed limit is 6 miles per hour for all the motorboats and yachts that occupy every available slip in the harbor.

The Paddle

The Patuxent River Trail is a waterway map of interesting places to visit, historical reference waypoints, and runs through four different counties. This waterway trail starts "inside" the harbor of Solomon's Island. Two other Solomon Island launch sites are just outside the harbor. The Route 4/Route 2 joint highway ends at the Thomas Johnson Bridge. Directly under the bridge is a fee-for-use public boat ramp area with multiple cement ramps for motorboats. On summer weekends the Patuxent River in this location is so churned up with boat wakes, it's like venturing into a washing machine. There is a special area for car-tops to leave a car parked next to the beach area, for a beach launch or to use the cement ramp.

The second launch site (no fee) is on Solomon's Island Causeway, or as it's more commonly called, the Narrows. This is a thin strip of land where the town's stores and restaurants are located; it's also where a small stretch of beach—across from the town's Catholic church (the locals identify the area)—sits on the Patuxent River. It's very bohemian, with kayaks of every color and type mixed in with families swimming and

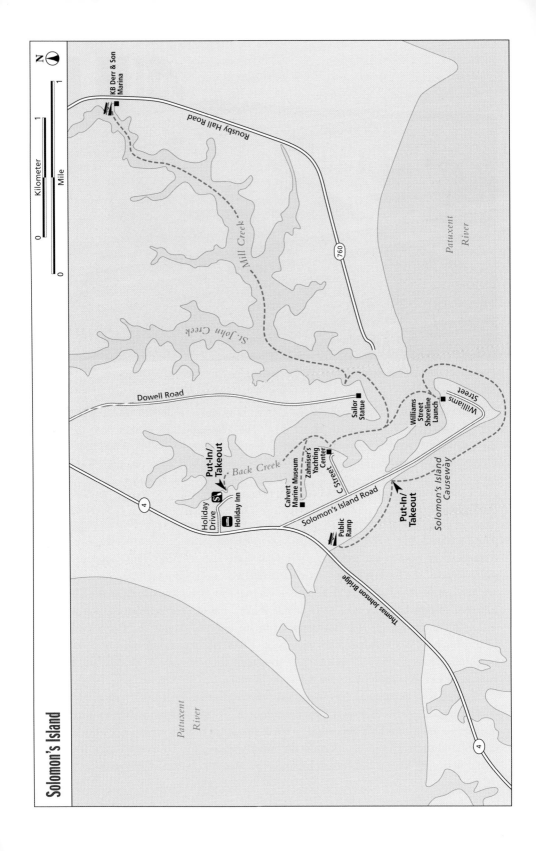

Solomon's Island

N

Kilometer

Mile

KB Derr & Son Marina

Rousby Hall Road

760

Mill Creek

St. John Creek

Patuxent River

Dowell Road

Put-In/ Takeout

Back Creek

Holiday Drive

Holiday Inn

Sailor Statue

Zahniser's Yachting Center

Calvert Marine Museum

C Street

Williams Street Shoreline Launch

Williams Street

Solomon's Island Road

Public Ramp

Put-In/ Takeout

Solomon's Island Causeway

4

Thomas Johnson Bridge

Patuxent River

4

picnicking. The water is not so rough paddling near the town's bulkhead walls and piers, but expect a few big waves now and again as you head for the inner harbor.

As you enter the harbor, steer to the left-side docks. Poke around the shoreline and look for a pile of oyster shells. You are now in the commercial section of the harbor where the professional fishing boats tie up. An old cement public boat ramp deteriorated so much that the town decided not to fix it and dumped discarded oyster shells on it. But just to its side is a great (free) shoreline beach launch area off Williams Street. This little forgotten and forlorn spot is the Patuxent River Trail's site #1 and is labeled as a public launch area. There's limited parking but it is a safe area. There are many places to launch from in the paddling loop, but this is a great starting point.

Keep to the left and paddle Back Creek. There are lots of marinas, but look for Zahniser's. This location has a nice waterfront restaurant, a pull-up dinghy dock by the swimming pool, and other amenities. Island Hideaway, on the Narrows, is special in that it has a private boat ramp on the harbor side and dockage for visiting guests. The Back Creek Inn B&B is in the harbor, and its waterfront location and strip beach are perfect for a long kayaking weekend stay.

The next location to look for is the Calvert Marine Museum with an excellent floating dinghy pier, a landing dock with picnic tables, and a first-rate family-oriented entertainment center with live seals swimming in a tank. Please do pay the entrance fee (good public restrooms if needed). Travel a bit farther to the Holiday Inn on the left, which has kayak rentals and a launch area plus an outdoor live rock-and-roll bar and grill in the evenings.

Going back to the fork in the harbor waterway, turn east. The tip of the small peninsula is called Turkey Bar and is owned by Calvert Marina. At the tip look for a memorial statue of a lone Navy man titled *On Watch*. Paddle a short way and find a little cove with a beach that makes a nice rest stop. About half a mile up, the creek divides again. Going straight the waterway is St. John Creek; it has a few interesting coves to explore. To the right, the waterway is Mill Creek, with good long coves to explore and a marina with a good ramp called KB Derr & Son near the headwaters. This is a long day of about 6.5 miles paddling, depending on where you started. KB Derr & Son is a good location for a two-car system for pullout or put-in.

13 St. Leonard's Creek

The creek is divided into a northern area and a southern area, with a private marina being the dividing line. The creek is a quiet, peaceful paddle in the off-season, but rough in summer.

County: Calvert County

Suggested launch sites:
  Jefferson Patterson Park
  Vera's White Sands Marina

Suggested takeout sites: Same

Length and float time: 1.5 miles per hour (medium paddle)
  Top to bottom—4 miles
  Vera's Marina to Patterson's Point—2 miles

Difficulty: Easy

Current: Mild, but heavy boat wakes during summer season

Fishing: Anglers might find croaker, spot, white perch

Season: Year-round

Fees or permits: Launch fee for Vera's White Sands Marina and Jefferson Patterson Park beach

Nearest city/town: St. Leonard

Boats used: Recreational boats; paddleboards only good in off-season due to wakes

Organizations: None

Contacts: None

Rest areas: Multiple on creek shoreline

Restaurant pullouts: Vera's White Sands Marina

Put-In/Takeout Information

Vera's White Sands Marina & Beach Club, 1200 White Sands Dr., Lusby, MD; (410) 586-1182; GPS N38 25.239' / W076 29.201'

Jefferson Patterson Park and Museum, 10515 Mackall Rd., St. Leonard, MD; (410) 586-8501; GPS N38 23.388' / W076 30.446'

Overview

St. Leonard's Creek is a 4-mile protected paddle from top to bottom with two access areas. One of these is at the mouth of the river, where there's a historical museum on the waterfront with a shoreline beach launch area. The second is a marina in mid-creek that is not kayak friendly due to past experiences and allows access from its ramp seven days a week off-season, but not on weekends during the summer.

The Paddle

The Patuxent River's upper region is narrow and long with limited motorboat activity. The lower region is wide and deep with motorboat and yacht activity year-round. The long creeks, like St. Leonard's, are a pleasure to paddle in the off-season, but paddlers need to be cautious during the peak summer months when motorboat

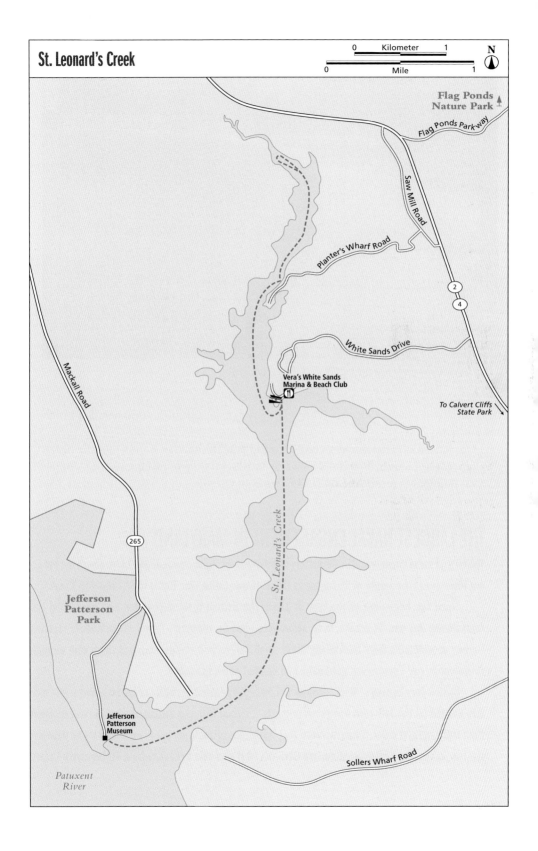

St. Leonard's Creek

Flag Ponds
Nature Park

Flag Ponds Parkway

Saw Mill Road

Planter's Wharf Road

White Sands Drive

2

4

Vera's White Sands
Marina & Beach Club

To Calvert Cliffs
State Park

Mackall Road

St. Leonard's Creek

265

Jefferson
Patterson
Park

Jefferson
Patterson
Museum

Patuxent
River

Sollers Wharf Road

0   Kilometer   1

0   Mile   1

N

This beach is home to famous battles and horseshoe crabs.

wakes cause a lot of challenges. This waterway is tidal, but it's a good paddle in high or low tide.

The Jefferson Patterson Museum is a good launch site year-round, plus the beach has horseshoe crab shells to take home as souvenirs. As you paddle north, there are several little coves to explore and a few beaches on the shorelines for rest stops. On

THE LARGEST NAVAL ENGAGEMENT IN MARYLAND

The largest naval engagement in the history of Maryland took place on June 26, 1814, where the Patuxent River meets the mouth of St. Leonard's Creek. It was called "The Battle of St. Leonard's Creek."

Since the beginning of the War of 1812, the British had commanded and controlled the Chesapeake Bay and its creeks. In an attempt to open St. Leonard's Creek, "Commodore" Joshua Barney assembled a local fleet of eighteen small barges and sloops, supplied them with enough firepower to call themselves gunboats, and headed down the creek.

Commodore Barney's "fleet"—supported on land by American militia units, including a gun battery located on the Jefferson Patterson property—clashed with the British. During the engagement from both land and water, it was recorded that "hundreds of shots per hour" were exchanged between the two forces. The British relented, and Barney's fleet was able to escape from St. Leonard's Creek.

the west side of the creek, boaters can see the same cliff formations created from the same shoreline erosion for which Calvert Cliffs is known.

Vera's White Sand Marina & Beach Club is famous for weekend entertainment and an excellent bar and grill restaurant. Colorful murals surround the performers' stage. The boat ramp is in good shape and the launching fee is modest. But previous kayakers must have caused problems, because the owner has negative signs specifically directed at kayakers. The party beach is off-limits at all times. The ramp is not open to kayakers during the summer weekends, as she needs every parking space and apparently kayakers do not generate a reliable stream of income as do other guests.

The northern half of the creek is a quiet pleasure paddle as you near the headwaters. There are two rest areas of note: Wagner Street on the west side has a community paved lot for storage of kayaks and a launch area, and Planter's Wharf on the east side has a deer path from the public road to the waterway.

Cecil County and the Susquehanna River

It's a long, pleasant drive from the Conowingo Dam to the downtown area of Port Deposit. We found lots of roadside pull-offs for shore anglers and adventurous kayakers. Use caution, though, as the waterways are filled with sharp, rocky terrain for any type of boats. Look for an unusual log cabin restaurant-tavern along the way. The Union Hotel was built in the 1790s and looked inviting for year-round dining exploration. Its website says the waiters are in colonial garb!

On the outskirts of Port Deposit, where the water becomes friendlier, lies a quiet memorial to an old-timer who owned a point of land that was his fishing camp. He was called the "Dean of the Susquehanna" due to his years of knowing where the rocks and fish were on the river just a bit north of his camp. With his passing the landing became Rock Run Park, with a single deteriorated ramp. Cleaned up with new benches and a level dirt parking lot, there is no mention of Mr. Townsend. But the locals and fishermen know the stories and his tales.

George Washington and other notable rebels slept here (paddle 14)!

14 Port Deposit to Perryville

The waterfront town of Port Deposit is a two-lane community, with two economically different sides of the road for 0.25 mile. Built into the mountainside are the older roadside homes from days gone by, with a few pizza and sub shops. On the waterfront side are sparkling new condominiums with piers and dockage for yachts. Perryville is a quiet residential town with some new waterfront condos with docking and pleasant suburban neighborhoods.

County: Cecil County
Suggested launch sites:
Rock Run Park at Townsend's Point
Port Deposit Marina Park
Perryville Community Launch
Perryville VA Medical Center
Perryville Community Park
Suggested takeout sites: Same
Length and float time: 1 mile per hour (slow paddle)
Rock Run Park to Port Deposit Marina Park—1 mile
Port Deposit Marina to Perryville Community Launch/Garrett Island—1.5 miles
Perryville Community Launch to Rodgers Tavern—0.5 mile
Rodgers Tavern to VA Medical Center ramp—1.5 miles

VA ramp to Perryville Community Park kayak launch (at high tide)—1 mile
Difficulty: Moderate
Current: Mild to strong
Fishing: Anglers might find in the Lower Susquehanna River largemouth, smallmouth, and striped bass, bluegill, pickerel, crappie, catfish, yellow and white perch
Season: Year-round
Fees or permits: Honor use fee at Port Deposit
Nearest city/town: Port Deposit and Perryville
Boats used: Sea kayaks and recreational boats on calm days
Organization: Cecil County Parks and Recreation
Contacts: None
Rest areas: Only at specified launch sites
Restaurant pullouts: None

Put-In/Takeout Information

Rock Run Park at Townsend's Point, 1 Rock Run Landing, Port Deposit, MD; GPS N39 36.781' / W076 07.564'

Port Deposit Marina Park, South Main Street and Bainbridge Road, Port Deposit MD; GPS N39 35.937' / W076 06.597'

Perryville Community Launch, North Roundhouse Drive, Perryville, MD; GPS N39 34.013' / W076 04.731'

Perryville VA Medical Center, Perry Point, MD; GPS N39 32.818' / W076 03.321'

Perryville Community Park, Marion Tapp Parkway, Perryville, MD; GPS N39 33.179' / W076 04.525'

Perryville ramp and Garrett Island

Overview

The paddling is on open water but hugging the shoreline is the best bet. The journey is broken into three sections.

The Paddle

Port Deposit to Perryville

Using the Port Deposit Marina Park ramp, paddle south along the coastline to Perryville's public ramp. This is open river travel, and like most rivers it can be smooth or choppy. With two public launch areas for anglers in good-size motorboats on both sides of the river, watch for choppy wake water on summer weekends. It's about a 1.5-hour paddle from town to town. The fun part of the trip is paddling around Garrett Island. This is a major undeveloped, environmentally protected, and forested island managed by the Blackwater National Wildlife Refuge. The island is off-limits to visitors except for a small area surrounding a sandy beach that is just across the channel from the Perryville Community ramp. If you add in going around the island, it's a comfortable 4-plus-hour round-trip paddle from town to town.

Perryville Community Launch to the Community Park at Mill Creek

Want a little more Perryville to paddle? Visit the Rodgers Tavern colonial museum

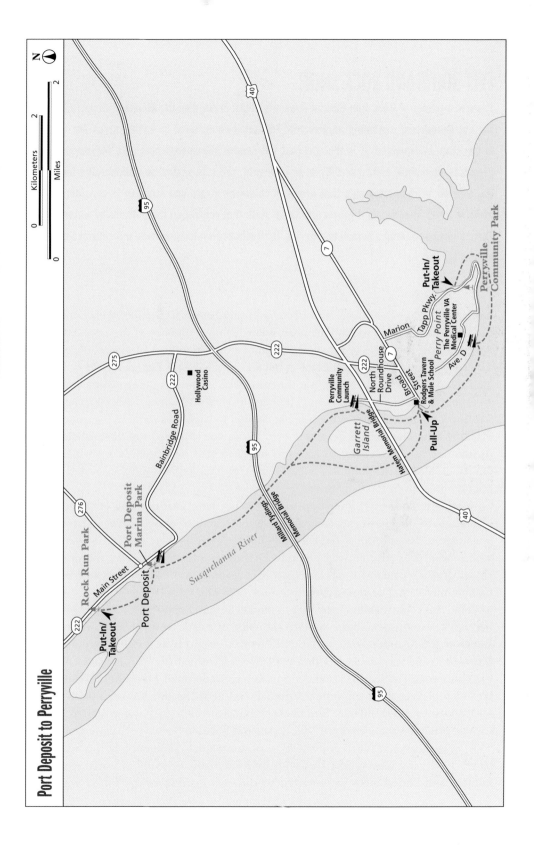

Port Deposit to Perryville

Kilometers
0   2

Miles
0   2

N

Rock Run Park

276

222

Put-In/
Takeout

Main Street

Port Deposit

Port Deposit
Marina Park

Bainbridge Road

222

275

Hollywood
Casino

222

95

95

40

Susquehanna River

Millard Tydings
Memorial Bridge

Garrett Island

Hatem Memorial Bridge

Perryville
Community Launch

North
Roundhouse
Drive

Broad Street

Pull-Up

Rodgers Tavern
& Mule School

222

222

7

Marion

40

95

7

Tapp Pkwy.

Perry Point

The Perryville VA
Medical Center

Ave. D

Put-In/
Takeout

Perryville
Community Park

FELT BOOTS AND ROCK SNOT!

There is a poster at Rock Run Park at Towson's Point, created by the Maryland Department of Natural Resources, reminding anglers that felt-soled shoes used in wading areas are illegal in the state of Maryland. It is thought that felt retains the microscopic alga *Didymosphenia geminata*, commonly known as Didymo or rock snot, and it is passed on while wading for fish. The Didymo, a freshwater alga that grows in coldwater rivers and streams, is considered an invasive water species, as it grows into large mats that remain on the bottoms of waterways. Though not considered a human health risk, it affects eco-system habitats and natural sources of food for fish.

during the summer with its waterfront pier and tie-up (0.5 mile), then continue paddling the coastline south. This open water is the confluence of the Susquehanna River and the Chesapeake Bay, which is sometimes smooth and sometimes choppy. The coast follows along the Veteran's Administration Medical Center and Perry Point Golf area. Look to the shoreline near the peninsula's endpoint to see a seating area and an unmarked public cement ramp. The ramp is well maintained with a locked gate arm and a grassy patch off to the side big enough to back up a minivan for launching a car-top boat. The water is deep here even during the lowest part of the tidal change. At low tide we recommend that boaters stop here and turn back. At high tide you can paddle around the point to the Perryville Community Park and the kayak launch site (1.5 miles from Rodgers Tavern).

Curiously enough, the medical base does not have guards at the entrance and seems to have a sparse worker and patient status. Dozens of empty houses and hospital buildings are found throughout the base. Look closely as there are "herds" of tame white-tailed deer roaming the grounds. Driving around the base, we found three closed driveways due to locks and gate arms leading into the adjoining Perryville Community Park. The closed gates drove my GPS unit crazy.

The Perryville Community Park includes Stump Point—the endpoint of the Perryville peninsula—and the western shoreline of Mill Creek. There is a dedicated launch area for car-top boats, and it's well marked with a launch sign. Ominously so too is the waterway marked with a park sign—it's called the "Susquehanna Flats." One almost has to see the extended sandbar to understand how the currents and silt buildup affect the environment, especially in the fall season. We saw hundreds of birds and at least five different bird flocks walking the inch-deep waterways. As far as the eye could see, the mouths of Mill Creek and Furnace Bay were shallow sandbars. This area of flats is a visual confirmation of the natural confluence of the Susquehanna River and Chesapeake Bay, with freshwater mixing with saltwater. Anglers, hunters, and birders alike are attracted to this area because of the varied wildlife.

The Community Park's kayak launch area is subject to the tides also, and when we visited in the fall at low tide, the shoreline was 30 yards from the cement landing. It's a comfortable 4-plus-hour round-trip paddle from Perryville Community Launch to the VA's unmarked boat ramp (a little longer if the tide is high); a boater also can visit the Community Park launch area (add 1 mile). At low tide, public facilities can be used by walking around the hospital's gate arm; it's 5 minutes to the Community Park's restrooms.

Perryville Community Park and Furnace Bay

The Conowingo Visitor Center directed me to a local professional guide who uses the Perryville Community Park as a frequent launch area for Furnace Bay and a small stream called Principio Creek for kayak tours in the spring and summer months. He recommended it as a sweet 2-plus-hour paddle in a semi-protected area in the summer season and at high tide. Kayaking Made EZ provides boats and equipment.

15 Bohemia and Scotchman Creeks

The Bohemia River, which becomes Bohemia Creek at the Route 213 bridge, is best known for the multitude of marinas found at the mouth in confluence with the Elk River. The creek is mild and has waterways to paddle.

County: Cecil County
Suggested launch sites:
   Bohemia Beach Park
   Hack's Point Marina
   Richmond's Marina
Suggested takeout sites: Same
Length and float time: 1.5 miles per hour on Great Bohemia Creek; 1 mile per hour on Scotchman Creek
   Great Bohemia Creek—3 miles one-way
   Scotchman Creek—1.5 miles one-way
Difficulty: Mild to choppy depending on season
Current: Mild

Fishing: Anglers might find in the Bohemia River largemouth bass, striped bass, bluegill, pickerel, crappie, catfish, yellow and white perch
Season: Year-round (but strongly recommend not on summer weekends)
Fees or permits: Launch fees at Hack's Point and Richmond's Marinas; none at Bohemia Beach Park
Nearest city/town: Chesapeake City
Boats used: Sea kayaks and recreational boats; paddleboards on Scotchman Creek
Organizations: None
Contacts: None
Rest areas: Multiple on shorelines
Restaurant pullouts: None

Put-In/Takeout Information

Bohemia Beach Park (north side of Route 213 bridge); GPS N39 27.813' / W075 52.114'

Hack's Point Marina, 1645 Glebe Rd., Earleville, MD 21919; (410) 275-9151; GPS N39 27.648' / W075 52.491'

Richmond's Marina, 1500 Glebe Rd., Earleville, MD 21919; (410) 275-2061; GPS N39 27.736' / W075 52.617'

Chessie Marine Sales (sales and rental of Hobie kayaks and paddleboards), 706 Augustine Herman Hwy. (Route 213), Elkton, MD 21921; (410) 620-2628

Overview

Great Bohemia Creek is wide with interesting horse farms along its banks. It's extremely popular for motorboat gatherings on summer weekends, so this is a recommended off-season paddle. Scotchman Creek is protected and has abundant wildlife that surprises paddlers during the spring mating season.

Access to Bohemia and Scotchman Creeks

The Paddle

The harbormaster in my hometown has been conducting an experiment, trying to charge kayakers and paddleboarders to also pay to use the city's boat ramps on an honor basis. He put up signs saying "There is no free lunch" and asking all boaters to put a fiver in the box. Bless his heart, but I'll use the adjoining beach if they hire another kid to sit in a chair and guilt me into paying a fee this summer. That being said, the best free place to launch in Cecil County at the mouth of the Bohemia Creek area is a dog beach. It's just across the Bohemia River bridge on the left—no sign, just a small six-car paved lot and a minor portage down a deer path to a medium strip of sandy beach with branches and washed-up logs (watch where you step). This is the year-round Bohemia Beach Park, and you will meet all kinds of people and dogs using the beach.

Adjoining the beachfront is a chain-link fence with a private property sign and a warning that there are two male bulls roaming this property, and smile, you are being filmed. I paddled up and down Great Bohemia Creek looking for the bulls, but maybe they found some other farmyard pleasures, as the land up and down the creek is devoted to farmland and horse farms. The El Dreco storm in 2011 uprooted many old-growth trees up and down the creek, which requires cautious navigation for car-top boaters who like to hug the shoreline. A nickname for the fallen trees by some guidebooks is "strainers," due to the long branches that seem to stretch out to snarl debris.

Bohemia and Scotchman Creeks

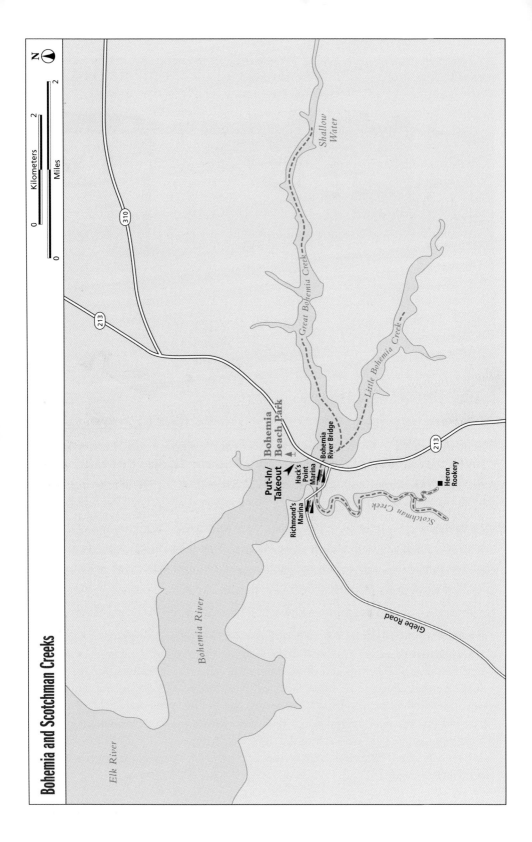

N

Kilometers

0   2

0   2

Miles

310

213

Elk River

Bohemia River

Great Bohemia Creek

Shallow Water

Little Bohemia Creek

Put-In/
Takeout

Bohemia Beach Park

Richmond's Marina

Hack's Point Marina

Bohemia River Bridge

213

Scotchman Creek

Heron Rookery

Globe Road

The creek is about 3 paddle-able miles long with another mile being shallow mudflats. The creek's coves have sea grass and are not navigable. The larger creek mouth joins with Little Bohemia Creek next door, which maps show as 2-plus miles, but locals say there is too much sea grass and shallow waters for a good paddle. During the summer Bohemia Creek's mouth is jammed with yachts and motorboats anchored and looking to cluster party all weekend long. Their Jet Skis tear up the water, and the wakes are rough to paddle. On Monday it's like visiting a different place. Scotchman Creek is skinny and too shallow for the Jet Ski folk, which is why it's still a wonderful wildlife preserve.

There are two marinas, Hack's and Richmond's, with ramps that are kayak friendly (fee to launch), both at Scotchman Creek's mouth. Maps show the main waterway only a mile long with a fork, but it seemed to go on much longer. The branch to the west is wider and pleasant. It comes to a stop at a downed tree blocking the way. Locals have made a deer path to portage around it. The branch to the east is where to go to explore wildlife firsthand. We encountered a rookery for gray herons that was as noisy as a Florida retirement center, with every bird clabbering louder than the other about their grandkids.

THUMP THUMP–MATING CARP

Paddling to the very headwaters of Scotchman Creek where the vegetation grows high, we found a school of extra-large carp swimming in circles stirring up the mud and darting between the grass. We could not put in a paddle without being knocked about. Then the carp started to deliberately swim into our boats. It scared us silly at first until we learned about the carp from a local naturalist watching from the bank. He burst into laughter at our momentary plight and congratulated us on witnessing a unique wildlife rite. It turns out the carp were mating, and the naturalist informed us that the females bang themselves against hard objects to loosen their eggs. Apparently it's becoming a common phenomenon for rangers and professional fishermen to see, but unfortunately, the mating rites are uprooting the protective shoreline grass. With the increase of the carp population in Maryland's rivers and creeks, this issue is now being addressed by car-top boater-hunters with bows and arrows blessed by Maryland's Department of Natural Resources.

Charles County

Joyce Simpson said she is proud of her Charles County heritage. "I am related to Thomas Greene, second provincial governor of Maryland, and also to the Bean family. They were the ones Mattawoman–Beantown Road was named for. Beantown was a small village that lay just south of the newly built train station. It was named Bean Station for a short time," she said. "In 1850, it was renamed Waldorf. Waldorf is a German word meaning 'village in the forest.' My other grandparents owned Trotter's Hotel on Route 5 South, so I've seen a lot of changes through the years and it seems to me that Waldorf is at a saturation point. I was at the 300th celebration ceremony at the Port Tobacco Courthouse when they buried a time capsule." Simpson added, "I turned to my friend and told her I'd be around for the 350th, and here I am."

Wading anglers in Wicomico River (paddle 16)

16 Allens Fresh Run

Formerly known as Zekiah Swamp Natural Environment Area, Allen's Fresh Natural Area comprises more than 250 acres owned by the state and managed by the Maryland Park Service. There are no signs around the bridge area indicating any management oversight at all. The Charles County Parks and Recreation and the Maryland Park Service out of Sweden Point does keep tabs on the location and gives advice. Bring a fishing rod and footwear for mud.

County: Charles County
Suggested launch site: Route 234 bridge (Budds Creek Road)
Suggested takeout site: Same
Length and float time: 1 mile per hour in the creeks; 2 miles per hour with the current going south; maybe 1.5 miles per hour against the wind going north
Difficulty: Mild to moderate
Current: Moderate due to wind and tide changes

Fishing: Anglers might find smallmouth, largemouth, spotted, white, and striped bass; crappie, walleye, catfish, trout
Season: Year-round, though headwaters do freeze to ice in winter
Fees or permits: None
Nearest city/town: La Plata
Boats used: Fishing kayaks and recreational kayaks
Organizations: None
Contacts: None
Rest areas: None
Restaurant pullouts: None

Put-In/Takeout Information

Allens Fresh Run, 10800 Budds Creek Rd. (Route 234), La Plata; GPS N38 24.915' / W076 56.349' (East side of road near bridge, look for colored tags on branches; unknown future of current dirt road used to drive kayaks to water's edge near bridge. West side of road has a paved apron with bushes hiding a path for portaging boats to water access.)

Overview

There are two unique Wicomico Rivers in Maryland: the Wicomico body of water on the eastern shore that divides Wicomico and Worcester Counties, and the Wicomico River that has its headwaters in Charles County. The eastern shore Wicomico River is 25 miles long and is a tributary of the Chesapeake Bay. The Charles County Wicomico River is about 13 miles long and is a tidal tributary of the Potomac River.

Wicomico derives from the words wicko mekee. In Native American the word means "a place where houses are built," such as the Indian towns along the shorelines that Captain John Smith referred to in his maps and journals. This adventure

Charles County was made for paddlers!

is on the Wicomico River that empties into the Potomac River at Cobb Island and St. Margaret's Island.

The Paddle

The guidance given to us by a park ranger was that both sides of the bridge could be used for access to the water. The slow-moving tidal waters combine with perfect food and shelter for yellow perch, which are abundant; the fish thrive and are an angler's night dreams. We were the only recreational kayakers and the only folks without fishing poles on the water.

The tidal waters are doable at low levels, but not recommended. Walking up and down the roadway looking for access, we found a short scramble down a well-worn wooded bank to a shallow branch of water that looked a bit stagnant. We held our breath, hoping to make it over one of the many washed-pebble sandbars that needed an inch or two more of water to be paddled over at low tide. Paddlers had left colored marking tape on the limbs of bushes to mark the way. Lots of mud, so maybe bring some paper towels just in case.

We paddled around to where the anglers were casting, and, after a few false starts around the sandbars, we did find the river pathway. We also found a nice shoreline with a deer path near the bridge that required more portaging but no mud. Lots of quiet laughter from the fishing pole crowd. Once we shook a few hands, we found

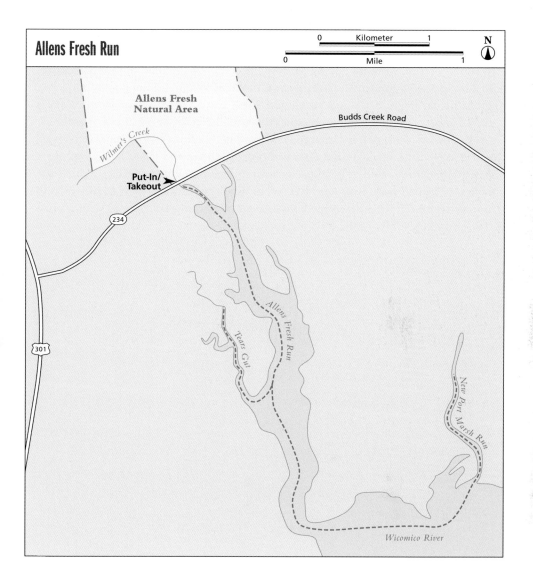

out that normally there is a little dirt road a bit farther east off Budds Creek Road, where boaters could drive to the water's edge with a kayak, but no one has been able to use the road for quite a while, as construction crews had closed it off with a 100-foot continuous dug-in chain fence. Apparently our ranger had not visited the site in a while.

The ADC map shows the Wicomico River turning into a narrow creek going north. More than one person recommended this narrow water trail for sport and recreation. However, after doing overhead photo research, the stream looks like it goes only 0.5 mile before becoming part of the woods rather than the 2 miles of heaven described by other kayakers. Maybe at high tide? Instead we paddled south into the river now nicknamed Allen's Fresh Run The marsh makes the shorelines seem flatter and the river wider than the maps indicate. With a strong wind promised in the weather forecast, we were hoping for some paddling protection but found ourselves in a bit of a wind tunnel. The small Tears Gut Creek is only 1.5 miles away and looks great for exploring coves and backwater marsh areas. The Newport Marsh Run is only 3 miles south and has a wide waterway with 1.5 miles of possible navigation.

Late in the afternoon we tried the now-empty fisherman's shoreline coming back and portaged the boats on the deer path over potholes and fallen logs. Look for a paved apron wide enough for three cars on the west side of the bridge; behind the bushes is a good path. Everyone seemed to have caught a fish or two, and a kayak fisherman we followed down the bank access was packing up and said with a smile that he'd caught "fifty of the little fellers."

17 Friendship Farm Park

The 13-mile-long creek, the Nanjemoy, is named after a Native American tribe. It is one of many navigable tidal creeks out of the Potomac River. Environmentalists say the Nanjemoy Creek area has the largest rookery in the Atlantic shores area.

County: Charles County
Suggested launch site: Friendship Farm Park
Suggested takeout site: Same
Length and float time: 4 miles round-trip; 1 mile per hour (medium paddle)
Difficulty: Mild to rough in single adventure
Current: Strong
Fishing: Angles might find catfish, largemouth bass

Season: Year-round
Fees or permits: None
Nearest city/town: La Plata
Boats used: Sea kayaks and recreational boats; caution with paddleboards
Organizations: None
Contacts: None
Rest areas: Private property ramps
Restaurant pullouts: None

Put-In/Takeout Information

Friendship Farm Park, 4715 Friendship Landing Rd., Nanjemoy, MD; GPS N38 27.242' / W077 09.036'

Overview

This waterway is a branch of Nanjemoy Creek. As the crow flies, the navigable length on the ADC map is 3 miles, but 2 miles is listed on tourist maps from Charles County and the Maryland Department of Natural Resources (DNR). This winding creek is sparsely developed, with forests on one side and sea grass on the other. It's doable in low tides but avoid the sea grass side of the creek, as the shoreline can be too shallow.

The Paddle

In April 2014 the Friendship Farm Park boat ramp was opened again after being modeled and updated. The two cement ramps and fishing pier look new and refreshed, although the separate kayak ramp remains the same. A few motorboats with anglers were the first to know and blasted their way down the larger portion of the creek to the Potomac River for some bigger fish to catch. The smaller branch of Nanjemoy Creek is directly to the side of the ramp. We encountered only a handful of anglers in skiffs, as water levels can drop as much as 24-plus inches between tides.

Our first encounter with the variable water levels was around the first bend. We paddled into a wide basin only to immediately find ourselves paddling in mudflats. We skirted the sea grass area and headed for the shoreline with houses and piers. The

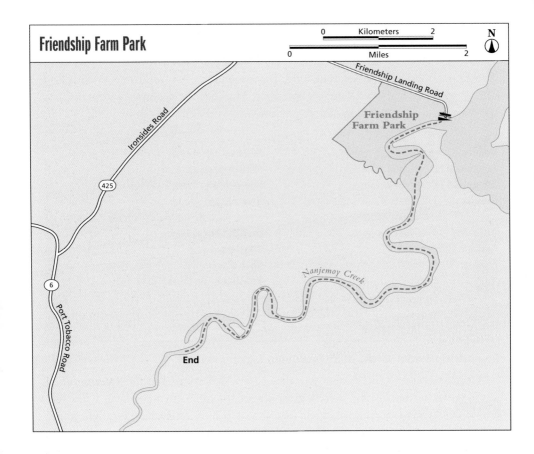

Friendship Landing Road

Ironsides Road

425

6

Port Tobacco Road

Friendship Farm Park

Nanjemoy Creek

End

water dropped again to 2 to 3 feet. We found the same throughout the journey. Our ADC and Bing maps showed the creek widening enough for a 3-mile paddle. The tourist maps made in conjunction with Charles County and the DNR showed a place to turn around about 2 miles from the launch.

The best part of the journey for us was the variety of wildlife and how timid they were to visitors. We recommend a long-range camera lens to capture images as they skedaddle at first glimpse of any boats. Large turtles sunning themselves on downed tree branches are visible in the morning and afternoon but seem to disappear in the evening. Around 4 to 5 o'clock is feeding time, and birds of all types come out to catch the evening updrafts and dive for fish. Gray herons are particularly abundant when the tide is low because their prey fish are easier to see and catch.

We normally paddle a leisurely 1 mile per hour, so about 2 hours in we checked the maps, and sure enough, we were at the turnaround basin indicated on the tourism maps. The next section of waterway seemed to get considerably narrower—but not necessarily as a warning not to explore farther. More adventurous boaters with a longer day will want to continue.

Wildlife is abundant and "friendly" here!

Going southwest, the current was very strong in sections and the breeze pushed us forward. The weather called for a gusty day of 10- to 25-mile-per-hour winds. We hoped the Nanjemoy Creek branch would be more of a protected area. We found two basin areas that, due to their wide and open geography, turned into wind tunnels. Be sure to leave extra time (and snacks and energy drinks) for the return trip. Rest breaks are only found by pulling up onto ramps built by private homeowners. The mudflats are not just silt buildup but also clumps of moss, which is not recommended for pull-ups (without getting stuck).

In one gusty section a "kind" motorboat skiff slowed down and inquired if we were ok and just how crazy were we? We waved back with a smile and the skiff sped off. At the very next bend in the creek the waterway again turned calm, and the 15 minutes of power paddling seemed to disappear from memory.

The tide was running low when we returned to the boat ramp, so I checked out the kayak ramp. Kayak ramps are based on a system of rollers and handlebars. My fishing kayak is 12 feet long and weighs 75 pounds without the extra equipment. Even after a long day's paddle, I usually can just paddle hard to get a good run on the rollers, then grab the handlebars on both sides to pull myself up in seconds in a smooth manner. Here, my boat never lined up straight on the rollers, and after three tries I was worn out from the effort. My muse was chuckling all the while. Perhaps this kayak ramp will work for you, but it did not for me.

18 Mallows Bay

This is a quiet paddle for singles or groups. Bring a picnic as it's not a full day of paddling. Some folks actually claim this is the best location they have ever paddled.

County: Charles County
Suggested launch site: Mallows Bay Public Ramp
Suggested takeout site: Same
Length and float time: Bay is only 0.75 mile long, but this is an extra-slow 2-hour exploration paddle
Difficulty: Easy
Current: None
Fishing: The day we visited all the anglers were catching monster catfish!

Season: Year-round
Fees or permits: None
Nearest city/town: La Plata
Boats used: Recreational boats and paddleboards
Organization: Charles County Parks and Recreation
Contacts: None
Rest areas: Multiple shoreline pull-ups
Restaurant pullouts: None

Put-In/Takeout Information

Mallows Bay Public Ramp, 1440 Wilson Landing Rd., Nanjemoy, MD 20662; GPS N38 28.137' / W077 15.822'

Overview

In 2010 Charles County, in coordination with the Maryland Department of Natural Resources (DNR), built this launch area specifically for canoes and kayaks to enjoy and to explore the Mallows Bay cove area. There is one cement ramp and one special kayak roller launch on the shoreline.

The Paddle

Mallows Bay is a historians' delight. If you have ever seen a grassy battlefield and felt great delight in viewing where history was made, then this is a trip you cannot afford to miss. But if you are looking for a high-energy adventure, or to see colorful bits of history, then you might be disappointed. From an overhead aerial view, the remains of ships sunken below the water's surface appear intriguing. To paddle around murky water only to see a couple of rusty beached ships falls short of expectations. The caretaker/weekend ranger hired by Charles County to meet and greet folks gave us a few pointers for our next visit.

- Come at low tide. The lower water level allows paddlers to see the sunken boat shapes better.

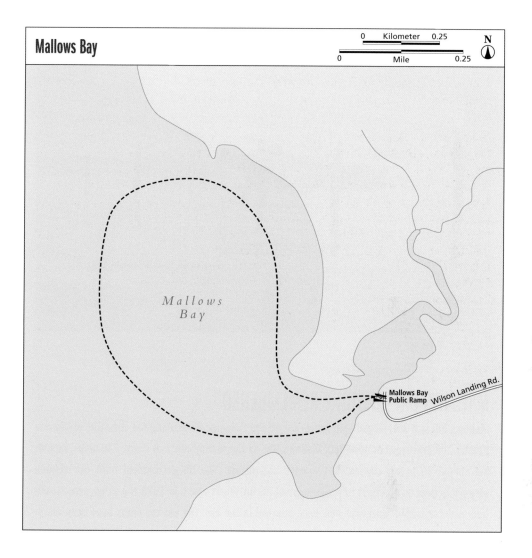

- Do not come after a hard rain or a storm. The stirred-up river and bay water carry soil or clay particles that will obscure your viewing.

- Explore the entire bay and shoreline, as there is no official paddling route. The overhead photos show ships and smaller boats together and apart, but all close to the shoreline.

- Remember that you are visiting history with its remains of wooden and metal ships, and not a marina of broken-down yachts. (The ranger is correct. I have researched and seen those marinas of old yachts, they are good substitutes for the mobile home trailers that are no longer welcome in Maryland.)

Hulk of a historic ship

MALLOWS BAY—HISTORY REMEMBERED

Mallows Bay is a submerged ship graveyard off the Potomac River along the coastline of Charles County. The graveyard archive lists Mallows Bay as the resting place of about 230 ships, including almost 90 poorly constructed wooden steamships. The US government built the wooden steamship fleet as an effort to preserve steel during World War I. In 1925 the ships were classified as deteriorated "surplus," and were interred in the bay. The sunken ships have been disregarded for fifty years. More were added later.

Due to recent interest, naval historians have archived them. Arial photos show that only a handful have survived and simply show as shadows. But a secondary benefit has been an underwater reef that supports the eco system for a growing aquatic community.

In 2010 Charles County, in conjunction with Maryland's DNR, took over a private club's access area and constructed a cement boat ramp and small pier to provide wider public recreational access to the Potomac River at Mallows Bay. Charles County advertises an unmarked paddling trail loop, calling it Mallows Bay Park and "salvage basin." The marketing has worked, as the location is a popular destination for canoes and kayaks to paddle among the ruins, although there is nothing to see but the shells of a couple of rusty ships—and a history remembered.

- Bring an overhead photocopy of where the sunken ships are located. Impress your paddling partner with your powers of observation!

Anglers will find themselves in heaven no matter what condition the water is in, as carp, sometimes monster size, like Mallows Bay as a feeding grounds because the ships are a perfect place for the seafood chain to flourish.

19 The Port Tobacco River

Maybe because the river was wide and the scenery was of undeveloped countryside, the paddle was quicker though no less enjoyable. This is a 3.5-mile adventure we did in a 4.5-hour day including visiting and walking around. If you start after lunch and come back to the Port Tobacco Marina on summer weekends, you just might catch the band playing on the docks during happy hour. An excellent cheap date, married or not!

County: Charles County
Suggested launch sites:
    Port Tobacco Restaurant & Marina
    Chapel Point State Park
    Goose Bay Marina
Suggested takeout sites: Same
Length and float time: 1.5 miles per hour
(medium paddle)
    Port Tobacco Marina to Chapel Point—2
        hours
    Chapel Point to Goose Bay Marina—1.5
        hours
Difficulty: Mild with some chop in summertime
Current: Mild

Fishing: Anglers might find largemouth and smallmouth bass, bluegill, pickerel, crappie, catfish, yellow and white perch, carp
Season: Year-round
Fees or permits: Goose Bay Marina and Port Tobacco Marina may charge launch fees
Nearest city/town: Port Tobacco City
Boats used: Recreational boats; paddleboards not recommended
Organization: Charles County Parks and Recreation
Contacts: None
Rest areas: Multiple along shorelines
Restaurant pullouts: Family restaurant at Port Tobacco Marina

Put-In/Takeout Information

Port Tobacco Restaurant & Marina, 7610 Shirley Blvd., Port Tobacco, MD; (301) 870-3133; GPS N38 29.818' / W077 01.574'

Chapel Point State Park, Chapel Point Road, Port Tobacco, MD; (301) 743-7613; GPS N38 28.240' / W077 01.884'

Goose Bay Marina, 9365 Goose Bay Ln., Welcome, MD; (301) 932-0885; GPS N38 27.205' / W077 03.172'

Overview

In 1685 Port Tobacco was a naval port of entry for the British Crown. Port Tobacco remained a major shipping port through the end of the American Revolutionary War, when its fortune changed. Today the area is sparsely developed with agriculture playing the major role. Like many rural state parks, fishing and hunting are the primary activities at Chapel Point State Park. Trailer parks have been disbanded and are no longer an active part of the residential equation, but RV camping resorts have

Chapel Point State Park, sandy shoreline

taken their place, and two locations on this boating loop typify that growing need and the results.

The Paddle

The headwaters of the Port Tobacco River are shallow, with mudflats even at high tide. Earlier maps show that the river goes clear to the town of Port Tobacco, but that is no longer feasible. The county and state put together a small paddling guide that names Port Tobacco Marina as part of that loop. The marina does have a launch fee, but it's usually waived for car-top boats in the off-season. There's also a good family seafood restaurant with seasonal live dockside entertainment on weekends.

We explored the headwaters around the marina, but did not get too far. What caught our attention was the adjoining RV campground. All the spaces were privately owned, and the RVs were parked in a semi-permanent manner, as Maryland law requires. For $30,000 to $40,000, the owner gets a small waterfront parcel with sewer, water, and electricity for their RV. The owners installed piers for their small motorboats and car-tops, and now have a country-style recreational second home. In researching campsites in Maryland that were on the water, we found fewer sites with "primitive tent" availability and more camping locations accommodating this semi-year-round business model.

The paddle south on the river can be smooth or choppy depending on the seasonal weather and the amount of motorboat traffic. It's a 2-mile paddle to the dirt

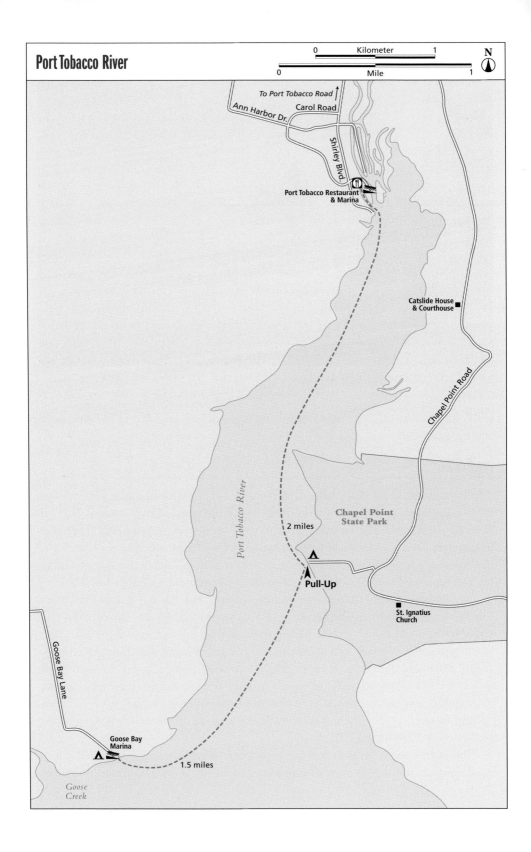

Port Tobacco River

0   Kilometer   1

0   Mile   1

N

To Port Tobacco Road

Ann Harbor Dr.

Carol Road

Shirley Blvd.

Port Tobacco Restaurant
& Marina

Catslide House
& Courthouse

Chapel Point Road

Port Tobacco River

Chapel Point
State Park

2 miles

Pull-Up

St. Ignatius
Church

Goose Bay Lane

Goose Bay
Marina

1.5 miles

Goose
Creek

road shoreline beach launch area at Chapel Point State Park. The park specializes in outdoor activity. Fishing on the shoreline is available year-round, but a tidal water license is required. Hunting is permitted in the 600-acre state park. The area provides suitable habitat for quail, squirrels, doves, rabbits, white-tailed deer, wild turkeys, and waterfowl. Chapel Point has a paddle-in campsite available seasonally and by permit only. The historic St. Ignatius Church, founded in 1641, is one of the oldest Catholic parishes in continuous service in the United States. The church is located adjacent to state park property, although on maps it's usually included in the shaded park area. As you paddle by the park, the church bells peel out loud and clear on the waterfront, and the church building stands out on the hillside.

Goose Bay Marina is only another 1.5 miles south. Docks and two cement boat ramps that are busy servicing motorboats morning to night, and RV campers nestled shoulder to shoulder, seem to be the best characterization of this happy place. This marina is also on the county/state paddling loop. The convenience store has grab-and-go supplies for last-minute shoppers. Another difference between the two marinas is the admittance of some tent campers and the closeness to the Potomac River for fishing boats.

When we arrived, lots of children were running around and they all stopped to stare at our orange- and reddish-colored kayaks as we pulled up. "Are they party boats?" one brave little girl asked. "They seem to have a fun look!" We couldn't help but smile and answered that she was correct—they are fun to party with.

Dorchester County

Dorchester County is the largest county in Maryland, with 983 square miles. The Dorchester County shoreline landscape is primarily salt marshes and tidal streams, all good kayaking waterways—especially with the county being 56 percent land and 44 percent water! Geographically the county has the Choptank River to the north, Talbot County to the northwest, Caroline County to the northeast, Wicomico County and River to the southeast, Delaware to the east and the Chesapeake Bay to the west. The county's marketing slogan is that Dorchester is "The Heart of Chesapeake Country."

Doesn't everyone know our crabs are works of art? It's worth a side trip to the famous Suicide Bridge Restaurant and Marina, an excellent family restaurant.

20 Cambridge–Choptank River

This city waterfront route encompasses a kayak-friendly hotel, a museum, a city fishing pier, a visitor center, a white sand beach, four public boat ramps, a long walking pier, a paddle downtown, historical locations, a grassy park with benches—and a bonus route to see an environmental lab in Cambridge that is working to save the oysters in the Chesapeake Bay.

County: Dorchester County
Suggested launch sites:
    Dorchester Sailwinds Visitor Center and Park
    Franklin Street Public Launch
    Trenton Street Public Launch
    Great Marsh Point Park
Suggested takeout sites: Same
Length and float time: 1.5 miles per hour (medium paddle)
    Hyatt Regency Hotel to the Great Marsh Point Park—3 miles one-way
    Hyatt Regency to Historical Society Museum—0.5 mile
    Museum to Sailwinds Visitor Center and Park—1 mile
    Franklin Street Public Launch to downtown Trenton Street Public Launch—0.5 mile
    Trenton Street Public Launch to Great Marsh Point Park—1 mile

Great Marsh Point Park to Horn Point Environmental Lab—4 miles
Difficulty: Choppy (Choptank River is wide, deep, and subject to winds and motorboat wakes)
Current: Mild on non-windy days
Fishing: Anglers might find in the Choptank River bluefish, croaker, flounder, spot
Season: Year-round
Fees or permits: None
Nearest city/town: Cambridge
Boats used: Sea kayaks or sit-in recreational boats
Organization: Dorchester County Recreation and Parks
Contacts: None
Rest areas: Multiple throughout trail
Restaurant pullouts: Hyatt Regency Hotel

Put-In/Takeout Information

Blackwater Paddle and Pedal (bikes and kayak rentals and tours)
Blackwater Refuge at 2524 Key Wallace Dr., Cambridge MD
Hyatt Regency Hotel at 100 Heron Blvd., Cambridge, MD
Dorchester Sailwinds Visitor Center and Park, 2 Rose Hill Place, Cambridge, MD; (410) 228-1000; GPS N38 34.326' / W076 03.870'
Franklin Street Public Launch, end of Franklin Street, Cambridge, MD; GPS N38 34.401' / W076 04.041'
Trenton Street Public Launch, Trenton Street, Cambridge, MD; GPS N38 34.119' / W076 04.354'
Great Marsh Point Park, end of Somerset Avenue, Cambridge, MD; GPS N38 35.097' / W076 04.676'

A family waterfront museum, the La Grange, with unique treasures

Overview

Dorchester County has many waterways to explore, but the Cambridge City–Choptank River route helps the veteran as well as the beginner paddler discover the city's proud current and historical characteristics. The Dorchester Sailwinds Visitor Center and Park, with its very visible artist rendering of a gigantic white sail, is one of the first welcoming signs from Cambridge to its guests. The center has information about the city's history and where to visit. Two locations well worth checking out are the Hyatt Hotel on the waterfront and the LaGrange Museum. Both are on the suggested Cambridge paddling routes.

The Paddle

Cambridge

This paddling route has lots of amenities to meet boaters' needs. The Dorchester Sailwinds Visitor Center and Park is the center of activity. Launching from the park's white sand beach cove to the east, boaters pass under Route 50 Memorial Bridge and immediately see the southern half of a discontinued bridge that has been made into a county fishing pier. The northern half is a dedicated state park fishing pier. As you pass by the residential shoreline, private piers are visible but not homes. The county built a public road through the neighborhood, but the original landowners retained the riparian rights and the shoreline remains private. At the end of the neighborhood is

Cambridge–Choptank River

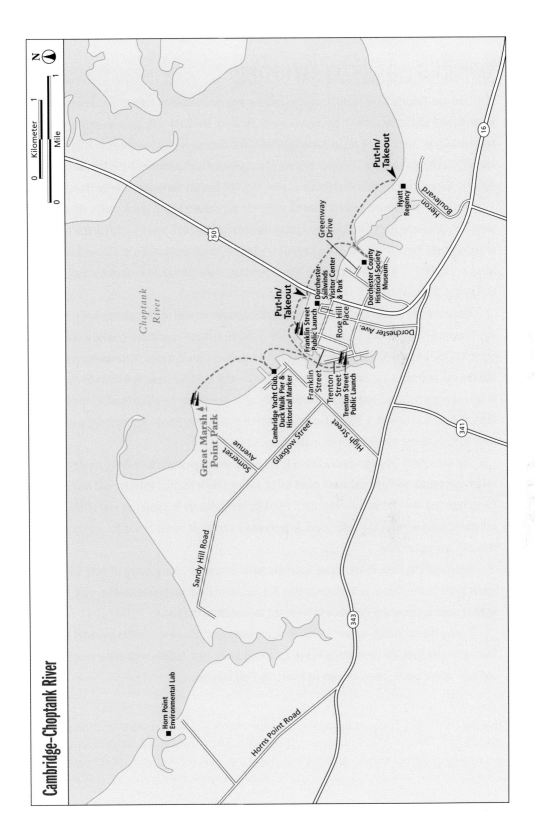

SAVING THE CHESAPEAKE BAY OYSTERS

Maryland and Virginia have been at odds in politics and environmental remediation issues even when the end goal is the same. In the case of oyster recovery, the State of Virginia recently released some promising numbers on oyster harvesting from the Chesapeake Bay. In the glory days of the late 1950s, Virginia harvested 4 million bushels of oysters. That total bottomed out in the mid-1990s with 17,600 bushels. In 2013 Virginia tallied over 405,000 bushels harvested from its shorelines.

Virginia's government appropriated $2 million to purchase 1 billion oyster shells, the equivalent of 4,000 dump trucks worth, to be spread throughout Virginia's rivers so that oyster larvae, or spats, could find a home and grow. Virginia is adamant about aquaculture and farms 100,000 acres of the state's water bottoms. The state then leases the area to fishermen for controlled harvesting. Virginia rotates its harvesting areas every two years.

Maryland also has an oyster recovery plan that focuses on wild oyster seeding and harvesting. The oyster tally in 2013 for Maryland was 340,000 bushels—triple the previous season—according to the Department of Natural Resources. Baby oysters grown in state-sponsored labs like the one in Dorchester County are fertilized in the wild and take about two years to develop. Maryland protects these beds by prohibiting fishing or harvesting on a fourth of its reefs with fines and years in prison. A 2011 study that focused only on Maryland recommended a drastic step: halt the oyster harvest entirely in the state.

The Horn Point Environmental Lab is a living classroom experience for young and old to see oyster cultivation up-close and learn more about saving this important industry and seafood in Cambridge and the Chesapeake Bay. Horn Point Oyster Hatchery is known as one of the largest oyster hatcheries on the East Coast. It produces a variety of oyster larvae for use in oyster research and restoration.

Efforts at the Horn Point Oyster Hatchery have resulted in the seeding of over 1 billion oyster spats to the waters of the Chesapeake Bay. Scientists and environmentalists work in the hope of slowing the oyster decline and restoring the health of the bay.

During the spawning season, March through September, the center offers weekday tours. Touring groups have the opportunity to see a working production facility, with oysters spawning and baby oyster larvae. Tours for kids last thirty to sixty minutes.

Shoal Creek, which allows boaters to visit the Historical Society Museum (entrance fee), which has a pier and shoreline pull-up area. The museum has an excellent collection of waterman tools, and a good history of Cambridge and local businesses that have come and gone. Don't miss the Native American dugout canoe, as it is an excellent, well-preserved, handcrafted work of art. Out of Shoal Creek and to the right is the Hyatt Regency Chesapeake Bay Resort. The hotel has contracted with a boat rental company to supply its guests with paddleboards and kayaks. Pull out onto the low-level piers or sandy beaches to purchase lunch in the grill or the snack bar at the marina.

To the west of Sailwinds Park are the Franklin Street public ramps. A little hard to find, they are located behind Dorchester General Hospital. The park ramps are low and wide with plenty of parking. Paddle around the point and left into a protected creek in the heart of the city. On the left is the Trenton Street public boat ramp for a rest stop if needed. Go back to the Choptank River; at the mouth of the creek to the left is the Historical Waterfront Park, which is one of the Harriet Tubman Trail designated areas and where slaves were once marketed. The long walking pier that runs parallel to the park and bulkhead is called the "Cambridge Duck Walk." From the Duck Walk to Great Marsh Point Park is 0.5 mile. The park has green grass, park benches, large cement boat ramps, and a tiny shoreline beach for car-top boats to launch from.

Horn Point

From Great Marsh Point Park to the Horn Point Environmental Lab is a 4-mile paddle; add another mile if you explore Jenkins Creek. The Horn Point location is part of the University of Maryland Environment Studies program. This is not a launch site, but there's lots of beach and possibly a cement incline/ramp for their working boats available. Boaters can make an appointment for a tour and see a hands-on Maryland success story for helping save the Chesapeake Bay oysters.

Frederick County

Frederick County is in the northern region of Maryland, bordering the southern part of Pennsylvania and the northeastern border of Virginia. The government seat of Frederick County is the city of Frederick, and just minutes to its north is the Catoctin Mountains. The Potomac River flows through the county's southern border and travels west from the Monocacy River 12 miles to the city of Brunswick.

The Monocacy Aqueduct is the C&O Canal's most famous icon, which is at the mouth of the Monocacy River where it flows into the Potomac River (paddle 21).

21 Monocacy River

There are ten access waypoints to the Monocacy River, described southward as the river flows; boaters can decide where to start and how long to paddle.

County: Frederick County
Suggested launch sites:
  Millers Bridge—Route 77
  LeGore Bridge
  Creagerstown Bridge Park
  Devilbiss Bridge
  Riverside Center Public Ramp
  Pinecliff Park
  Monocacy National Battlefield Waterway—
    Gambrill Mill Access
  Buckeystown Community Park
  Monocacy River NRMA
  Monocacy Aqueduct
Suggested takeout sites: Same
Length and float time: 42 miles; 2 miles per hour with current (fast paddle)
Difficulty: Mild to difficult
Current: Mild to strong depending on parts of river

Fishing: Anglers might find in the Monocacy River carp, catfish, crappie, largemouth and smallmouth bass, panfish, suckers, trout
Season: The Monocacy is usually runnable in the spring and early summer up to mid-July, and from late fall through winter unless extreme drought conditions exist. Water levels should read at least 19 inches minimum to kayak safely.
Fees or permits: None
Nearest city/town: Frederick
Boats used: Long sea kayaks would not be useful in tight-turn whitewater areas
Organization: Frederick County Parks and Recreation
Contacts: None
Rest areas: Multiple shoreline pullouts
Restaurant pullouts: None

Put-In/Takeout Information

Millers Bridge—Route 77, 10700 Rocky Ridge Rd., Woodsboro; GPS N39 36.264' / W077 17.669'

LeGore Bridge, LeGore Bridge Road, Woodsboro; GPS N39 34.818' / W077 18.816'

Creagerstown Bridge Park, 12014 Penterra Manor Ln., Thurmont, MD; GPS N39 33.835' / W077 21.098'

Devilbiss Bridge, Devilbiss Bridge Road, Walkersville, MD; GPS N39 30.444' / W077 22.654'

Riverside Center Public Ramp, 1801 Monocacy Blvd., Frederick, MD; GPS N39 26.621' / W077 22.974'

Pinecliff Park, 8350 Pinecliff Park Rd., Frederick, MD; GPS N39 23.353' / W077 22.715'

Monocacy National Battlefield Waterway—Gambrill Mill Access, Gambrill Mill, Frederick, MD; GPS N39 22.171' / W077 23.282'

Buckeystown Community Park, 7221 Michaels Mill Rd., Buckeystown, MD; GPS N39 19.628' / W077 24.950'

Water levels on the Monocacy River change seasonally.

Monocacy River NRMA, Route 28 and Park Mills Road, south of Frederick, MD; GPS N39 14.603' / W077 26.343'

Monocacy Aqueduct, mouth of Monocacy Road, Dickerson, MD; GPS N39 13.471' / W077 26.998'

Overview

The Monocacy Water Trail is a paddle and exploration of the lower 42 miles of the river from Millers Bridge at Route 77 to the Potomac River. It is not an adventure to be done in a single day. The water levels change drastically throughout the year. Veteran paddlers say the Monocacy is runnable during the spring and early summer, then again in the late fall through winter. The water levels are also closely tied to weather conditions. Floodwaters and extreme droughts are common. Water levels should read at least 19 inches minimum for boating safely.

That being said, the peculiar character of the river should be discussed. The first thing I learned on my first visit is that the Monocacy River flows downhill. Just because the water levels in one part of the river are so shallow it barely covers your feet does not mean that the mouth of the river near the Potomac River could not be paddled and explored going upriver to the next access point. The width and depth of the waterway also is similar to a navigable inland creek, with rocky bottoms, downed trees, and pile-ups of branches caught in midstream boulders. Year-round the river has anglers casting and youngsters splashing.

The Chesapeake Bay Gateways Network is a major organization that publishes maps and brochures about waterways throughout Maryland. Their map of the Monocacy uses the boat-on-a-trailer icon for all access waypoints, whether they are ramp or shoreline launches. Also, the icons are placed in general areas and without specific addresses or GPS coordinates and should *not* be used for finding launch sites by boaters. Specific site descriptions follow.

The Paddle

The first northernmost access location used by most organizations is Millers Bridge on Route 77. There is no site management, no identification signs, and no facilities. There is room for three cars on the street parking area and a short portage through a wooded area on a deer path. The shoreline launch area has massive tree roots and gravel. The water level can be very low, as it is the farthest point from the Potomac River.

The second location is the LeGore Bridge site off LeGore Bridge Road. Again, there is no site management and no identification signs. I parked at the top of the dirt road, at first not knowing what to expect. It turns out the dirt road is wide enough for one car to drive up or down its length and the drive is not too long. At the bottom is a semi-cleared area with no facilities. Kids looking to smoke and drink a beer where mom and dad won't hassle them are frequent guests. The fishing is not very good here, I am told; there are boulders in the river, and the rocky shoreline requires some fancy footwork to portage a boat to the water. It's great flat land to pitch a tent for a weekend paddle trip—just know that the locals will be visiting at all hours.

Creagerstown Bridge Park, managed by Frederick County Parks and Recreation, is a quiet little public park with a playground for kids, a small paved area for parking, and a small cement boat ramp. The launch is only for car-top boats, and the water level can be shin deep with river gravel shorelines. The site is found on the Maryland Department of Natural Resources (DNR) website for boat launches.

The Devilbiss Bridge access (also on the DNR website) is labeled incorrectly as having a boat ramp. There is a small paved parking area managed by Frederick County Parks and Recreation, but no facilities. Paddling is allowed March to October with launching by permit only November through February. The shoreline has small Class I rapids to the left of the launch area—with small rocks and boulders year-round. Older pictures show a wide gravel path to the shoreline, a gentle incline but medium portage for car-top boats. We suggest a machete just to make the walking path wide enough to walk on.

Biggs Ford Road and Bridge is not a legal access area, but privately owned property with a swinging locked fence at the top of the road. It's noted on maps due to a cement barrier in the middle of the river that must be portaged around when the river is shallow (possible rest area and emergency exit from river).

The Riverside Center in downtown Frederick is also known locally as the "Walmart launch site" due to the closeness of the recreation spot to the shopping

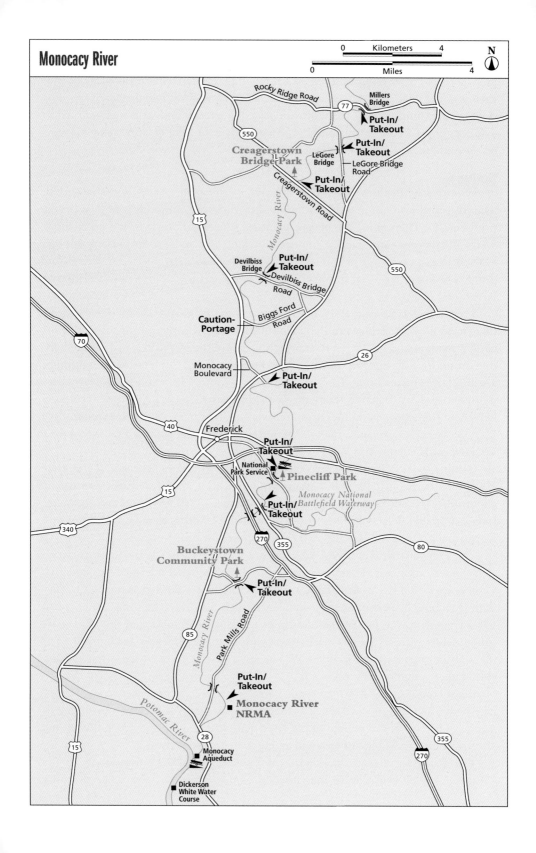

Monocacy River

Kilometers 0 — 4
Miles 0 — 4

N

Rocky Ridge Road

Millers Bridge

77

Put-In/ Takeout

550

Creagerstown Bridge Park

LeGore Bridge

Put-In/ Takeout

LeGore Bridge Road

Creagerstown Road

Put-In/ Takeout

Monocacy River

15

550

Put-In/ Takeout

Devilbiss Bridge

Devilbiss Bridge Road

Biggs Ford Road

Caution- Portage

26

70

Monocacy Boulevard

Put-In/ Takeout

40

Frederick

Put-In/ Takeout

National Park Service

Pinecliff Park

Monocacy National Battlefield Waterway

15

Put-In/ Takeout

270

355

80

340

Buckeystown Community Park

Put-In/ Takeout

Monocacy River

85

Park Mills Road

Put-In/ Takeout

Monocacy River NRMA

Potomac River

28

355

15

Monocacy Aqueduct

270

Dickerson White Water Course

DICKERSON'S OLYMPIC WHITEWATER COURSE

Near the mouth of the Monocacy River on the Potomac River, near Dickerson, Maryland, is the Dickerson Whitewater Course. The Mirant Power Company owns and maintains the facility, which was engineered as a release for the power plant's used water.

The cement water shoot was designed for use by canoe and kayak paddlers training for the 1992 Olympic Games in Spain and is renowned as the first pump-powered artificial whitewater course built in North America. Today the course and water shoot are still active and the only course anywhere with heated water. The Dickerson Whitewater Course remains active as a training center for whitewater slalom racing, swift-water rescue training, and other whitewater activities. It is closed to the public and access requires membership in the Bethesda Center of Excellence. It's fun to see and is photo worthy.

center. The site is managed by the City of Frederick and is found on the DNR website. There is a cement incline that almost reaches the water level and has a molded block on its tip like a ball on the end of a stairway banister. Is this to keep boats from going too far down the ramp? I can only guess. Lots of kids play here in the knee-deep water during the hot summer.

Pinecliff Park's boat ramp is in a grassy community playground area. The ramp is made of bricks, and the tip of the launch is missing a few. The site is managed by the Frederick County Parks and Recreation, which has issued a warning of Class I rapids to the Monocacy Aqueduct. This ramp is found on the DNR website.

The National Park Service manages the Monocacy National Battlefield Waterway. The Gambrill Mill museum and park access to the Monocacy River are not on the Route 355 Urbana Highway, but on a side road with signs. There is a boardwalk from the parking area to an inclined pathway to the water's shoreline. Boat wheels are highly recommended for long portage. There is a medium-size parking lot, swimming is allowed, and the location is found on the DNR website. The Monocacy Water Trail map shows a water access icon on the Route 355 Urbana Bridge. There is a small parking lot and a deer path to the water's edge at this location, but use caution as the deer path is almost a sheer drop of 20 feet or more. The National Park Service has a new museum and gift store a mile up from the Urbana Bridge on Route 355. They are quite unhappy with the map's misplaced boat ramp icon, as they were not contacted about their part on the river and have been receiving unfavorable comments.

Buckeystown Community Park is a small-town recreational area with benches, tot-lot, and facilities. The park's Monocacy River shoreline runs for 50 yards, and there are two well-worn deer paths over flat rocks and boulders to the water's edge. Several rock ripples making Class I rapids were observed in the ankle-deep water.

Frederick County Parks and Recreation manages the site and it also is found on the DNR website.

The Park Mills Bridge–Monocacy River National Resource Management Area (not on the DNR website) does not have a boat ramp but is a shoreline access area. Facilities are available, and there is a hardpacked, shoulder-width walking path with a long portage to a sand-gravel beach area. Boulders create constant whitewater rapids under the bridge. This is the last launch area south before the Monocacy Aqueduct Park 3.5 miles away. This is the only section of the river that can be recommended as a safe paddle north from the Monocacy Aqueduct to "almost" the Park Mills Bridge! This is a good 4-hour paddle in high or low tide.

The Monocacy Aqueduct boat ramp is part of the C&O Canal system route and is found on the DNR website. Site management is by the National Park Service, and there are permanent restrooms and a large parking lot. The water is tidal, but even in shallow water seasons the river is doable. The original C&O Canal system included eleven stone aqueducts designed to carry the canal across the major river tributaries that drain into the Potomac River along the canal's route. The Monocacy Aqueduct is the largest of the eleven aqueducts erected along the C&O Canal, and is often described by historians as one of the finest canal features in the United States.

Bonus: Potomac River–Dickerson Route

If you'd like to explore more, turn east onto the Potomac River toward the power plant at Dickerson. There is a man-made cement whitewater course that is pumped with warm drainwater from the power plant. It is not open to the public per se, as potential users must qualify first and be a member of specific groups. Visually exciting, the current from the drain-off is constant year-round, with or without paddler participation. This will finish off an interesting day.

Harford County

In early colonial days, Havre de Grace was under serious consideration for the location of the nation's capital rather than the District of Columbia. Its location at the top of the Chesapeake Bay with its deep water for shipping and trade was favorable, and its distance from the Atlantic coastline would make it secure in times of war. Today Harford County has environmental issues that affect its present and future growth, such as sediment and fertilizer runoff that encourages unwanted submerged aquatic vegetation (SAV), or sea grass, and soil contamination from military use of chemical agents.

As reflected in this exhibit at the Havre de Grace Decoy Museum, Harford is a fowl hunter's dream come true (paddle 22).

22 Havre de Grace

This adventure has seven waypoints as access to the Susquehanna River along Havre de Grace City and offers a longer paddle to a minor county launch area for sea kayakers.

County: Harford County
Suggested launch sites:
  City Yacht Basin
  Frank J. Hutchins Park
  Jean Roberts Memorial Park
Suggested takeout sites: Same
Length and float time: 1 mile per hour (slow paddle)
  3 miles round-trip in town
  1.5 miles to Swan Harbor
  1 mile to E&M Tydings Park
Difficulty: Mild
Current: Mild in off-season
Fishing: Anglers might find largemouth and smallmouth bass, bluegill, pickerel, crappie, catfish, yellow and white perch, carp
Season: Year-round

Fees or permits: Honor system off-season; City Yacht Basin has marina master's office
Nearest city/town: Havre de Grace
Boats used: Sea kayaks for extra-long route, otherwise recreational boats; maybe paddleboards
Organization: Harford County Parks and Recreation
Contacts: None
Rest areas: Multiple along coastline
Restaurant pullouts: City Yacht Basin has a seasonal snack bar
  Tidewater Grille has its own piers
  Jean Roberts ramp has a seafood diner across the street and close access to downtown stores and restaurants

Put-In/Takeout Information

The Marina & Yacht Yard (commercial), 723 Water St., Havre de Grace MD; (410) 939-2161; GPS N39 32.4061' / W076 05.420'

Jean Roberts Memorial Park (public), Ostego and Water Streets, Havre de Grace, MD; GPS N39 33.189' / W076 05.451'

Frank J. Hutchins Park (public), Congress Street, Havre de Grace, MD; GPS N39 32.864' / W076 05.090'

Wettig's Boatyard (commercial), 11 Congress Ave., Havre de Grace MD; (410) 939-3260; GPS N39 32.881' / W076 05.209'

City Yacht Basin (public), 352 Commerce St., Havre de Grace, MD; GPS N39 32.268' / W076 05.535'

Swan Harbor Park (out of town), 401 Oakington Rd., Havre de Grace, MD; (410) 939-6767; GPS N39 30.208' / W076 06.764'

Eleanor & Millard Tydings Park (out of town), 900 Tydings Ln., Havre de Grace, MD; GPS N39 30.205' / W076 06.758'

The first access from the Susquehanna is for car-tops!

Overview

Havre de Grace is the northern waterfront city in Harford County. The city's location is literally at the confluence of the Chesapeake Bay and the Susquehanna River. What happens in the river happens to the city.

The Conowingo hydroelectric dam, which is a few miles north, created a two-tier river that over the years has become a two-sided sword environmentally. The held-back water, which is identified as being created from "fresh" water sources, has become a sore point of pollution and bacteria behind the upper-tier waters of the dam. Water is allowed to flow regularly into the lower tier, but storms occasionally flush out the backwater and wreak havoc along the immediate waterfront, which can echo for weeks throughout the rest of the Chesapeake Bay in a negative manner. But the Susquehanna River freshwater that is allowed into the Chesapeake tidal basin creates a unique fishing and wildlife area. This relationship is explained well in two first-class museums for families in Tydings Memorial Park: the Decoy Museum and the Martine Museum along the town's waterfront trail.

Havre de Grace is a fun little city with history, waterfront from top to bottom, a main street that is only 3 blocks long, two first-rate water-oriented family museums, and two places to rent kayaks. Like many small communities, to survive, businesses do not just provide one service, but look for as many ways to entice you and encourage you to visit and spend a dollar. In the middle of the downtown main street is the city

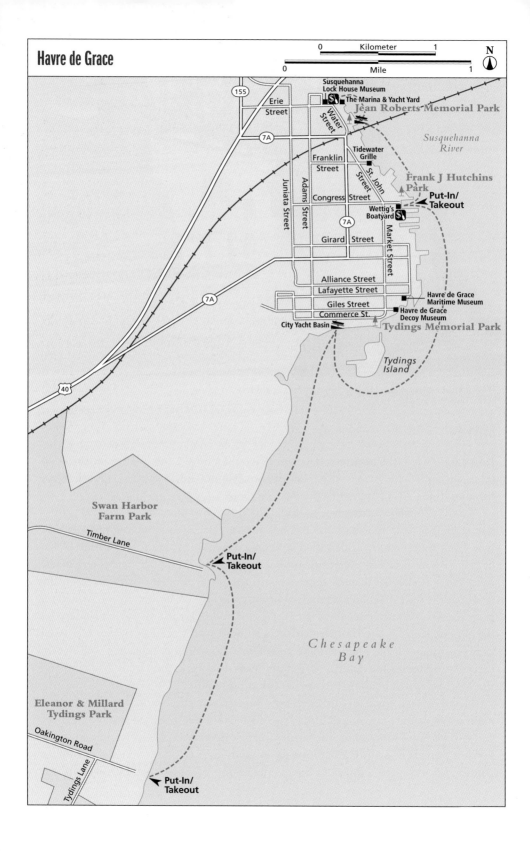

Havre de Grace

N

Kilometer
0   1
0   1
Mile

155

Erie
Street

Susquehanna
Lock House Museum

The Marina & Yacht Yard

Jean Roberts Memorial Park

Water Street

7A

Susquehanna
River

Franklin
Street

Tidewater
Grille

St. John Street

Frank J Hutchins
Park

Congress Street

Put-In/
Takeout

Juniata Street

Adams Street

7A

Wettig's
Boatyard

Girard Street

Market Street

Alliance Street

Lafayette Street

Giles Street

Havre de Grace
Maritime Museum

7A

Commerce St.

City Yacht Basin

Havre de Grace
Decoy Museum

Tydings Memorial Park

Tydings
Island

40

Swan Harbor
Farm Park

Timber Lane

Put-In/
Takeout

Chesapeake
Bay

Eleanor & Millard
Tydings Park

Oakington Road

Tydings Lane

Put-In/
Takeout

THE CONOWINGO VISITOR CENTER

The Conowingo Visitor Center sits near the Conowingo Dam, with three hardworking staff members employed by the Exelon Power Company, located in upper Harford County a few miles up from Havre de Grace. They are guides and seem to know a little bit about almost everything happening in and around the Susquehanna River. Two of the staffers are kayakers themselves and are very helpful in understanding the lower-tier river and launch sites. A wall map explains the various access areas on the river, and inside a larger room are museum-caliber explanations of the history and fishing, along with pictures of eagles. The Susquehanna Valley seems to be a perfect environment for eagles, and they are flourishing. The Exelon company has a yearly contest and awards prizes for the best eagle photos, which are used for monthly pictures in their calendar. Ever want to argue artwork? In 2014 the best photo was the clearest and most striking, but arguably not the most action-packed or the most environmentally inclusive. The visitor center also supports a public swimming pool during the summer season. Good PR work.

logo painted in a huge circle. That's city pride. We found a couple of bookstores; one in particular had a comic book section that collectors would cry for, and numerous oddball decorations were for sale including life-size *Star Wars* statues! The antiques store, also on the main street, has not just the usual good antique furniture, but also things found in your crazy uncle's attic, if you had one. There are two bakeries in town: one just selling authentic meringue cookies and the other a mom-and-pop bakery making donuts, bread, and little sweet fruit turnovers they call "fritters."

The Paddle

Jean Roberts Memorial Park is in the northern section of town, located next to a railway bridge, with a small but well-maintained cement ramp designated for car-top boats. There are a lot of parking spaces and both a year-round and a portable restroom. A block away to the north is the Havre de Grace Marina & Yacht Yard. This private marina seems to have a little bit of everything but advertises kayak and paddleboard rentals. We saw a cement ramp that was not being used other than for docking, and low-floating piers with an area for kayak storage and put-in. Adjoining the marina is the town's canal museum and a mom-and-pop restaurant called Prices Seafood. The town offers many restaurants and types of cuisine, with one restaurant on the waterfront, called the Tidewater Grille, with its own piers for visitors.

Midway going south on the city paddle is the Frank J. Hutchins Memorial Park. It has a short dock with a few finger piers. A paddleboat ferry is docked here, and there is a special car-top access ramp with just a bit of portage. Next door is Wettig's Boatyard, which has several rental sit-in and sit-on-top kayaks, a canoe, and a boat to take tourists parasailing on the Susquehanna River! Mr. Wettig built his own kayak ramp and described the traffic on the river to us with the extra caution about sea grass growing in the shallow coastal areas.

The last city takeout and put-in is Millard E. Tydings Memorial Park and City Yacht Basin. City Yacht Basin has a fee-for-use cement ramp primarily for boat trailers, but all the hunters and anglers we chatted with were friendly and in good spirits. Havre de Grace is only 30 minutes north of Baltimore City, but the Ravens football purple-and-black-colored shirts give way to camouflage and hunting gear apparel throughout the city. There is a burger and fries restaurant on the parking lot of City Yacht Basin, but it seems to be seasonal. The permanent public restrooms are open year-round. The two family museums, Havre de Grace Decoy Museum and Marine Museum, are on the waterfront park and within walking distance (entrance fees are charged).

The round-trip city paddle from north to south and back again takes about 2 hours nonstop, which leaves lots of time to sightsee and visit. If you are a speed demon and want more paddling, keep going south. Another hour will take you to the county-managed Swan Harbor Farm Park with its beach landing for a rest. For extreme power paddling, proceed to Eleanor & Millard Tydings Park, another mile south. It will be a long paddle back along the open waters of the Chesapeake Bay with possible strong afternoon breezes and wind. Boaters should probably consider this a two-car destination point.

23 Mariners Point Park

Harford County rubs elbows with Baltimore County in the waterways. Leeching chemicals from the US Army's Aberdeen Proving Ground have played havoc with the sea grass growth. Still, the Environmental Protection Agency has said the water and the fish are ok to drink and eat. Stay calm and paddle on.

County: Harford
Suggested launch site: Mariners Point Park
Suggested takeout site: Same
Length and float time: 1.5 miles per hour (medium paddle)
Difficulty: Mild to medium
Current: Strong
Fishing: Anglers might find in the Gunpowder River largemouth and striped bass, pickerel, crappie, catfish, yellow and white perch, bluegill, carp
Season: Year-round

Fees or permits: Fee to use ramps; free at kayak step launch area
Nearest city/town: Joppatowne
Boats used: Paddleboards for Fosters Branch and the marina area in Gunpowder Cove; recreational boats; sea kayaks advantageous in afternoon winds
Organizations: None
Contacts: None
Rest areas: Many shoreline rest areas
Restaurant pullouts: None

Put-In/Takeout Information

Mariners Point Park (kayak/canoe launch), 100 Kearney Dr., Joppatowne, MD 21085; (410) 612-1608; GPS N39 24.054' / W076 21.065'

Overview

The Bird River can be hard to traverse because the long-stemmed, brown-green sea grass grows up to the water's surface. A channel is cut through during summer and fall for motorboats. Gunpowder Creek and branch trails are a 4-hour round-trip paddle.

The Paddle

The first visual of the park is a fun, tall, bright yellow rain-coated seaman statue. It's worth a picture, but do it now; you won't remember to take it on your way out. The second sight is a bevy of cement ramps and a massive lineup of motorboats waiting in line to launch. The park administrator will check you out; when he sees your car-top boat, he'll send you on your way deeper into the park peninsula to the canoe/kayak launch area. As you zigzag around the massive parking lots, you begin to wonder if it's you or the administrator who has lost his mind. If you are lucky, there will be other canoes and kayaks on the far edge of a grassy knoll. If not, look for a small white sign that identifies the launch.

Car-tops use wide steps to waterfront access here.

Back up the car to the grassy knoll and unload. The portage is not that far, but dragging boats down a set of stairs is not fun and is rough on the boats. If the tide is out, there will be a small beach on which to get organized and launch. If the tide is high, the bottom step is your platform; carefully load up and push off. Parking is a block away from the launch area. If the lot is not jam-packed, you might be safe in taking up a whole parking area slated for a car and trailer. I've done that several times and have not been yelled at yet. On summer weekends expect lots of company. It's best to organize the boat and family before portaging down the steps, as you will be urged along by others.

Once you are on the water, go left and hug the shoreline. The channel will be filled with motorboats going out and coming in. Pretend you are walking against the traffic and the shoreline is your sidewalk. Once out of the main stream, keep paddling left and catch your breath. Up on the park's peninsula is a massive buoy marker on dry land. It's also quite impressive and worth a picture.

A little creek named Fosters Branch opens up, and for 0.5 mile the paddle is quiet and serene. The creek is dredged every ten years, a friendly homeowner along the waterway told me. Now comes the cheap thrill. At the end of the neighborhood are two tunnels over which the Joppa Farm Road lies. This is a safe paddle but a little tight. Go in one side, make a very sharp turn and come out the other side. It takes only minutes but is a great camera shot of you and your friends. Paddle back out to the main thoroughfare.

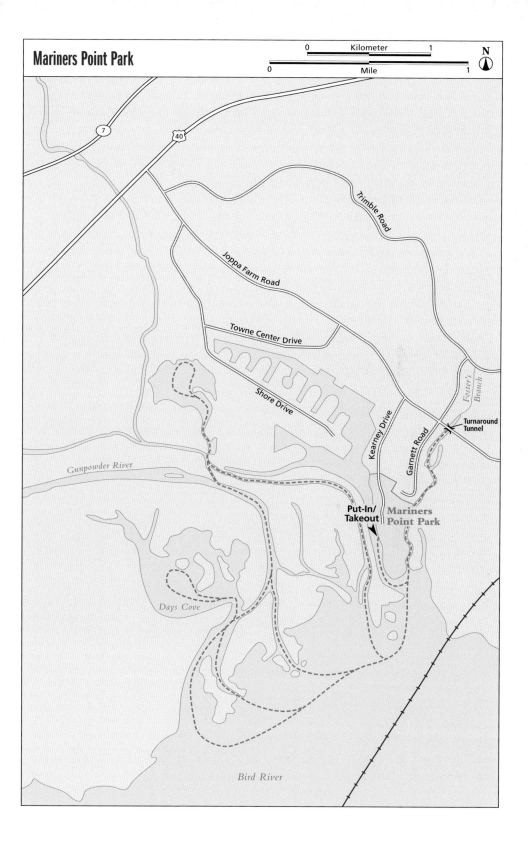

Mariners Point Park

0 Kilometer 1

0 Mile 1

N

7

40

Trimble Road

Joppa Farm Road

Towne Center Drive

Shore Drive

Kearney Drive

Garnett Road

Foster's Branch

Turnaround Tunnel

Gunpowder River

Put-In/ Takeout

Mariners Point Park

Days Cove

Bird River

You will notice the motorboats are traveling in a straight beeline heading for the railroad. Most are just following the guy in front, trying to get out to where the bigger fish swim. The smarter ones know the US Army Corps of Engineers dredged out a channel through the sea grass field, enabling boats to travel. Yes, I said sea grass "field." The Bird River is a bird's nest of vegetation that can grow right up to the surface. It makes paddling harder—not impossible, just a bit more frustrating. Please don't get caught fishing in those waters outside the railroad—the army has police patrolling the shoreline, and I hear it's a fairly big fine.

Paddling along the railroad is rough water but doable. A better plan is to paddle around the few small islands, then find the route going north—a skinny little passageway that meanders for about half a mile and then opens up into a basin. We found a clearing on a shoreline bank to pull up on for a picnic lunch and quick dip in the water. Usually local kids fish here on weekends. Come back out of the basin and look for the cutover on the right side.

For a good day paddle, take the cutover into a larger creek. Continue south to a quiet basin called Days Cove for a rest, or keep traveling till you find the Bird River again. (There are several pathways from the creek to the river—the ones farthest to the left are the quickest routes. It's about 1 mile, or an hour's paddle back.)

Kent County

As an Eastern Shore county, Kent is embraced by water on three sides with the Chesapeake Bay to its west and its northern and southern borders drawn by the Sassafras River and the Chester River, respectively. Kent County is an independent location and not to be confused with the Kent Island in Queen Anne's County located just across the Bay Bridge. Founded in 1706, Chestertown is the government seat. Located at the head of the Chester River, it became one of six "Royal Ports of Entry" for the English colonies in Maryland.

In the eighteenth century Chestertown was considered Maryland's second-leading port, trailing only Annapolis, despite Kent County being Maryland's smallest county. Today Chestertown is no longer a major shipping port, but it still can claim to be second—only to Annapolis again—in its number of existing eighteenth-century homes in Maryland!

Smalltown heart, Bigtown welcome, even for geese (paddle 24)!

24 Chestertown–Chester River

To fully enjoy the northern Chester River, we recommend two days of a one-way paddle. Of course, at any time, the paddler can merely watch the clock, check the tides and winds, and turn around and have a great day on the water. But if you want to have a "full" day of adventure—pack an extra energy drink and arrange for a pickup in one of the mid-river launch/pullout sites and do the rest another day. If you can do the two-day paddle, camp at Duck Neck Campground and go the distance to Chestertown the next day.

County: Kent and Queen Anne's Counties
Suggested launch sites:
    Kent–Shadding Reach (launch site)
    QAC–Crumpton Public Landing
    QAC–Deep Public Landing
    QAC–Duck Neck Campground (public landing)
    Kent–Buckingham Wharf (public launch)
    Chestertown–Chestertown Marina (public ramp)
Suggested takeout sites: Same
Length and float time: 1.5 miles per hour (medium paddle)
    Shadding Reach to Crumpton–3 miles
    Crumpton to Deep Public Landing–2 miles
    Deep Public Landing to Duck Neck Campground–1 mile
    Duck Neck to Buckingham Wharf–2 miles
    Buckingham Wharf to Chestertown–3 miles
Difficulty: Medium to rough and choppy depending on wind and weather

Current: Medium
Fishing: Anglers might find in Chester River largemouth and striped bass, bluegill, pickerel, crappie, catfish, yellow and white perch
Season: Year-round
Fees or permits: None for Kent County, but must have permit to launch from Queen Anne's side
Nearest city/towns: Crumpton and Chestertown
Boats used: Sea kayaks and recreational boats; paddleboards only on creeks and calm water days
Organization: The Chester River Association, chesterriverassociation.org
Contacts: Kent County and Queen Anne's County Parks and Recreation
Rest areas: Multiple public and a few shoreline beaches
Restaurant pullouts: Fish Whistle waterfront restaurant in Chestertown Marina area

Put-In/Takeout Information

Kent—**Shadding Reach** (upper river), Shadding Reach Road, Chestertown, MD; GPS N39 15.088' / W075 52.865'

QAC—**Crumpton Public Landing** (upper river), Market Street, Crumpton, MD; GPS N39 14.349' / W075 55.842'

QAC—**Deep Public Landing** (mid-river), Deep Landing Road, Pheasantfield, MD; GPS N39 14.434' / W075 57.625'

QAC—**Duck Neck Campground** (public landing; mid-river), 500 Double Creek Point Rd. (campground), MD; (410) 778-3070; GPS N39 14.609' / W075 58.743'

Chester River has lots of character, some areas choppy, some areas always smooth.

Kent—**Buckingham Wharf** (public launch; mid-river), Buckingham Road, Chestertown, MD; GPS N39 14.273' / W076 00.877'

Chestertown Marina (public ramp), 211 S. Front St., Chestertown, MD; GPS N39 12.345' / W076 03.892'

Overview

The Chester River is about 43 miles long. It forms the water border between Kent County and Queen Anne's County. For boating, the head of the Chester River begins at Millington Waterfront Park on the Queen Anne's County side and ends at the mouth of Chesapeake Bay.

We spoke with a kayaking chef on her day off, who lives in Millington. The tides do make the Chester River extremely shallow in that area, especially in drought times, but it was doable with a little portaging over two or three sandbars.

The most notable creeks are Langford and Morgan on Kent County's north side and the Corsica River and Southeast Creek on the Queen Anne's County's south side. The southern Chester River becomes wide and deep, and competition with motorboat activity becomes more than just a challenge. Langford Creek also falls into this category. My wife and I have explored parts of Langford and found weekend recreational boating to be haphazard—we do not recommend it. At the headwaters of the Corsica River is the Centreville Wharf with a good ramp and dockage. A kayak rental company there offers a multitude of services and even teaches kayak fishing to juniors during the summer.

Chestertown–Chester River

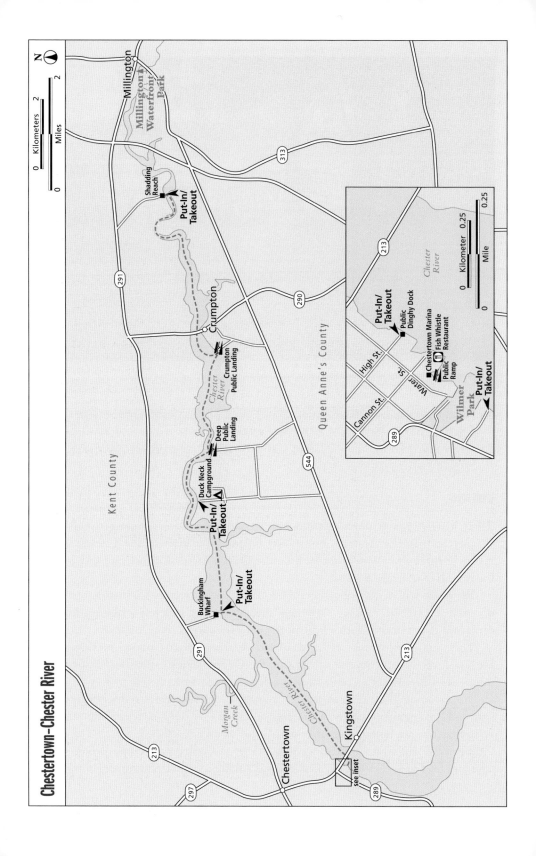

Kilometers
0   2

Miles
0   2

N

Millington

Millington Waterfront Park

313

Shadding Reach
Put-In/Takeout

291

Crumpton

Chester River

Crumpton Public Landing

Deep Public Landing

Duck Neck Campground
Put-In/Takeout

290

544

Kent County

Queen Anne's County

Buckingham Wharf
Put-In/Takeout

Morgan Creek

291

213

297

Chestertown

Chester River

Kingstown

213

289

see inset

Inset

213

Put-In/Takeout
Public Dinghy Dock

Chester River

High St.

Chestertown Marina
Fish Whistle Restaurant
Public Ramp

Water St.

Cannon St.

Wilmer Park
Put-In/Takeout

289

Kilometer
0   0.25

Mile
0   0.25

CHESTERTOWN, A FRIENDLY TOWN AND PROUD OF ITS COLONIAL HISTORY!

Chestertown, the seat of government for Kent County, is a waterfront city and as such has several launch sites for car-top boats. The town's charm is more than its friendly residents. Washington College is located here, and there's easy access to the water for locals and tourists. The town has great pride in its colonial history. Local lore claims that in 1774, the town colonists boarded a British ship anchored in the Chester River and threw its load of tea overboard. Chestertown reenacts this mimicking of the Boston Tea Party and its act of defiance with costumes, flag waving, songs, and celebration. It's lots of fun that resonates throughout the year.

High Street Park is filled with ducks, geese, gulls, and another waterfowl—an incredible sight. The sign says, "Don't Feed the Birds." Use the public dinghy dock to launch your boat. Nearby on the same waterfront is the Canon Street launch, a low-floating pier. There's paved parking for ten cars and no facilities (and no birds to poop on the car). The Chestertown Marina public ramp is a fee-for-use ramp, constructed for heavy use by motorboat trailers and such. There are two museum-caliber ships to see (where the colonial festival takes place). The Fish Whistle is the town's waterfront family restaurant and is adjacent to the marina.

Two blocks down is Wilmer Park, where the town holds its outdoor community parties and events; there is also a free shoreline launch area for car-top boats. Some boat portage is required over the long grassy area. The park was named after a Chestertown mayor who served during the Civil Rights era. The Washington College Boat House has an adjoining private shoreline and ramp area with storage for the college's crew rowing boats. They are friendly and gracious. We were invited to use this beach when the college was using Wilmer Park for one of its many social functions. No portage of boats is needed at this launch location.

The Paddle

The first recognized public launch on most maps is the Kent County Shadding Reach launch site. A simple dirt road with pine trees on both sides of the roadway leads to the launch site. The fragrance of fallen pine needles creates an aroma that is hard to forget. The road ends with a rough, worn-out cement step down. The water level is acceptable, but in extremely low tides the Chester River could be only inches deep traveling the 2-plus miles north to Millington Waterfront Park. (*Caution:* On the Eastern Shore, when a body of water is tidal and only moderate in depth, as the tide current changes to low tide, sometimes nature expedites the flow, and a paddler can become stuck with only inches of water depth and mudflats in every direction within a matter of minutes.)

Traveling southwest for 3 miles the next landmark is the Route 290 bridge; Queen Anne's Crumpton Public Landing—a public boat ramp and a small sandy beach—is just beyond. Fishing and crabbing are allowed, and there is a seasonal restroom. The waterway is a bit breezy here due to the wide basins, and in the afternoon the wind may add challenges coming back. Crumpton is the only town on the Queen Anne's side of the river and may be a good turnaround or pullout area for the first half of the journey. Less than 2 miles farther is the Deep Public Landing, a well-maintained public boat ramp and bulkhead, also in Queen Anne's County. (Look for the shoreline beach alongside this ramp. The ramp is made of coarse, rough cement, and it looks like the obliging next-door neighbor is kayak friendly.) The river narrows and the water becomes very calm, which makes it an excellent area for paddleboarding.

Just a mile farther on the south side is Duck Neck Campground and public landing. This is a very informal waterfront RV and tent campground. (**Caution:** Do not attempt to drive to the Duck Neck public ramp.) The Duck Neck Campground is perfect for a two-day paddle. Kent County's Buckingham Wharf launch site is 2 miles farther and earned its name from earlier days of agricultural shipping and steamships. Now the site has a mixed hard-pack cement and beach ramp with a small paved parking lot. It is close to Morgan Creek, which we recommend as a day's adventure. Paddle 3 miles more to your final destination—Chestertown.

25 Morgan Creek

Just outside Chestertown on Morgnec Road is a dirt roadside turnoff with lots of grassy area for parking. This waterfront area is directly on Morgan Creek and about a 15-minute paddle from the confluence of the Chester River. This is a long, winding, peaceful, and protected creek. There are few home sites and good launch sites. Use Buckingham Wharf on the Chester River for extremely low-tide launching possibilities into the creek

County: Kent County

Suggested launch sites:
  Morgnec Road
  Rileys Mill Road
  Buckingham Wharf

Suggested takeout sites: Same

Length and float time: 1.5 miles per hour (medium paddle)
  Morgnec Road launch to creek's mouth—0.5 mile
  Morgnec Road launch to Rileys Mill Road launch—1.5 miles
  Morgnec Road launch to Urieville Community Lake—3 miles
  Chestertown to Morgnec Road launch—2 miles

Difficulty: Easy

Current: Mild

Fishing: Anglers might find in Chester River largemouth and striped bass, bluegill, pickerel, crappie, catfish, yellow and white perch

Season: Year-round

Fees or permits: None

Nearest city/town: Chestertown

Boats used: Recreational boats and paddleboards

Organizations: None

Contact: Kent County Parks and Recreation

Rest areas: Multiple coves and private piers to lean on; Rileys Mill Road is halfway point

Restaurant pullouts: None

Put-In/Takeout Information

Kent—**Morgnec Road at Morgan Creek,** Route 291–Morgnec Road, Chestertown, MD 21620; GPS N39 14.158' / W076 02.215'

Kent—**Rileys Mill Road,** Rileys Mill Road, Chestertown, MD 21620; GPS N39 15.335' / W076 02.472'

Kent—**Buckingham Wharf** (public launch; mid-river), Buckingham Road, Chestertown, MD 21620; GPS N39 14.273' / W076 00.877'

Overview

The creek can be a 4- to 6-hour paddle depending on where you launch from, and even longer depending on how "full" a day of paddling you want. The Morgnec roadside turnoff is a gathering place for anglers, who place several rods off the banks, sometimes local guys hanging out with a beer in hand, and always families who believe that children should learn to fish. The banks can be muddy, and the tidal

Morgnec Road launch

change is sometimes as much as 24 inches. We recommend packing a roll of paper towels for your feet and cleaning off the boat's bottom later on. Buckingham Wharf's public launch, 1 mile away, is the closest launch on the Chester River to the creek's mouth, but for a long "full" day, launch from Chestertown and pass under the Route 213 bridge for an additional colorful 2-hour paddle to the confluence.

The Paddle

Morgan Creek seems to be known as a fishing spot, but as a regular paddler, I know it as a consistently smooth, quiet, and protected water trail (great for paddleboards). This creek is paddleable even at low tide, and the shoreline vegetation seems to change seasonally and with each twist and turn. A few powerboats venture up the creek to the sparsely developed area where their own piers and homes are located. There are a few sand- and mudbars in the center of the water trail, which will momentarily surprise paddlers; this is a long waterway and the currents are mild, but sediment buildup can happen in all creeks.

The Rileys Mill Road public shoreline launch is about the creek's midpoint. We have never passed this area without seeing at least one fisherman or fishing family trying their luck. The low-level shoreline makes a rest stop easy, but the adjoining lot with a homeowner peering down and checking out the activity makes a "trip into the trees" a bit suspenseful. Bring a picnic blanket, as the grassy/sandy area can be moist and the blanket is useful protection for shy folk answering the call of nature.

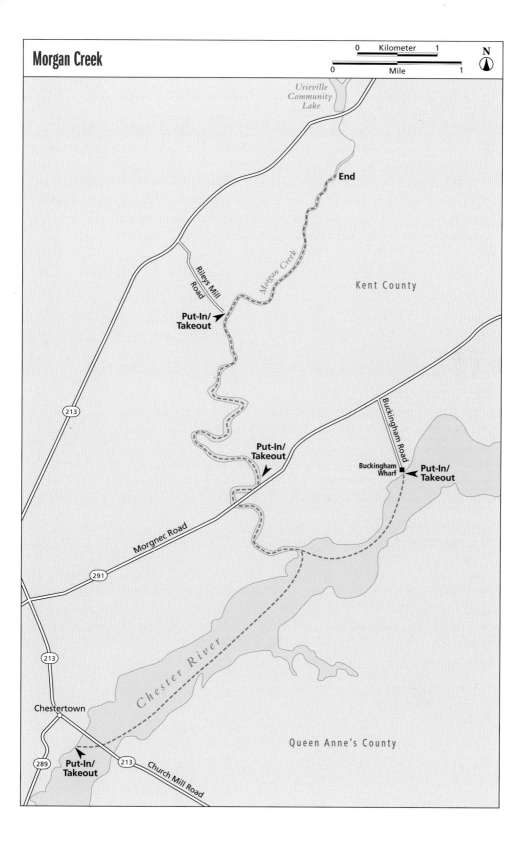

Morgan Creek

Kilometer
Mile

N

Urieville Community Lake

End

Rileys Mill Road

Morgan Creek

Kent County

Put-In/ Takeout

213

Buckingham Road

Put-In/ Takeout

Buckingham Wharf

Put-In/ Takeout

Morgnec Road

291

213

Chester River

Chestertown

289

Put-In/ Takeout

213

Church Mill Road

Queen Anne's County

The creek narrows at times then blossoms into basins. We found a private pier with a picnic table on the creek with a good pull-up shoreline. Imagine our surprise to find the beach area land-mined with prickly nut balls from the surrounding trees. Bring water shoes for moments like these!

The creek travels clear up to a roadway, and on its other side is a public fishing pond. We always ran out of time enjoying the paddle and the ever-changing environment before making it to the headwaters.

Paddling back to the Morgnec launch is easy. Watch the clock and check the tides and wind. The Chester River (if you started at Buckingham Wharf) can be mirror-smooth easy or challenging. In the fall plan to get off the water by 4:30 p.m., as it gets very dark on the open waterways no matter how beautiful the sunset.

26 Sassafras River–East and West

The Sassafras River offers many kayak avenues for adventure. Aggressive paddlers who want to travel fast and explore many creeks should concentrate on the western side and start from Betterton Park or the Fredericktown public ramp. Recreational kayakers looking for a quieter day might start from the Foxhole launch site, paddle around Hen Island and Creek. Paddleboarders will have a good time exploring the marinas and creeks around the Route 213 bridge area.

County: Kent and Cecil Counties
Suggested launch sites:
    Kent–Betterton Park and Public Ramp
    Kent–Foxhole Launch
    Kent–Turners Creek Public Ramp
    Cecil–Fredericktown Public Ramp
Suggested takeout sites: Same
Length and float time: 1.5 miles per hour (medium paddle)
    Eastern side: Fox Hole Launch to Route 213 bridge–3 miles one-way
    Western side: Fredericktown Ramp to Turners Creek Ramp–5 miles one-way
    Western side: Turner's Creek Ramp to Betterton Park–5 miles one-way
Difficulty: Mild to difficult depending on wind and boat wakes
Current: Medium
Fishing: Anglers might find in Sassafras River largemouth and striped bass, bluegill, pickerel, crappie, catfish, yellow and white perch
Season: Year-round
Fees or permits: None

Nearest city/town: Betterton, Fredericktown, and Georgetown
Boats used: On western side, sea kayaks; on eastern side, recreational boats and paddleboards
Organizations: Cecil County and Kent County Parks and Recreation
Contacts: None
Rest areas: Multiple throughout river
Restaurant pullouts:
    Kent–Kitty Knight House (historic inn and restaurant; part of Georgetown Marina with kayak rentals), 14028 Augustine Herman Hwy., Georgetown, MD; (410) 648-5200; GPS N39 21.656' / W075 52.819'
    Cecil–Granary Marina and Restaurant, 100 George St., Fredericktown, MD; (410) 275-1603; GPS N39 21.806' / W075 53.292'
    Cecil–Skipjack Cove Yachting Resort (kayak rentals), 150 Skipjack Rd., Georgetown, MD; (410) 275-2124; GPS N39 21.965' / W075 53.464'

Put-In/Takeout Information

Kent—**Betteron Park and Public Ramp,** Still Pond Road (Route 292), Betterton, MD; GPS N39 22.256' / W076 03.752'

Kent—**Foxhole Launch, Fox Hole Road,** Galena, MD; GPS N39 22.462' / W075 49.750'

Kent—**Turners Creek Public Ramp,** Turner's Creek Road, Kennedyville, MD; GPS N39 21.464' / W075 58.988'

When in bloom the flowers take up about one-third of the Turner's Creek surface area.

Cecil—**Fredericktown Public Ramp,** Fredericktown Road, Georgetown, MD;
 GPS N39 21.783' / W075 53.197'

Overview

The Sassafras River is about 22 miles long, but is divided by a low drawbridge in the Georgetown area into an east river and a west river, with each side of the river in a different county, and both with very different characteristics.

Kent County's Georgetown is only a little knob of residential homes, a historic inn, and a hub of services from the Georgetown Marina off the Route 213 bridge that runs through it. But to know the Sassafras River is to know this landmark area. In 1812 the British fleet was sailing in and out of Maryland's rivers, burning homes and buildings. All but two waterfront buildings on the Sassafras River were destroyed—those belonging to Ms. Kitty Knight's family. The legend goes that she personally had an interview with the admiral; he was so taken with the woman and her charms that those two buildings were spared. They are now used as a tavern and inn. Reenactments of the confrontation take place in uniforms and colonial gowns on the inn's doorsteps, and it is said that Ms. Kitty's ghost frequents the inn and orders room service from room #4! The marina also sports an ice cream shop and a shop for boat parts and gifts, hosts lots of waterfront weddings, and rents kayaks during the season from its beach.

Across the bridge is the larger waterfront village of Fredericktown on the Cecil County side of the river. Fredericktown has five marinas and the only public cement ramp in the area. All the marinas can accommodate car-top boaters as visitors, but only Duffy has an excellent white sand beach for lounging and launching from. The Skipjack Marina, which calls itself a resort, is the largest and offers kayak rentals and launches from low-floating dockage, as well as lots of snack shops and dining possibilities.

The Paddle

Sassafras River East

The east end of the river travels toward the river's head. The farthest boating point is the Foxhole public launch site on the Kent County side. This is a rough, undeveloped shoreline area with no facilities and an elongated beach during low tide. It's popular with families for shoreline fishing. We have yet to see a keeper being caught, but there are lots of smiles year-round. The water depth keeps out most motorboats in this section of the river till about Hen Island and Creek. This is a fairly small, forested island, with excellent fishing around its shorelines. There is a skinny creek on the Cecil County side without a real name, and it is fun to paddle for a good hour round-trip into the backlands.

The Sassafras River is clean enough to swim in, so boats just need a piece of beach to pull up on. Kayakers always seem to find the little coves (maybe because they paddle so close to the shorelines). A little cove off Hen Island is just big enough to hide a couple of kayaks for a picnic on its river-smooth pebble beach. We always bring spring floaters—thin oval tubes with foldable wires inside that blow up and a mesh in the center—which are great for getting wet in shallow waterways and beach areas where real swimming isn't going to happen.

There is one marina on the eastern side of the Sassafras River—Gregg Neck Boat Yard. Although it does have a wide gravel-based ramp/incline, the marina is not really set up to accommodate traveling guests, much less car-top boaters. This is a resting home for yachts that have become permanent homes for older waterfront folk whose boats are about the same age as their residents. As trailer parks are disappearing, these marinas for year-round residents are becoming more prevalent. Before the drawbridge on the Kent County side is Mill Creek, a protected, quiet water trail perfect for paddleboarding in low or high tides; it's about a slow hour round-trip paddle. And as you approach the bridge, look on the left side for the two-story waterslide installed by a Georgetown resident. We chatted with three generations of family eating a Sunday picnic and watched the kids climb the ladder, catch their breath, and then tear down the fiberglass slide. The round-trip paddle from Foxhole to the Route 213 bridge takes 5 hours with stopping to explore a few coves. This is a semi-protected area with limited motorboat wake waves, but there is a wind that picks up in the late afternoon. So watch the clock, check the afternoon waves and wakes from motorboats, and be aware of the breezes. It's easy to lose time here.

Sassafras River–East and West

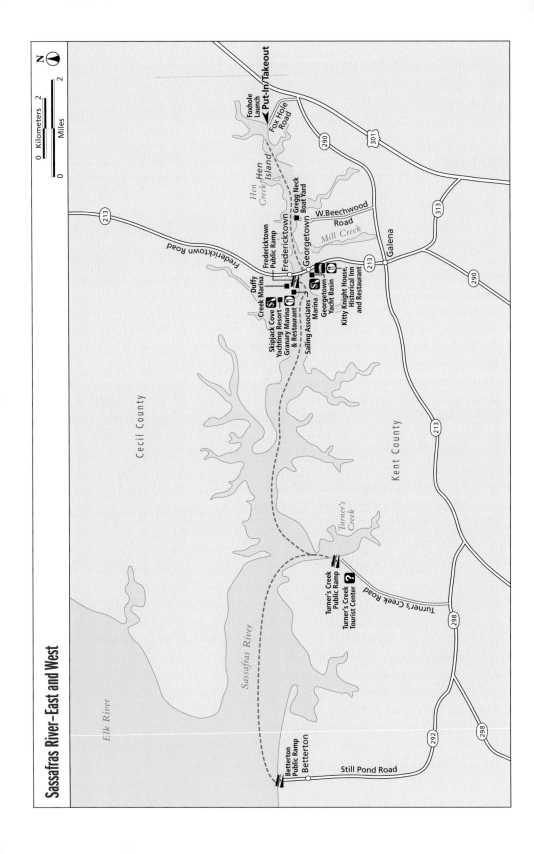

Elk River

Sassafras River

Cecil County

Kent County

213

Frederricktown Road

213

290

Duffy Creek Marina

Skipjack Cove Yachting Resort
Granary Marina & Restaurant

Sailing Associates Marina

Fredericktown
Fredericktown Public Ramp

Georgetown
Georgetown Yacht Basin
Kitty Knight House, Historical Inn and Restaurant

Gregg Neck Boat Yard

Hen Hen Creek Island

Mill Creek

W.Beechwood Road

Galena

313

290

301

Foxhole Launch
Put-In/Takeout
Fox Hole Road

Turner's Creek

Turner's Creek Public Ramp
Turner's Creek Tourist Center

Turner's Creek Road

298

292

298

213

Betterton Public Ramp
Betterton

Still Pond Road

N

0   Kilometers   2

0   Miles   2

Sassafras River West

There are several prominent marinas adjacent to or near the Route 213 bridge for kayakers to note:

- Georgetown Yacht Basin—kayak rentals, boat store, ice cream parlor
- Duffy Creek Marina—the best private beach for swimming and car-top launching
- Granary Marina and Restaurant—visiting low pier for pullout or tie-up only
- Skipjack Cove Yachting Resort—kayak rentals and restaurant

There are several coves and creeks to explore along the coastlines of both counties going west. Dyer Creek is peaceful but only as a short sidebar paddle; nearby Hall Creek is very protected and has quiet water even with summer boat wakes on the river.

From the Fredericktown Public Ramp to Turners Creek is a 5-mile one-way paddle. Turners Creek has a public ramp and shoreline launching for car-top boats. There is also a first-rate family museum about Captain John Smith, explaining his exploration of the region. Turners Creek is taken over with lily pads, and during the plant's flowering stage while you paddle the unimpeded side of the waterway, your eyes and senses are saturated. It's a short, 90-minute round-trip paddle but quite unforgettable.

There are several wide and medium-length creeks to explore between Turner's Creek and Betterton Park. But from one public ramp to the other is a 5-mile straight paddle. Betterton Park is at the mouth of the Sassafras River, which joins the Chesapeake Bay and the Elk River. This park offers a white sand swimming beach, a bathhouse, a boat pier, a sandy beach shoreline launch area, and a mixed-surface boat ramp. The Route 213 bridge to Betterton Park is a 6- to 7-hour one-way paddle on a good day. This should be a two-car operation done with partners or a group. The river on the west side of the bridge is deeper and wider, and motorboat traffic is constant. There are lots of little creeks and coves along both sides of the river, but we recommend sticking to the Kent County side and not crossing the river when it seems choppy.

27 Still Pond and Churn Creeks

Still Pond and Churn Creeks are protected paddles with only the occasional gust of wind. The depth of the water for most of each creek is about 4 to 5 feet, with extended sandbars at their mouths. The old Coast Guard Station is an excellent mid-point for lunch, sunbathing, and swimming, with a small but well-maintained cement ramp. Which creek is better? Both deliver a good day of quiet paddling, but Churn Creek is a little less likely to attract jet skis.

County: Kent County
Suggested launch sites:
    Old Coast Guard Station at Still Pond
      Creek
    Still Pond Creek Launch
Suggested takeout sites: Same
Length and float time: 1.5 miles per hour (medium paddle)
    Old Coast Guard Station to Still Pond
      Creek Launch—2.5 miles one-way
    Old Coast Guard Station to headwaters of
      Churn Creek—2.25 miles one-way
Difficulty: Easy
Current: Mild

Fishing: Anglers might find on Still Pond Creek largemouth and striped bass, bluegill, pickerel, crappie, catfish, yellow and white perch
Season: Year-round
Fees or permits: None
Nearest city/town: Worton
Boats used: Recreational boats and paddleboards
Organization: Kent County Parks and Recreation
Contacts: None
Rest areas: Multiple shoreline pull-ups
Restaurant pullouts: None

Put-In/Takeout Information

Old Coast Guard Station at Still Pond Creek (part of Arts at Still Pond Station), Still Pond Neck Road, MD 21678; (410) 778-7370; GPS N39 20.100' / W076 07.877'

Still Pond Creek Launch, Still Pond Creek Road, Worton, MD 21678; GPS N39 19.234' / W076 05.254'

Overview

Historians found that the Still Pond Creek area was used by Native Americans as a successful breeding ground for oysters. It's now a well-developed urban creek with side to side homes that offers a well-protected, calm water paddle during the off-seasons, and it's perfect for picnics on either end.

The Paddle

Most of the online descriptions of Still Pond Creek are based on maps; none are based on observations from actually paddling the creek year-round. The Still Pond Creek

These creek beaches are cool, enticing, and perfect for paddlers!

launch area is just a minor cement apron off a bend on a local neighborhood road. It wasn't built to be a boat ramp for motorboat trailers, but lord knows they try. The launch area has street parking for three cars and a gentle incline for car-top boaters.

The mouth of Still Pond Creek is a draw for motorboats and yachts to join together in clusters and party the whole weekend during the summer. The yachts bring Jet Skis and the motorboats bring water skis. Talk about rough water from wakes. Come Monday morning, however, the water is calm, and the 2.5-mile paddle from the Still Pond Creek launch to the Old Coast Guard Station is peaceful and highly recommendable in low or high tide.

The Old Coast Guard Station at Still Pond Creek is a shadow of what it once was: a full office building with dockage for several boats and a gated driveway to protect the federal employees. The building now houses a shared community art center and a few offices for a minor government agency. No port-a-potties are available, only bushes and trees (bring your own paper). The gate is open 24-7, and the cement boat ramp is still in good working order. One Coast Guard boat remains on duty and travels about, with the sailors now encamped in a house just outside the fence. There is a sandy beach with massive stone water breaks to protect the shoreline area. The water around the beach is only inches deep but is great for adults and kids to splash about in. Kayaks can pull up and enjoy the soft sand. Just across the open-water basin that leads to the Chesapeake Bay, on the left, is a small opening to another body of water. Churn Creek has no public access but has an old-time 1950s lake feeling and appeal—less developed and with more trees. The tiny mouth of the creek is maybe

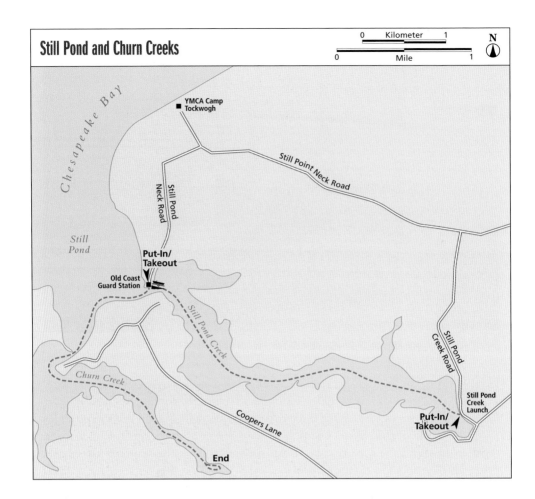

YMCA Camp Tockwogh

Chesapeake Bay

Still Point Neck Road

Still Pond Neck Road

Still Pond

Put-In/ Takeout

Old Coast Guard Station

Still Pond Creek

Churn Creek

Still Pond Creek Road

Still Pond Creek Launch

Put-In/ Takeout

Coopers Lane

End

30 feet wide and during summer weekends is decorated with beach chairs from other motorboat folks who like the white sand beaches. Churn Creek is shorter in actual length than Still Pond Creek, even with the 4.5-mile round-trip to and from the Coast Guard Station. Gratefully the Jet Skis and waterskiing crowd is not found here. The headwater area is mudflats, but the paddle is nice year-round in low or high tide. Several sandbars are available to pull in for a rest or a picnic.

Montgomery County

Montgomery County was important in the abolitionist movement, and the Potomac River provided many runaway slaves with access to freedom via the Underground Railroad. A notable resident was Josiah Henson, who wrote about his experiences in a memoir, which became the basis for Harriet Beecher Stowe's *Uncle Tom's Cabin* (1852). Josiah, the inspiration for the character Uncle Tom, was a slave in Montgomery County, and a slave cabin where he is believed to have spent time still stands at the end of a driveway off Old Georgetown Road.

The Potomac River supports a large ecosystem which includes white egrets (paddle 28)!

28 Pennyfield to Riverbend Park

The Potomac River flows south so paddling north is not for recreational boaters. This is a good place for a two-hour two-car shuttle system, staying on the Maryland side of the river. But plan ahead and paddle to Riverbend Park in Virginia for a short and mild whitewater experience and a delightful calm water basin with a trail walk to the Great Falls. A well-earned memory and a terrific day of paddling! This is a camera event.

County: Montgomery County, Maryland, and Fairfax County, Virginia
Suggested launch sites:
    MD–C&O Canal Pennyfield Lock
    MD–C&O Canal Swains Lock
    VA–River Bend County Park
Suggested takeout sites: Same
Length and float time: 1.5 miles per hour (medium paddle)
    C&O Pennyfield Lock to Riverbend County
    Park–5.5 miles one-way
Difficulty:
    Potomac River–west to east: fast paced with occasional submerged boulders (several whitewater class one rapids)
    Potomac River–south to north: heavy growth of sea grass and strong currents to paddle against; Riverbend to Swains Lock paddle not recommended for recreational boaters

Riverbend basin—calm and quiet waters
Current: At times strong and forceful
Fishing: Anglers along the Potomac River might find catfish, crappie, largemouth and smallmouth bass, panfish, sunfish, suckers, walleye
Season: Year-round; best paddling during high tides
Fees or permits: Riverbend County Park has an entrance fee collected at gate
Nearest city/town: Gathersburg
Boats used: Sea kayaks and recreational boats; paddleboards only at Riverbend basin
Organization: Montgomery County Department of Parks
Contacts: None
Rest areas: Multiple along route
Restaurant pullouts: Riverbend Park has a snack shop in visitor center

Put-In/Takeout Information

MD—**C&O Canal Pennyfield Lock,** 12420 Pennyfield Lock Rd., Tobytown, MD; GPS N39 03.416' / W077 17.633'

MD—**C&O Canal Swains Lock,** Swains Lock Road, Travilah, MD; GPS N39 01.887' / W077 14.605'

VA—**Riverbend County Park** (kayak and canoe rentals), 8700 Potomac Hills St., Great Falls, VA; (703) 759-9018; GPS N39 01.091' / W077 14.724'

Overview

Looking for more than a 3-hour adventure one-way on the Potomac River? There are boulders and outcroppings to contend with on the Maryland side of the upper

Potomac River has strong currents and mini rock islands.

Potomac River going south, but on the Virginia side, if you have not crossed over, there are a couple of Class I whitewater rapids depending on the tide. There is no turning back, no rope on the boat and walking and pulling it back. Just smile and sit tight, the thrill is short and veteran sea kayakers may even yawn in your face, but for weekend recreational boaters it's like a roller coaster!

The Paddle

The C&O Canal "pathway-park" is owned by the National Park Service. Rangers patrol and maintain the canal itself when water is present, but in this location water access to the Potomac is funded and maintained by Montgomery County.

Access is through a tunnel called a "stone viaduct." The tunnel is watered from a tiny tidal creek named Muddy Branch. There is no portage needed as the cement ramp incline reaches to the waterline. The tunnel is about 5 feet in diameter and about 20 feet long. At low tide, boaters have had to walk their boats through the tunnel and then climb in to paddle the short shallow distance to the Potomac River. The river current can be strong and pulls south. Sea grass grows here, and the floor of the river is gravel with crystal-clear water. Paddle north to the mini islands or rock outcroppings in an area called Blockhouse Point, and to the left side of the river where the current is not so forceful. Boaters can pull up on a shell-filled shoreline and marvel at the cornucopia of colors and shell shapes.

Head south and dodge between the larger and smaller islands. The extended large island is named Watkins and is about 3 miles long. We found several boats pulled up

Pennyfield to Riverbend Park

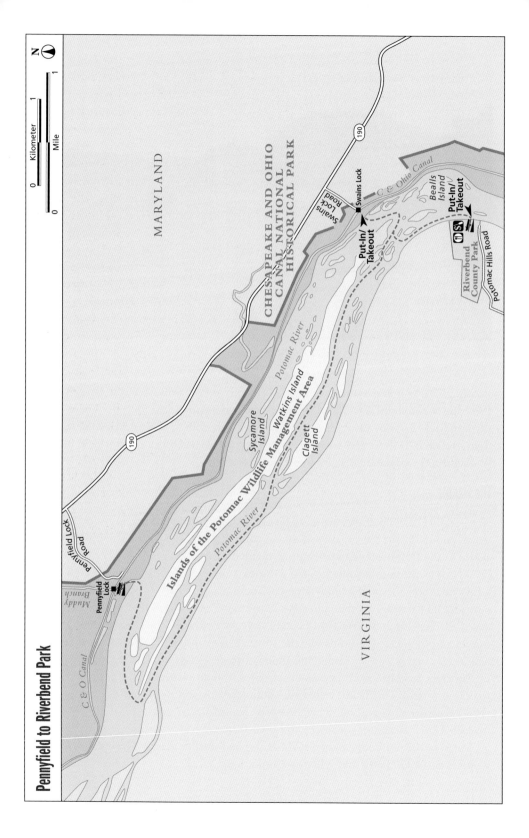

and enjoying a quiet rest on the island's shoreline. I am told there is a paddling passage through to the Maryland side of the river again for a shorter adventure, but cannot confirm this on ADC maps. This is a lazy, quiet water area, and other kayakers tell me it's a great place to swim and picnic. Hug the left side of Watkins Island and you'll see a passage at the island's end to Swains Lock—4.5 miles of one-way paddling. The water here is filled with mini rock outcroppings, but the current can be gentle near the shoreline. Swains Lock has no cement ramp, and the launch area is no more than a muddy shelf from which a boat can be lowered into the water. Years ago the Swains building had running freshwater and a concession stand where boats were rented. No more. The family gave up its rights to the location and now the canal lock is filled with stagnant water and a few fish the local boys try to hook. Tent camping is allowed here, and there are year-round port-a-potties.

For more adventure keep going south. From Swains Lock look out for boulders; from the Virginia side hold tight and paddle a few whitewater rapids. The best part is that the water calms down immediately; a short paddle later Virginia's Riverbend County Park is on the right. There is a cement ramp and lots of shoreline where kayaks and canoes are rented. A visitor center has snacks, restrooms, and a mini museum. By the cement ramp is a wooden log that is being hollowed out and fired into a Native American canoe. Riverbend Park has an annual Native American festival with dancing, singing, and crafts, and there's a walking path to the Great Falls National Park—Virginia side. Since the water in the basin is quiet and smooth, there are lots of boaters. Paddleboarders have a safe place to spend hours without being challenged by other aggressive boaters. The most memorable characteristics of the basin are the gigantic submerged boulders that boaters must paddle around. The edges are smooth and bumping into one might give boaters pause, but it's very safe. I checked the whole perimeter and found safety buoys marking off limits water regions where the Potomac River travels over a dam. This is an excellent end-of-a-trip location with activity to do after the water adventure. Remember it's a two-car one-way paddle.

29 Rocky Gorge Reservoir

There are three public access points into this long, winding waterway. The atmosphere here is more relaxed, and boaters and anglers are not challenged by motorboats or their wakes. Seven miles point to point gives boaters lots of opportunities to explore for several days.

County: Montgomery, Howard, and Prince Georges Counties
Suggested launch sites:
  Montgomery—Browns Bridge Ramp
  Howard—Scotts Cove Ramp
  Prince Georges—Supplee Lane Ramp
Suggested takeout sites: Same
Length and float time: 7 miles one-way; 1.5 miles per hour (medium paddle)
  Supplee Lane Ramp to Scotts Cove Ramp—0.75 mile
  Scotts Cove Ramp to Route 29 bridge—1.75 miles
  Route 29 bridge to Browns Bridge Ramp—3 miles
  Browns Bridge to Snell's Bridge—1.5 miles
Difficulty: Mild
Current: Mild

Fishing: Anglers at Rocky Gorge might find muskie, largemouth, smallmouth, and striped bass; rainbow and brook trout, northern pike, bluegill, catfish, pumpkinseed, walleye, crappie, yellow perch
Season: Closed in winter months
Fees or permits: Daily fee collected from ranger station; yearly permits sold
Nearest city/towns: Scaggsville and Laurel
Boats used: Sea kayaks, recreational boats, and paddleboards
Organizations: Montgomery, Howard, and Prince George's County Departments of Parks and Recreation
Contacts: Washington Suburban Sanitary Commission
Rest areas: Multiple throughout route
Restaurant pullouts: None

Put-In/Takeout Information

Browns Bridge Ramp (Montgomery County), 2220 Ednor Rd., Silver Spring, MD 20905; GPS N39 08.731' / W076 57.785'

Scotts Cove Ramp (Howard County), 11000 Harding Ln., Laurel MD 20723; GPS N39 08.073' / W076 53.494'

Supplee Lane Ramp (Prince George's County), 16904 Supplee Ln., Laurel, MD 20707; GPS N39 07.455' / W076 53.046'

Overview

The waterway's name is Rocky Gorge Reservoir, and it is partly located within an area in Prince George's County named T. Howard Duckett Park. This tends to create some confusion, but usually only in the eastern section of the reservoir. Sometimes the word "reservoir" is used interchangeably with the word "lake." Recreational boating activities are the same, but swimming is not allowed in the reservoir as water

Rocky Gorge in the fall at a northern bridge

managers struggle to keep the bacteria count low because this water supply is used for residential drinking water and must be kept to a higher standard than most lakes, regardless of size. The Rocky Gorge Reservoir is below the Triadelphia Reservoir, and the same Patuxent River that feeds one reservoir feeds the other with runoff. The Patuxent River Trail actually counts the waterway access points as trail markers into both reservoirs.

The Paddle

Reservoirs should have a stable water level year-round, or so I thought. Like an extra-large bathtub? Well it turns out that reservoirs have drastic water-level changes, some of which are natural and some man-made, that affect the look and use of the waterways. In addition to the Patuxent River feed, the water accumulates from natural water runoff from the surrounding communities and winter precipitation. According to the park ranger, the water is drained during the year to keep the body of water from overflowing the dam retainers and also to kill vegetation that tends to grow and adds pollution to the water.

These fluctuations are apparently not newsworthy, and boaters are given little if any public notification. But the fluctuation can be as much as 6 feet during a regular use period. The Browns Bridge launch area in Montgomery County, known for its miles of wilderness, slow easy currents, and rainbow shades of color on the granite boulders and vegetation to the west, is the most vulnerable to this water-level change.

Rocky Gorge Reservoir

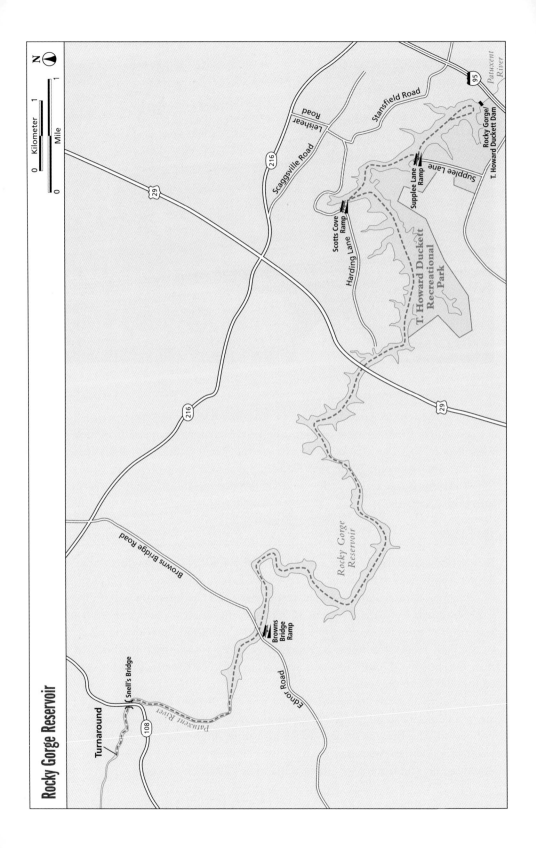

We have taken photos of a full waterway and later the same year when drained. The boat launch incline is almost 20 feet farther and the last 6 feet are mudflats. When this happens, it's nice to know the water is deeper at the other end of the waterway. Supplee Lane launch has a dual cement ramp, a well-paved parking lot, and tree-lined acreage. This ramp is closest to the dam and, as the water level drops, is the last to be affected. Scotts Cove Ramp, less than a mile away, has leased its surrounding shoreline to users who want to store their boats to a secured post year-round. This area is more of a family-use park with a ramp to the side. Very colorful, but when the water levels are low, it too suffers.

Why lament for a thirsty reservoir? Because the other six months of the year this is the most reliable and protected location to paddle on a windy or weather questionable day. There are no powerboats to churn up the relatively smooth and calm water. The boater is able to enjoy the changing seasons' vegetation and weather without much ado other than an extra jacket or fleece. The lack of competition on the waterway gives a whole new meaning to lowering your blood pressure. The length of this reservoir allows boaters to enjoy the waterway from many different access points.

30 Triadelphia Reservoir

The reservoir is 800 acres of freshwater with four launch sites and protected water as well as wide basins. This is a long stretch of paddling that is safe and has beautiful foliage.

County: Montgomery and Howard Counties
Suggested launch sites:
    Montgomery County—Triadelphia Launch
      Ramp
    Montgomery—Greenbridge Ramp
    Howard—Big Branch Ramp
    Howard—Pigs Tail Ramp
Suggested takeout sites: Same
Length and float time: 1.5 miles per hour
(medium paddle)
    4.5 miles long; from Triadelphia ramp to
      Greenbridge ramp (one way)
Difficulty: Easy
Current: Mild

Fishing: Anglers might find at Triadelphia Reservoir crappie, largemouth bass, pickerel, walleye
Season: Closed during winter months
Fees or permits: Daily launch fee requested; yearly lease for shoreline boat mooring
Nearest city/town: Columbia
Boats used: Sea kayaks and recreational boats; paddleboards welcome
Organizations: None
Contact: Washington Suburban Sanitary Commission
Rest areas: Multiple shoreline pull-ups
Restaurant pullouts: None

Put-In/Takeout Information

Triadelphia Launch Ramp (Montgomery County), NW 2600 Triadelphia Lake Rd., Brookeville, MD 21036; GPS N39 14.012' / W077 02.598'

Greenbridge Ramp (Montgomery County), 3310 Greenbridge Rd., Brookeville, MD 20833; GPS N39 11.937' / W077 00.791'

Big Branch Ramp (Howard County), 14810 Triadelphia Mill Rd., Dayton, MD 21036; GPS N39 13.952' / W077 01.673'

Pig Tail Ramp (Howard County), 5600 Greenbridge Rd, Dayton, MD 21036; GPS N39 13.108' / W077 00.374'

Overview

The surrounding grounds of the reservoir are in Patuxent River State Park—classified as the Triadelphia Watershed. The site is managed by the Washington Suburban Sanitary Commission (WSSC) and is extremely self-sufficient. The reservoir does have water drawdown periods, which affect the use of the access points from Howard County, but the drive to the other side in Montgomery County is short and not terribly inconvenient. The Brighton Dam is also a bridge to be crossed. On the Montgomery side is the Brighton Dam Information Center, a small wooden ranger building where a special visitor map of the Triadelphia Reservoir and the Rocky Gorge Reservoir can be

Pig Tail is a quiet car-top ramp on Howard County's side of the reservoir.

obtained. The center also collects the daily fee requested by the WSSC for launching fishing and car-top boats. This is an honor system backed by Department of Natural Resources rangers who check for receipts on the windshields of cars with trailers, and who chase out folks who are swimming. Gasoline engines in fishing boats are not allowed on the reservoirs, but battery-powered engines are permitted.

The Paddle

The Greenbridge launching area in Montgomery County has a heavy-duty cement ramp and ample parking for motorboat trailers, and is in the reservoir basin's wide midsection. This is a big body of water that attracts anglers, whether they catch fish or not! Where you launch from says a lot about your boat as well as your needs. Anyone can launch from here, but the typical user is heavily oriented toward the fishing crowd. Shoreline fishing is allowed, and the trails from this area are filled with weekend families looking for recreation (a fishing permit is required for adults).

The Pig Tail launching area in Howard County is modest and shallow. The cement ramp allows for a slowpoke to launch without any pressure from folks looking to get into the water next! A first-timer might be a little concerned about the shallow water level, but even in low water boaters can get out and not worry about tidal waters; the water level will be the same when they come back—honest. Most kayakers tend to hug the shorelines, as the reservoir basin is still wide here and is affected by wind and weather.

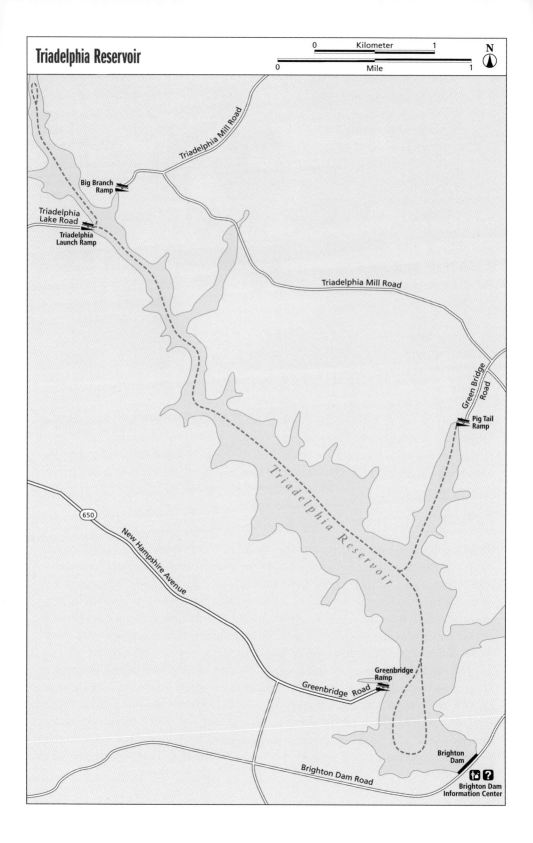

The Big Branch ramp on the northern Howard County side of the reservoir is the most affected by any water drawdown. Although it is a well-maintained location directly off the main roadway, we have yet to find enough water in the reservoir to cover the mudflats around the boat ramp. It is used so little that many maps do not even put the location on their grid.

The Triadelphia launch ramp is off Triadelphia Lake Road in Montgomery County. This area is more like a family park, with ample parking, a large fishing pier, a playground, and picnic tables. The cement ramp is in good condition, and a car can back right up to the water in high or low reservoir water levels. The northern waterway has a skinny creek that heads north for about a mile. Bring a camera and a picnic. Heading south the waterway stays comfortably protected by granite boulders and lush tree growth for about a mile before opening up into the wider basin that defines the lower waterway in the reservoir. It's all good paddling, just be aware that the wider basin is affected more by wind and weather.

Prince George's County

Upper Prince George's County is a part of the vast and sprawling metropolitan Washington, DC area, The National Harbor is a prime example of land developed for conventions and now an MGM casino and entertainment complex. The original concept was to give the often cramped District of Columbia another avenue of growth. The National Harbor's Ferris wheel is a copy of the London Eye. Ferryboats travel back and forth from George Washington's Mount Vernon plantation museum to the docks, and the dock supports a kayak and paddleboat rental company.

The National Harbor entertainment center on the waterfront (paddle 31)

31 Piscataway Creek to National Harbor

The Piscataway Creek is a large calm water basin with two water/nature trails leading to their headwaters. For more advanced paddlers: travel north, hugging the shoreline. Visit a historical landmark or pull up at the National Harbor for lunch and a ride on the new Ferris wheel that overlooks the Washington, DC, skyline! Finish the one-way trip by paddling across the Potomac River to the Belle Haven Marina near Alexandria.

County: Prince George's County
Suggested launch sites:
   Farmington Landing at Piscataway Park
   Fort Washington National Marina
   Belle Haven Marina (VA)
Suggested takeout sites: Same
Length and float time: 1.5 miles per hour (medium paddle)
   Fort Washington Marina to Fort Washington Lighthouse–1 mile
   Fort Washington Lighthouse to Fort Foote Beach–4 miles
   Fort Foote Beach to National Harbor–1.5 miles
   Fort Foote Beach to Belle Haven Marina–1 mile
   National Harbor to Belle Haven Marina–2 miles
Difficulty: Mild on creek; medium on shoreline; choppy and rough crossing river

Current: Choppy to rough in Potomac River depending on motorboat activity, wind, and weather
Fishing: Anglers may find in this section of the Potomac River smallmouth, striped, and largemouth bass; tiger muskie, crappie, catfish, redbreast sunfish, walleye, pickerel, yellow and white perch, bluegill, sunfish, carp.
Season: Year-round
Fees or permits: Honor system launch fee at Fort Washington and National Harbor Marinas
Nearest city/town: Fort Washington
Boats used: Sea kayaks and recreational boats; paddleboards on Piscataway Creek
Organization: Prince George's County Parks and Recreation
Contacts: None
Rest areas: Multiple throughout route
Restaurant pullouts: Proud Mary Restaurant (family style), Fosters Restaurant, McCormick & Schick's (upscale dining)

Put-In/Takeout Information

Farmington Landing at Piscataway Park, Wharf Road, Accokeek, MD; GPS N38 41.667' / W077 00.830'

Fort Washington National Marina and Proud Mary Restaurant (Atlantic Kayak Company—boat rentals also located here), 13600 King Charles Terrace, Ft. Washington, MD; (301) 292-6455; GPS N38 42.155' / W077 01.455'

Belle Haven Marina (kayak rentals), George Washington Memorial Pkwy., Alexandria, VA; (703) 768-0018; GPS N38 46.587' / W077 02.899'

The marina has a boat ramp, family restaurant, and kayak rentals.

Overview

Piscataway Creek is a tributary of the Potomac and is tidal for its final 2 miles. Records show two variant names for Piscataway Creek: Pascattawaye Creek and Puscattuway Creeke, named by the local Native Americans who originally settled there. A major icon, Fort Washington Lighthouse was built to guide ships of old and the yachts and motorboats of today and, of course, to wish good luck to boaters and kayakers entering Piscataway Creek from the Potomac River.

The Paddle

Piscataway Creek is about 2.5 miles long, and its headwaters divide into two separate branches. Fully half the Piscataway Creek basin becomes a mud flat at low tide. The basin fills and empties twice a day, of course, but in between, the water and the boating are great. During high tides the headwater branches allow kayaks to paddle to the nearby roadways. While exploring the southern branch, we found abundant wildlife so tame they literally crossed in front of our boat. Bring a camera!

The Farmington Landing is a county launch area, but use with caution: The last few times we visited, we did not find this to be a family-oriented or safe location. We suggest the Fort Washington National Marina as a better alternative. They ask for an honor system ramp fee, but the cement ramps are well maintained and the water is deeper here no matter the tidal waters. A seasonal office for Atlantic Kayak Company is also found here. They offer a variety of kayaks to rent, and specialize in group

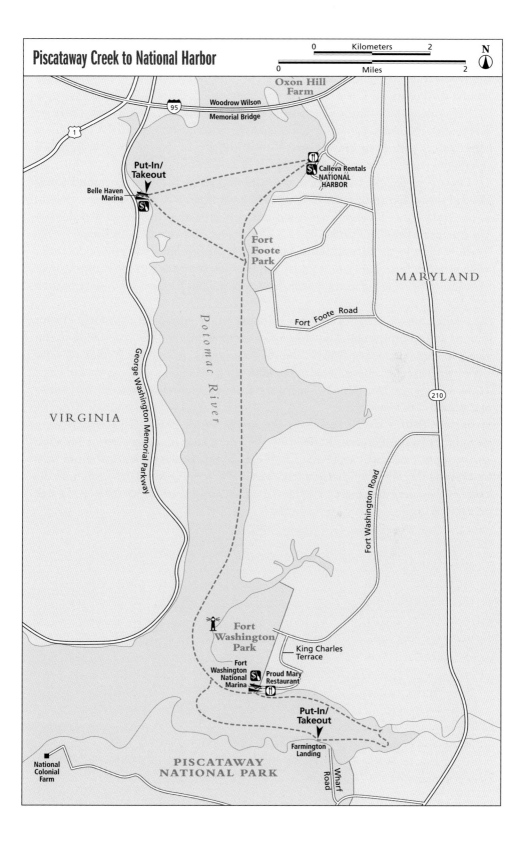

Piscataway Creek to National Harbor

Oxon Hill Farm

95

1

Woodrow Wilson Memorial Bridge

Put-In/ Takeout

Belle Haven Marina

Calleva Rentals
NATIONAL HARBOR

Fort Foote Park

MARYLAND

Fort Foote Road

Potomac River

George Washington Memorial Parkway

210

VIRGINIA

Fort Washington Road

Fort Washington Park

King Charles Terrace

Fort Washington National Marina

Proud Mary Restaurant

Put-In/ Takeout

Farmington Landing

National Colonial Farm

PISCATAWAY NATIONAL PARK

Wharf Road

Kilometers

Miles

N

wilderness tours and group metro Washington, DC, tours. The marina also offers the Proud Mary Restaurant for family dining. This is a perfect 2- to 3-hour paddle around the Piscataway Creek circumference and paddling to the creek's headwaters

For a longer adventure, paddle north from the Piscataway Creek mouth. There are several nice residential coves to explore, and the National Park Service at Fort Foote offers a deer path from the waterfront up to the top of the hill to view historical interpretive signs and actual cannons (free).

Boaters can paddle straight up to the National Harbor to enjoy year-round activities and waterfront restaurants. In May 2014 a world-class Ferris wheel was installed at the end of the dockage. Year-round this new attraction highlights Washington's vistas to visitors and locals alike. There is a kayak rental office with launching from the beach or from kayak floating ramps. The boating opportunities and pull-up locations will change as National Harbor grows and expands. According to the harbormaster/manager's office, they offer no specific launch or pullout facilities for visiting boating guests.

Oxon Cove and Oxon Hill Farm is a short paddle north of the National Harbor and has a caution warning. This cove looks very inviting, and the connecting stream that goes eastward looks navigable, but the tidal waters are extreme. Within a 4-hour period the basin becomes a mudflat. The park has good roads to drive groups of boaters to the basin for launching by special arrangement, but this is for a one-way paddle and is subject to water levels.

Rather than a return paddle to Piscataway Creek, the Belle Haven Marina, directly across the Potomac River from the Fort Foote location, offers a variation to the route that might work for a two-car system. This NPS marina is run by a kayak-friendly contractor that also rents kayaks. There is a user fee to launch from the cement boat ramp and a unique indoor/outdoor green grass carpet shoreline launch area for car-tops.

32 Patuxent River-Northern

It's possible to paddle from Queen Anne's Launch to Selby's Landing where Captain John Smith sailed up the Patuxent River. Follow the Patuxent Water Trail south with multiple launch sites and turnaround locations for a short or long paddle. (I included two other launch sites farther north on the map, but they do not have navigational integrity, and we do not recommend them at this time.)

County: Prince George's County (PGC) and Anne Arundel County (AAC)

Suggested launch sites:
- (PGC) Queen Anne's Launch
- (AAC) Wooton's Landing–Wetlands Park
- (AAC) Patuxent Wetlands Park at Wayson's Corner
- (PGC) Jackson's Landing aka Jug Bay Landing
- (PGC) Selby's Landing

Suggested takeout sites: Same

Length and float time: 1.5 miles per hour (medium paddle)
- (PGC) Queen Anne's Launch to (AAC) Wooton's Launch–1.5 miles
- (AAC) Wooton's Launch to (AAC) Patuxent Mobile Home Park–3.25 miles
- (AAC) Patuxent Mobile Home Park to (AAC) Patuxent Wetlands Park–1.25 miles
- (AAC) Patuxent Wetlands Park to (PGC) Mount Calvert historic site–2 miles
- (PGC) Mount Calvert site to (PGC) Iron Pot Campsite–½ mile
- (PGC) Mount Calvert site to (PGC) Jackson's Landing Ramp and ranger office–¾ mile
- (PGC) Jackson's Landing to (PGC) Selby's Landing–1.5 miles
- (PGC) Selby's Landing to (AAC/Calvert) Lyons Creek–1 mile

Difficulty: Easy

Current: Mild

Fishing: Anglers may find in this section of the Patuxent River largemouth and smallmouth bass, bluegill, pickerel, crappie, catfish, yellow and white perch, carp

Season: Year-round

Fees or permits: None

Nearest city/town: Upper Marlboro

Boats used: Recreational boats and paddleboards

Organizations: PGC and AAC Departments of Parks and Recreation

Contacts: None

Rest areas: Multiple

Restaurant pullouts: None

Put-In/Takeout Information

(PGC) **Queen Anne's Launch** (Patuxent Water Trail Site #52), 18405 Queen Anne Rd., Upper Marlboro, MD; GPS N38 53.106' W076 40.570'

(AAC) **Wooton's Landing**—Wetlands Park (Patuxent Water Trail Site #49), 4632 Sands Rd., Harwood, MD; GPS N38 51.369' / W076 41.180'

(AAC) **Patuxent Wetlands Park** at Wayson's (Corner Patuxent Water Trail Site #47), 1500-1570 Mt. Zion, Marlboro Road, MD; GPS N38 48.687' / W076 42.635'

Osprey are numerous on the creeks and the northern Patuxent River.

(PGC) **Jackson's Landing** aka **Jug Bay Landing** (ranger and visitor station with
   kayak and canoe rentals) (Patuxent Water Trail Site #42), 16000 Croom Airport
   Rd., Upper Marlboro, MD; (301) 627-6074; GPS N38 46.378' / W076 42.556'

(PGC) **Selby's Landing,** part of Patuxent River Park (Patuxent Water Trail Site
   #40), 16000 Croom Airport Rd., Upper Marlboro, MD; GPS N38 45.155' /
   W076 41.992'

Overview

The Patuxent River has long been the shared borderline of several Maryland counties: Anne Arundel, Calvert, St. Mary's, and, of course, Prince George's. Most marine
map guides conclude their maps of the Patuxent River around the area where Calvert County adjoins Anne Arundel County. The waterway associated with this map
area is Lyons Creek, where Captain John Smith turned his shallop around in 1608.
For kayakers going north or, like this adventure, heading south, this waterway was
custom-made, like a well-kept secret!

The Paddle

On the upper end of the Patuxent River, the first put-in point for years has been
the Queen Anne's Launch site. This is a well-maintained, low-floating metal pier that
requires a boater to travel a tangle of back roads to find. The water is deep with a mild
current in both low and high tide. Should someone tell you they paddled up to the

OSPREYS BACK FOR SPRING

In 2014 Two ospreys were fitted with mini GPS tracking units by the Earth Conservation Corps (an urban ecology organization) to find out where Maryland-born ospreys winter and to track their movements to better understand the birds' habits and to help protect the species. The birds, named Rodney and Ron, were tracked to South America. One spent the winter around a lake in the Venezuelan state of Arpure; the other chose to winter in Brazil at an oxbow lake near the Amazon River.

Teflon straps secured the lightweight solar-powered satellite transmitters to the ospreys' backs. The device transmitted data on altitude, headings, and speed. The birds head south because inland fishing waters can freeze during the northern winter and coastal fish tend to stay away from the surface where ospreys can't catch them. The Earth Conservation Corps raised $20,000 and hired Rob Bierrgard, a raptor expert who has been tracking ospreys for over a decade. The two birds were captured in the spring using a special mesh laid in their nests over the seasonal new eggs. Once gently secured, the birds' GPS units were turned on once an hour for 12 hours a day. Ron journeyed about 3,500 miles and Rodney about 2,900 miles.

The annual cycle is typically five months in wintering in the south, one month migrating north, five months in the nesting area, and another month migrating south. Most ospreys like to nest on top of pilings. Look at pilings with navigational signs on the water and there is a good chance you will see branches bundled between the signs. Many communities will put out flat platforms for ospreys to build their nests on. (Woe to unattended sailboats or yachts, as we have seen ospreys build nests on the upper levels of boats when other habitats are taken!) The babies hatch within six weeks from the time the eggs are laid; we have seen little heads sticking out of the nests between mid-April and May.

Governor's Bridge and back, look at their character and see if they fit the "Jungle Jim explorer type with a machete who will portage their boats over trees and boulders in the shallow streams" kind of person. Because that's the landscape above Queen Anne's Launch. The launch areas look appealing but the waterway stops short.

The next site is Wooton's Launch, about 1.5 miles downriver. This is also a low-floating metal pier. About a mile farther, on the west side, on weekends boaters will hear model airplanes buzzing around the river's edge. This is a sanctioned club meeting on county property. The only time you will see a member is when the planes crash into the trees on the river's edge. There is a deer path up to the staging area with port-a-potties. Guests are welcome but not necessarily invited, if you follow my drift. Look for the power lines strung across the river for the location.

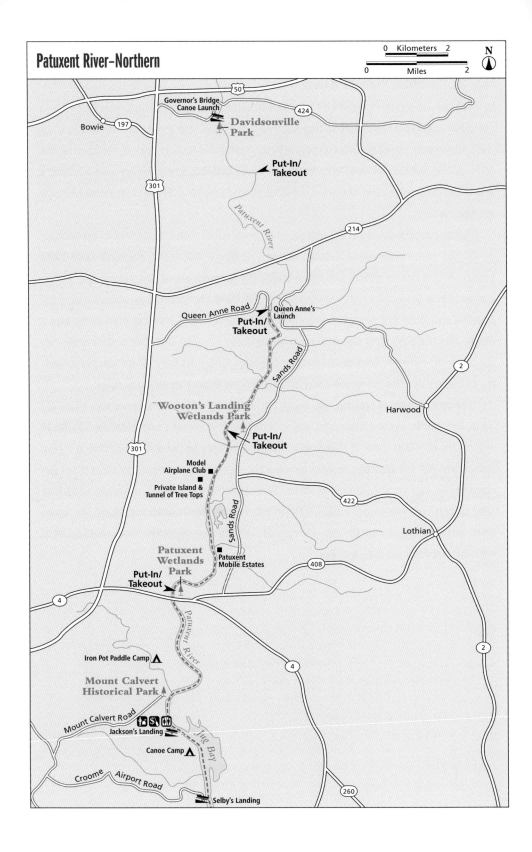

Patuxent River-Northern

0   Kilometers   2

0   Miles   2

N

50

Governor's Bridge
Canoe Launch

424

**Davidsonville
Park**

Bowie

197

**Put-In/
Takeout**

301

Patuxent River

214

Queen Anne Road

Queen Anne's
Launch

**Put-In/
Takeout**

Sands Road

2

**Wooton's Landing
Wetlands Park**

Harwood

**Put-In/
Takeout**

301

Model
Airplane Club ■

Private Island &
Tunnel of Tree Tops

Sands Road

422

Lothian

**Patuxent
Wetlands
Park**

■ Patuxent
Mobile Estates

408

**Put-In/
Takeout**

4

Patuxent River

4

2

Iron Pot Paddle Camp ▲

**Mount Calvert
Historical Park**

Mount Calvert Road

Jackson's Landing

Jug Bay

Canoe Camp ▲

Croome   Airport Road

260

Selby's Landing

The next leg of the journey is where most of the wildlife can be found. Look for turtles on downed trees and singing birds. Snake Island is a tiny strip of private land where folks like to camp. On weekends the old boys have been caught dashing between trees in their birthday suits; one or two many bottles and way too happy. Next is a canopy of interlocking treetops and a rookery of blue birds singing as you pass by. In a couple more miles is the Patuxent Mobile Home Park. This is a private site but they are generous, polite folks wanting to use their picnic benches. Don't use as a pullout area unless it's an emergency, please. *Caution:* The current has made the paddle easy to this point. Look at your watch and add another half hour to paddle back; this location is highly recommended as a turnaround point.

Boaters can paddle another mile south to Patuxent Wetlands Park at Wayson's Corner. This is the midpoint for a long paddle route and an excellent pullout location for a comfortable 6-mile one-way paddle using a two-car system. The next pullout area is 3 miles away, and paddlers should plan to be off the water by 5 p.m.

From Patuxent Wetlands Park to the Mount Calvert historic site is a 2-mile no-stopping paddle. The land texture and characteristics change after the Route 4 bridge. The trees recede, and pussywillow and other grasses hug the shores. Look for redwing blackbirds and hawks. The Mount Calvert site has a low-floating metal pier, but it's just as easy to pull up on shore. Look to the west and on a large branch of water is Iron Pot Campsite, a 0.5-mile paddle in and only accessible by water. The branch goes a bit farther for a short exploration. From the Mount Calvert site to Jackson's Landing Ramp and ranger office is only a 0.75-mile paddle. Kayaks and canoes are rented here year-round by appointment. The basin is called Jug Bay, and Jackson's Landing is often referred to by this nickname.

Jug Bay is a tricky paddle, as the tidal waters will fool you. The large basin seems endless, but at low tide only the center is safe for motorboats as well as kayaks to travel. On the east side of Jug Bay are several Anne Arundel County research offices and wetland study areas, found on the Patuxent Water Trail as marked sites. They're interesting to paddle by, but do not attempt to launch or use as a rest area. The director told me of several boaters who got stranded at low tide and could not get back across the shallow mudflats. Follow the channel markers closely for safety. Near the mouth of Jug Bay is a water-accessible campsite with a long, walk-out, low-level pier that sits in the mud.

From Jackson's Landing to Selby's Landing is a 1.5-mile paddle across Jug Bay. Selby's Landing has a proud history of being one of the first African American airplane landing strips operated by a former Tuskegee Pilot. Also in the marsh area directly adjoining Selby's Landing is Matapoini Creek and the White Oak Campsite. Matapoini Creek travels into the Merkle Wildlife Sanctuary and only stops at low tide 0.25 mile past the pedestrian bridge and walkway that runs through the park. Selby's Landing to Lyons Creek (where Captain John Smith was supposed to have sailed up the Patuxent in his explorations) and the Merkle Wildlife Sanctuary is only a 1-mile paddle away. Lyons Creek is not a long paddle but is worth the time to see at low or high tide, something most marine charts won't tell you.

Queen Anne's County

Kent Island is the doorway into Queen Anne's County from the Bay Bridge. It is the split in Maryland from the Chesapeake Bay that gives rise to the Eastern Shore region. Kent Island was created by tides and currents that cut it from the mainland. A wide and deep boating channel called the "Kent Narrows" separates Kent Island from the rest of Queen Anne's County.

For car-top boaters, the island has most of the county's ramps and launch sites. As an interesting note, this is the largest island in the Chesapeake Bay. Historically Kent Island was originally settled by the Matapeake Ozinie Indians and later by William Claiborne as an extended trading post for Maryland's English settlement.

Economically it was Kent Narrows that became Queen Anne's County's busiest seafood processing area. Archives detail the area having as many as twelve packing-houses. Today the area is known for restaurants and crab houses that serve up the fresh catch brought in year-round by local fishermen.

Queen Anne's County public landing parking permits are required for parking at all landing facilities throughout the county. For a current list of vendors where daily or annual permits may be purchased, visit www.parksnrec.org/hiker-biker-trails/landings-piers/.

Waterfront bar and grill on Narrows (paddle 33)

33 Goodhands to Ferry Point

Queen Anne's County has fifteen launch sites that fall under its parks and recreation department. These are well-maintained boat ramps as well as shoreline mudflats. A car-parking permit is required by all cars parked in one of the launch areas whether you are launching a car-top boat or not. Park police ticket daily throughout the year.

County: Queen Anne's County
Suggested launch sites:
  Goodhands Creek Public Landing
  Chesapeake Exploration Center
  Kent Narrows Public Landing
Suggested takeout sites: Same
Length and float time: 1.5 hours per mile (medium paddle)
  Goodhands Creek Landing to Kent Island Yacht Club—1.5 miles one-way
  Chesapeake Exploration Center to Ferry Point—1.5 miles one-way
  Kent Island Yacht Club to Chesapeake Exploration Center—1.5 miles one-way
Difficulty: Mild to rough depending on motor-boat traffic and weather
Current: Medium

Fishing: Anglers may find in this area bluefish, catfish, weakfish, white perch
Season: Year-round
Fees or permits: A current permit must be displayed by each vehicle parked at any Queen Anne's County launch (this includes car-top boat launching at ramps too). For up-to-date list of vendors, visit www.parksnrec.org/hiker-biker-trails/landings-piers/
Nearest city/town: Kent Island
Boats used: Sea kayaks and recreational boats
Organization: Queen Anne's County Parks and Recreation
Contacts: None
Rest areas: Multiple throughout route
Restaurant pullouts: Yes

Put-In/Takeout Information

Kent Island Kayaks (bike, kayak, and fishing pole rentals, tours), 110 Channel Marker Way, Grasonville, MD; (410) 991-8468 or (877) KI-KAYAK (545-2925)

Passion Paddle Sports (rental service for canoes, kayaks, and specializing in paddle-boards), 325 Cleat St., Stevensville, MD; (443) 458-4259 or (866) 735-5926

Goodhands Creek Public Landing, Goodhands Creek Road, Chester MD; GPS N38 57.785' / W076 15.882'

Chesapeake Exploration Center (QAC Visitor Center and DNR office), 425 Piney Narrows Rd., Chester MD; (410) 604-2100; GPS N38 58.527' / W076 14.942'

Kent Narrows Public Landing, Piney Narrows Road, Chester MD; GPS N38 58.300' / W076 14.938'

Overview

This adventure shows off Queen Anne's waterfront to the max. Kent Island is a hub for tourists, and you have the choice of a good sightseeing paddle, a little private

Beach, boats, and picnics at Ferry Park

beach with walk-around camera time, or to speed demon through the tourist areas and soak up some wildlife marsh area before heading to the beach cove (or not); lots of possibilities.

The Paddle

Goodhands Creek Public Launch is a typical cement ramp launch area in Queen Anne's County with plenty of parking for cars, trucks, and boat trailers. Make sure your parking permit is on the windshield or dashboard. Backing up to unload is usually not a problem, but during peak season when parking is tight and motorboats are anxiously waiting to launch, maybe portaging boats a few feet from parked cars might be neighborly. At high or low tide, paddling is good and doable. Scenic trees and shorelines are the main characteristics here. Follow the horizon to the left. As you come out of the bay, the water opens up wide; hug the coastline if big boats are making wakes, but the water usually stays fairly calm year-round.

The first peninsula of land you see is the home of the private (and extremely friendly) Kent Island Yacht Club. A small kayak beach is on the bay side for an emergency potty run or a picnic lunch on their launch site. As you paddle around the long, cement breakwater protection barrier, the water becomes turbulent with boating traffic. If you have a whistle or a bike horn, keep it handy, as the big-boy boats do not always see kayaks. Paddle to the left under the bridges to Ferry Point for a shorter trip to the park beach and you may skip the next paragraph!

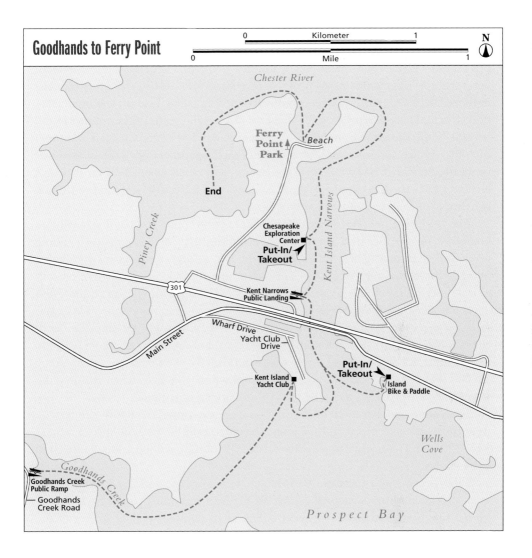

Kilometer

Mile

N

Chester River

Ferry Point Park
Beach

End

Piney Creek

Kent Island Narrows

Chesapeake Exploration Center
Put-In/ Takeout

301

Kent Narrows Public Landing

Wharf Drive
Yacht Club Drive

Main Street

Put-In/ Takeout

Kent Island Yacht Club

Island Bike & Paddle

Wells Cove

Goodhands Creek
Goodhands Creek Public Ramp
Goodhands Creek Road

Prospect Bay

Paddle to the right if you are a speed demon and want the longer paddle-only adventure. Here boaters will find a multitude of bars and grills for tourists elbowing each other for waterfront among the coves and marinas. We found a beach safe enough to pull up on for temporary rest and recreation but not as a put-in or takeout area around the Wells Cove area. Also found here is Island Bike and Paddle, a boat rental company that uses a floating launch platform for kayaks. You can poke into Oyster Cove and come full circle paddling Marshy Creek. Here you will see Chesapeake Bay Environmental Center (CBEC) land and perhaps a kayak or two from a kayak rental company at this location. The CBEC still retains the "Horse Head Environmental Center" nickname because the peninsula, from an aerial shot, has the shape of a horse's head. Now paddle out of the basin and head back into traffic.

Because of closeness of the two sides of the shores, this area is called the "Narrows." It is also the defining area of Kent Island and its two adjacent connecting bridges. On the left shore is Kent Narrows Public Landing, a well-paved and multiple-run cement ramp area for heavy traffic motorboat use. Kayaks are also welcome, but boaters need to move fast, as the crowd of trailers is usually lined up taking boats in and out during peak season. There is a pavilion for shelter if the weather turns stormy. Keep to the left side of the shoreline to reach the Chesapeake Bay Exploration Center and tourism office, which also has a small local office of the Department of Natural Resources (waterfront police if you will). There are two cement ramps chained off for their use, but local folks use the ramps for kayak launches and easy parking. Good restrooms, benches, picnic tables, and tourism brochures are found here.

The land becomes waterfront tall grassland as you round the peninsula. Motorboats pick up speed as they see the open water, and their owners grip their fishing rods a little tighter. Paddle a little more to the left; around the corner is your afternoon destination, Ferry Point Park—a kayak resting area but not a launch or takeout location according to the Queen Anne water trail map. This is a quiet, protected cove with shallow waters. No motorboats enter here, and most big waves fade before reaching this cove. A long, wide stretch of white beach awaits. Unstrap the beach chairs and reapply the suntan lotion. One small word of caution is advised: Locals use this location as a dog park and throw sticks and such for their pets, and because they are pets they leave behind . . . presents. So look where you walk when roaming the wooded park area. Good sweeping vistas for photographs is a plus.

Depending on how much time you have spent exploring, the return paddle may need to be straightforward and focused, as an afternoon breeze will kick in around 3 to 4:30 p.m. The normal 2-plus-hour flatwater journey will be a little longer and more taxing.

I always bring an extra can of an electrolyte drink and snack for teatime. These semi-healthy stimulants will pick you up for the hard, rewarding paddle back to your launch site. If an afternoon rainstorm comes in by surprise, pull in to any of the marinas or other stops mentioned. Folks around this area are understanding and will take care of you.

34 Southeast Creek and Island Creek

These creeks are on the Queen Anne's County side of the Chester River. The Southeast Creek public ramp is near the confluence with the Chester River. Rolph's Wharf Marina, with a bed-and-breakfast inn, is on the Chester River just north of the creeks and is an easy paddle.

County: Queen Anne's County
Suggested launch sites:
  Rolph's Wharf Marina
  Kennersley Point Marina
  Southeast Creek Public Landing
Suggested takeout sites: Same
Length and float time: 1 mile per hour (slow paddle)
  Southeast Creek Public Landing—1 mile from the mouth with 2 miles more going east
  Island Creek is near the mouth—2 miles south to Granny Finley Branch fork
Difficulty: Easy

Current: Mild
Season: Year-round
Fees or permits: Queen Anne's County requires permits at public locations; www.parks nrec.org/hiker-biker-trails/landings-piers/
Nearest city/town: Church Hill
Boats used: Sea kayaks and recreational boats; paddleboards only on Indian Creek
Organizations: none
Contact: Queen Anne's County Parks and Recreation
Rest areas: Multiple quiet coves
Restaurant pullouts: Rolph's B&B Inn

Put-In/Takeout Information

Centreville Outdoors at The Wharf (CD Outdoors LLC) (rental service for kayaks and paddleboards; delivery fee), 101 Waterway, Centreville, MD; (410) 991-8468
Rolph's Wharf Marina—Bed & Breakfast Inn, 1008 Rolph's Wharf Rd., Chestertown, MD; (410) 778-6347; GPS N39 10.431' / W076 02.223'
Kennersley Point Marina, 223 Marina Ln., Church Hill, MD; (410) 758-2394; GPS N39 09.152' / W076 02.350'
Southeast Creek Public Landing, Southeast Creek Road, Church Hill, MD; GPS N39 09.469' / W076 01.552'

Overview

This adventure starts from the confluence of the Chester River and goes from the mouth into the wider Southeast Creek, which winds down into a smaller branch, or into Island Creek, which is narrow and better protected. Both are first-rate paddles that are strongly affected by the morning and evening weather, wind, and tides.

There are some quiet times paddlers just can't explain.

The Paddle

Southeast Creek is wide and the land geography is fairly flat. This is an important fact to note, as the afternoon breeze has a "tunnel" effect, and paddling against the wind can become a challenge. The creek maintains its depth in the main channel at high tide as well as low tide. The creek does have protected twists and turns during the second hour of paddling east. Check your watch, the tides, and wind for your return paddle back. (***Caution:*** Sometimes this creek's water can be choppy.)

Island Creek is off Southeast Creek near the Chester River mouth, or confluence. It can be accessed from the Southeast Creek Public Landing launch or the Kennersley Point Marina directly on Island Creek. The marina has a shoreline beach and mini sand ramp. This creek is narrower, with high land banks, and is forested the entire length going south. Even with an afternoon breeze, the water never gets above a small ripple and makes an excellent paddleboarding area. The depth of the creek is moderate and doable only to the Island Creek Bridge, two-thirds the travel adventure during low tide. On the southern side of Island Creek Bridge, the water trail changes its name to Granny Finley Branch.

Our paddle was cut short due to the fast change in the creek's depth during the low tide period. (***Caution:*** On the Eastern Shore, when a body of water is tidal and only moderate in depth, as the tide current changes to low tide, sometimes nature expedites the flow, and a paddler can become stranded within a matter of minutes

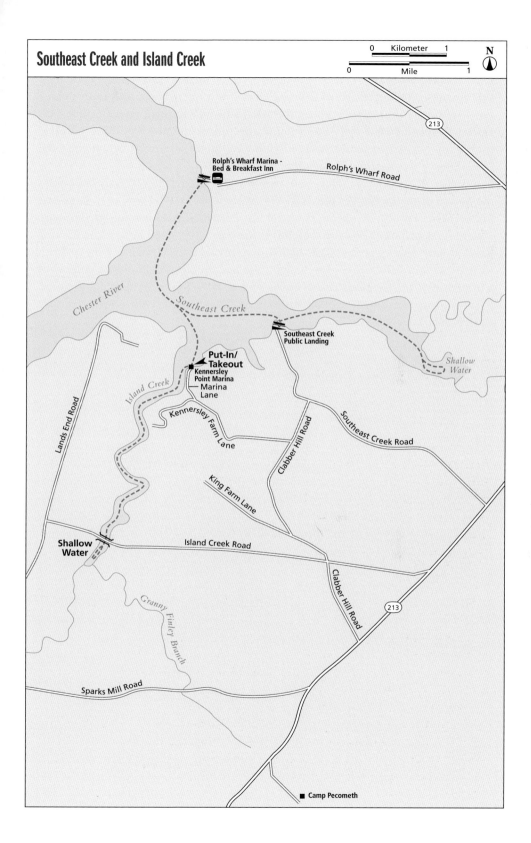

Southeast Creek and Island Creek

0 Kilometer 1
0 Mile 1

N

213

Rolph's Wharf Marina - Bed & Breakfast Inn

Rolph's Wharf Road

Chester River

Southeast Creek

Southeast Creek Public Landing

Shallow Water

Put-In/ Takeout

Kennersley Point Marina

Marina Lane

Lands End Road

Island Creek

Kennersley Farm Lane

Clabber Hill Road

Southeast Creek Road

King Farm Lane

Shallow Water

Island Creek Road

Clabber Hill Road

213

Granny Finley Branch

Sparks Mill Road

Camp Pecometh

with only inches of water depth and mudflats in every direction.) A local who kayaks Granny Finley's said that at high tide the trip to the creek's headwaters is fairly long and rewarding. He remembered seeing a variety of scarce wild animals in that elongated area. Again, check your watch, the tide, and winds on your return paddle. This creek is a rewarding and safe 3-hour round-trip to and from the low wooden bridge back to the marina or public ramp. Only during high tide should you attempt the extra distance into Granny Finley's Branch.

Rolph's Wharf Marina with the River Inn Bed & Breakfast is just a mile from the mouth of the creeks. We met Skip the owner as he and the staff were preparing for the Memorial Day weekend. The pool was clean, fresh, and inviting (pay for use). The bar and grill on their sandy beach is Party-ville USA! They use a reconditioned flat-bottomed fishing boat with its hull buried in sand for their bar, and the grill is a massive outdoor barbecue cooker. Rolph's also has a good-condition boat ramp with a minimal use fee for launching boats, as well as skiffs for crabbing and a pontoon boat for gentle motorboat explorations to rent. What a good weekend place to start and finish an adventure.

St. Mary's County

Called the "Birthplace of Maryland," St. Clement's Island was the place where Leonard Calvert and his English adventurers first touched Maryland soil. Today the island is a state park with hiking trails, picnic tables, information boards, and a boat dock and fishing pier. The park is half a mile from the shoreline but accessible only by boat.

After they landed at St. Clement's Island, the English explorers sailed the *Ark of London* and the *Dove* up what is now called the St. Mary's River. They were sold/given the Indian village along with 30 square miles of land around it. This established Maryland's first permanent settlement, St. Mary's City. The city served as Maryland's capital for the next sixty years. The original city was all but forgotten after the capital moved to Annapolis in 1695.

Saint Mary's College campus is small, but represents the heart of the county (paddle 35).

35 Great Mills to St. Mary's College

This 7-mile one-way shuttle adventure using two cars goes from the headwaters of the St. Mary's River to St. Mary's College Boatyard and Historical Park—a fun full day if the stream has enough water!

County: St. Mary's County

Suggested launch sites:
Great Mills Canoe/Kayak Launch
St. Mary's Boatyard (shoreline beach)

Suggested takeout sites: Same

Length and float time: 1.5 miles per hour (medium paddle)
Great Mills to Tippy Witchity Island (privately owned)—3.25 miles one-way
Great Mills to St. Mary's College Boatyard—7 miles one-way

Difficulty: Moderate to difficult. During dry season the shallow creek has sandbars and downed trees that may require portaging. Strong current during rainy season

Current: Usually flat, calm water

Fishing: Anglers might be able to find spot and perch in this area

Season: Year-round

Fees or permits: None

Nearest city/towns: Leonardtown, Great Mills, and St. Mary's City

Boats used: Smaller recreational craft like kayaks and canoes

Organization: St. Mary's County Recreation and Parks

Contacts: None

Rest areas: Multiple shorelines

Restaurant pullouts: None

Put-In/Takeout Information

Coltons Point Marina (boat ramp) (rents and sells kayaks and day tours for St. Clements Island), 3800 Kopels Rd., Coltons Point, MD; (301) 769-3121

Great Mills Canoe/Kayak Launch, 20228 Point Lookout Rd., Great Mills, MD; GPS N38 14.247' / W076 29.945'

St. Mary's College Boatyard (shoreline beach), off Route 5, Trinity Church Road, St. Mary's College, MD; GPS N38 11.356' / W076 25.955'

Overview

On March 27, 1634, a group of 300 English settlers arrived on two ships—the *Dove* and the *Ark*—and founded St. Mary's City. Governor Leonard Calvert led the group of settlers, who originally had landed up the Potomac River's north shore on St. Clement's Island. March 25, celebrated as Maryland Day, is an official state and county holiday.

According to archaeologists and historians, the original St. Mary's was laid out according to the baroque town plan, which called for the settlers to live within the township and included community buildings such as a church, stores, and homes. The layout directed outlying farms, fields, woods, and orchards to be laid out in a grid or

The paddle route is as fun as the sign.

strips of land. After the initial establishment, however, most residents preferred to live on their farming plantations in the surrounding countryside. The primary cash crop was tobacco. Governor Calvert hoped the settlement would be the capital of the new Maryland colony, but that of course went to Annapolis.

Today the old St. Mary's City area is laid out as a living museum with the home-sites dug out and a few buildings reconstructed, to showcase the simple buildings the colonials would have built.

It is interesting to note that the previous occupants of the land were a Native American tribe called the Yaocomico. Their chief, Tayac Kittimundiq, a sub-tribal leader in the Piscataway Indian Nation, gave the land to the newcomers. At the museum grounds, interpretive signs try to explain to visitors the vast differences in the two cultures. For a period of time, the two groups coexisted peacefully.

The Paddle

This adventure is memorable, but it requires lots of preparation, the right day, and favorable weather. Exploring the headwaters of a creek or river can take a boater up some mighty skinny waterways. My partners and I usually can go where the water is at least 12 inches deep and there is some possibility of a turnaround area without having to paddle backwards for the last mile or so to deeper water. So imagine a launch area that is already at the headwaters, and the current is going downhill taking you

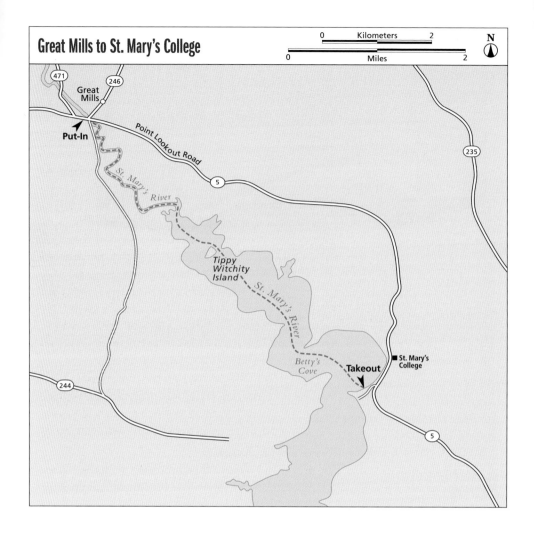

with it! Navigable creeks going both ways are not always possible, and although the county and state say boaters can come and go both directions in this tiny stream, I would seriously have a plan B in my pocket.

Most headwater streams get more water in the spring and in the fall. Summer is when the use demand is high, but sometimes a drought and low water levels just won't cooperate. My kayak has a fishing boat design that is loaded with safety and comfort amenities with a heavy bottom for stability. Portaging over sandbars and logs is not my cup of tea, and this route merits caution for the first mile. The rest of the trip is fine, but at low tide, mudflats are common in all creeks and rivers. If you start out at high tide, remember that in 4 to 5 hours the water level may drop and make the stream or creek look and the paddle feel very different, especially if the current is going downhill naturally and you must paddle against it to go back.

Look for some islands in the river as it opens up. The largest island—Tippy Witchity—is privately owned but is typically used as a halfway marker. The takeout is at the St. Mary's College Boatyard. As boaters travel through the basins, the largest is Betty's Cove; from here the college's mini marina of docks with indoor-outdoor carpeting as padding for the constant use of boats by students is easy to spot. Look to the far left; a sandy beach is out of the mainstream of activity but still close enough to the boatyard court. The beach is adjacent to the college's cement boat ramp. The county has some arrangement with the college for visitor use of the facility, but this does not include parking! Every parking lot the college owns posts dire warnings of cars being towed if they do not have a proper parking sticker. The county says this a drop and go location. Parking is a mile away in the Campus Center—Lot K on the left.

St. Mary's City is not really a city by head count; it's a small college town without the town. How such a small area was built without a thought about parking for guests and users is part of the mystery and character. Drive around the brick buildings of the campus for a taste of a clean, safe place to send your kids. Take the historical walk in the outside museum area and find lots of good information on the interpretive panels along the pathways. The highlight is a handcrafted ship that is a good copy of the original colonial ship, the *Dove*. The tourist guides fire a small cannon for the schoolkids that shoots out confetti mixed with gunpowder—quite a jaw-dropper and lots of smiles all around.

There is a pull-up beach next to the ship docks with a picnic table; be polite and maybe you won't get chased away. There is also a historical inn that serves food during the season, and nothing else but empty picnic tables—lots and lots of picnic tables. Leonardtown is about 30 minutes away and is the missing small town, with some interesting non-chain family restaurants that look inviting.

36 St. Inigoes Landing and Creeks

Two protected creeks are perfect for recreational boats and good long paddles for faster sea kayaks; paddleboarding is possible with caution.

County: St. Mary's County
Suggested launch sites:
  St. Inigoes Landing
  BluHaven Marina
Suggested takeout sites: Same
Length and float time: 1.5 miles per hour (medium paddle)
  Smith Creek loop—4.75 miles
  Jutland Creek loop—6.75 miles
Difficulty: Easy
Current: Mild
Season: Year-round

Fees or permits: None
Nearest city/town: Leonardtown
Boats used: Sea kayaks and recreational boats (waterways are a little too open with lots of commercial traffic in creeks to recommend paddleboarding)
Organization: St. Mary's County Recreation and Parks
Contacts: None
Rest areas: Multiple throughout creek areas
Restaurant pullouts: None

Put-In/Takeout Information

St. Inigoes Landing (public ramp and shoreline), 46621 Beachville Rd., St. Inigoes, MD; GPS N38 06.696' / W076 24.935'

BluHaven Piers Marina (ramp and rentals), 48409 Smith Dr. (PO Box 513) Ridge, MD 20680; (301) 872–5838; GPS N38 07.628' /W076 23.696'

Launch from cement ramp or sandy beach

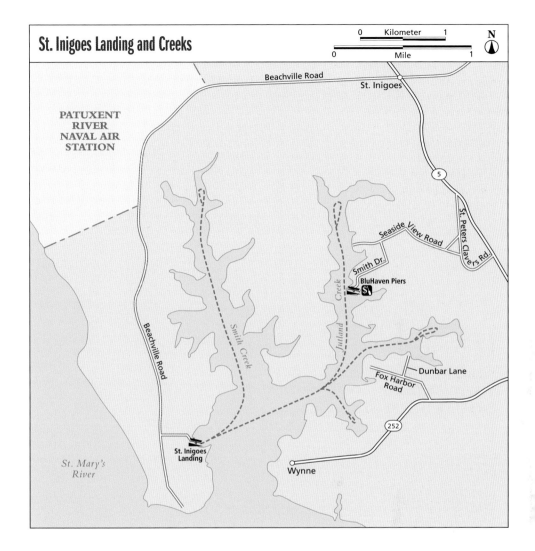

Overview

The landing at St. Inigoes has been updated and looks fairly new and welcoming. It's a well-maintained area with seasonal restrooms and amenities.

The Paddle

These creeks are mostly protected paddling areas in that they are not subject to the open waters of the St. Mary's River, which are wide and deep in this location. Smith Creek explores the shoreline of the St. Inigoes State Forest. Boaters will see farmlands, woodlands, and natural preserve areas. Your exploration of Smith Creek is about 4.75 miles long.

Jutland Creek has a shallow headwaters basin where ducks and geese congregate and raise families in relative safety; it's especially good viewing with binoculars during the spring hatching season. The Jutland Creek loop is 6.75 miles long. BluHaven Piers Marina is kayak friendly, has a ramp, and rents kayaks.

37　Port of Leonardtown Park and Winery

Leonardtown, like many small to medium Maryland towns with colorful characteristics, has invested strongly in its waterfront for tourism. The Leonardtown Wharf is a waterfront park for both locals and tourists. The park made its debut in 2008, and the revamped and remodeled Port of Leonardtown Park and Winery opened in 2009. Leonardtown is also known for its oyster-shucking championship at the annual state fairgrounds and perhaps its Mennonite farming community, where members sell homemade and home-grown products.

County: St. Mary's County

Suggested launch sites:

  Port of Leonardtown Public Park

  Leonardtown Public Wharf Park

  Camp Calvert Public Landing

  Abell's Public Wharf

Suggested takeout sites: Same

Length and float time: 1.5 hours per mile (medium paddle)

  Port of Leonardtown Park to Leonardtown Wharf—2.5 miles

  Leonardtown Wharf to Camp Calvert Park—0.5 mile

  Camp Calvert Park to Abell's Wharf—3 miles

Difficulty: Mild to rough

Current: Mild to strong

Fishing: unknown

Season: Year-round

Fees or permits: None

Nearest city/town: Leonardtown

Boats used: Sea kayaks and recreational boats

Organization: St. Mary's County Recreation and Parks

Contacts: None

Rest areas: Multiple throughout route

Restaurant pullouts: Winery has sausage, cheese, and crackers to purchase

Put-In/Takeout Information

Port of Leonardtown Public Park (year-round winery and ramp) (Patuxent Adventure Center—seasonal kayak rentals, 410-394-2770), 23190 Newtowne Neck Rd., Leonardtown, MD; GPS N38 18.191' / W076 39.449'

Leonardtown Public Wharf Park (plastic car-top pull-up ramp) (Patuxent Adventure Center—seasonal kayak rentals, 410-394-2770), 22500 Washington St., Leonardtown, MD; GPS N38 17.159' / W076 38.264'

Camp Calvert Public Landing (shoreline launch), 22530 Camp Calvert Rd., Leonardtown, MD; GPS N38 17.048' / W076 37.754'

Abell's Public Wharf (boat ramp and shoreline launch), 21620 Abells Wharf Rd., Leonardtown, MD; GPS N38 15.633' / W076 38.711'

Overview

The winery, housed in an old state highways garage that has been adapted for this new use and fitted with state-of-the-art wine production equipment, is now producing its

Fun place for families, friends, and romantic dates

first wines. The facility shares acreage with the McIntosh Run canoe/kayak launch and the Port of Leonardtown Public Park. McIntosh Run is a tidal run that flows through a 53-acre wildlife conservation area and out into Breton Bay.

The Paddle

The Port of Leonardtown Public Park and Winery name sounds more impressive that the actual building and waterway. The creek is a good kayak paddle with a decent small-craft cement ramp; a kayak rental company is on-site during the season; and there's lots of parking on tiny washed-stone pebbles. The winery is housed in a small, plain, and unimaginative building, but the atmosphere inside is cozy, and the wine-tasting bar is long and accommodating. There are tables and chairs and refrigerated sausage logs and chunks of cheese with boxes of crackers to make a meal—a great date and wine-tasting experience. Our hostess knew her stuff and poured twelve samples (six per person for a nominal fee), and customers sipped slowly. They sell a lot of wine. Boaters can launch from this location and/or return here depending on how long they want to paddle.

The county says the water trail is safe for beginners, and for the first 2 miles the waterway meanders through canopies filled with wildlife such as bald eagles, orioles, and wild turkeys. Farther along, the waterway opens up to large marshes and duck blinds. Leonardtown Wharf has a visitor center; about half a mile up the main road

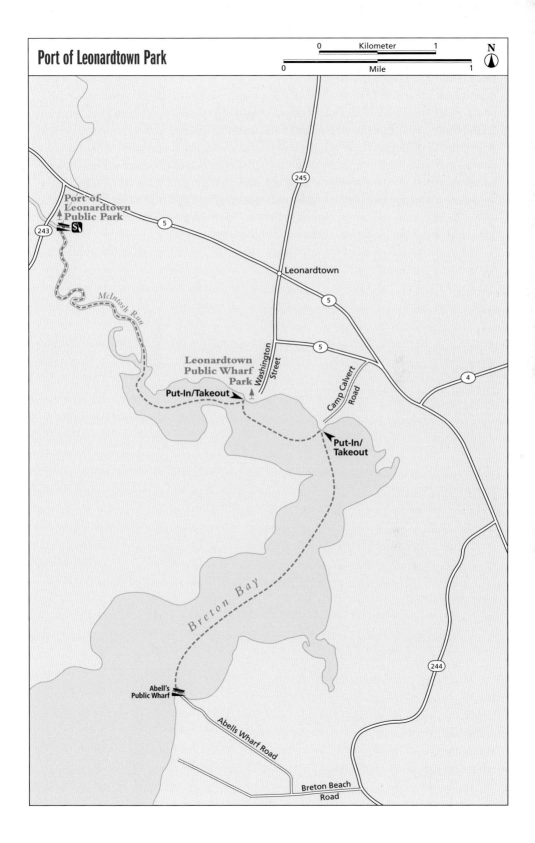

is the downtown area with family restaurants and interesting stores. The wharf is a brick bulkhead with a plastic launch/incline for car-tops and is easy to use. If the downtown noise and brick bulkhead do not appeal, paddle about another 0.5 mile to Camp Calvert Park. This small, unassuming waterfront park has a strip of sand on its shoreline and a few picnic tables hidden under large shade trees. Street parking is minimal, but the atmosphere is quiet and friendly. Hug the shore, continuing through Breton Bay, and 3 miles later is Abell's Wharf with a cement boat ramp and a sandy beach shoreline. Some maps show a shaded park grounds just before the ramp. This is an ongoing anthropological dig in an old Indian village and not a tourist attraction, although I am sure they are proud of their state-sponsored work and might welcome folks with a genuine interest.

Talbot County

Talbot County is considered the midway section of Maryland's Eastern Shore region. To the north lies Queen Anne's County with the Wye River as Talbot's border. To the east lies Caroline County and to the south Dorchester County with the Choptank River, all bordering Talbot County. The Chesapeake Bay is to the west. The county's geography is a study of the creeks, rivers, and coves that travel deep into the county's territory from all directions.

The county government seat is Easton, the only major city in the county to have public water and sewer services, which has enhanced its growth and desirability as a prime residential location for the entire Eastern Shore. There are some well-known visitor centers that have attracted statewide attention, emphasizing the county's character and promoting cities and towns like Tilghman Island, St. Michaels, and Oxford.

Bed and Breakfasts, like this one in St. Michaels, can be found throughout the Eastern Shore (paddle 39).

38 Oxford Town

Oxford is a small, historical waterfront town that enjoys company, but is not specifically tourism oriented. The town boasts a restaurant-inn with character, a waterfront bed-and-breakfast, a seasonal ferry, several marinas, a long, white sand community beach, town parks with bands that play on seasonal weekends, and a calm-water harbor that is perfect for paddleboards.

County: Talbot County
Suggested launch sites:
 Bellevue Landing
 Ferry Park
 Community Beach
 Town Parking Lot
 Schooners Landing
Suggested takeout sites: Same
Length and float time: 1 mile per hour (slow paddle)
Difficulty: Easy on Town Creek; choppy and rough on Tred Avon River
Current: None in Town Creek; swift on Tred Avon River

Fishing: Anglers may find in Oxford Town waters bluefish, weakfish
Season: Year-round
Fees or permits: None
Nearest city/town: Oxford Town
Boats used: Recreational boats and paddleboards in Town Creek; sea kayaks in Tred Avon River
Organization: None
Contact: Talbot County Parks and Recreation
Rest areas: Multiple
Restaurant pullouts: Multiple

Put-In/Takeout Information

Easton Cycle and Sport (bike and kayak rental deliveries); (410) 822-7433

Bellevue Landing, 5536 Bellevue Rd., Royal Oak, MD 21662; GPS N38 42.173' / W076 10.898'

Ferry Park (small cement car-top ramp), West Strand, Oxford, MD 21654; GPS N38 41.596' / W076 10.477'

Community Beach (shoreline launch), East Strand, Oxford, MD 21654; GPS N38 41.662' / W076 10.221'

Town Parking Lot (shoreline launch), East Strand, Oxford, MD 21654; GPS N38 41.690' / W076 10.160'

Schooners Landing (Oxford Town public cement ramp; mix of restaurant and public ramp—parking limited), end of Tilghman Street, Oxford, MD 21654; GPS N38 41.582' / W076 10.120'

Sandaway Bed & Breakfast, 103 Strand Rd., Oxford, MD 21654; GPS N38 41.530' / W076 10.544'

Oxford's public beach is called the Strand, and all community events that involve getting wet are held here.

Overview

The one public boat ramp, which is owned by Oxford Town, adjoins a family seafood restaurant called Schooners. Parking is limited, and the launching fee rate for "all boats" has irritated many visitors and local residents. Kayakers can avoid the fees with other available launch opportunities. The Tred Avon River is wide and deep, making currents and weather major factors in exploring Oxford Town's shoreline and other nearby creeks unless your boat is a sea kayak or you are a bold recreational boater!

The Paddle

The ferry that crosses the Tred Avon River is seasonal and is used to transport people, cars, and bikes. The river is only 0.5 mile wide and would make an interesting paddle on a calm day.

Next to the Oxford Ferry pier is a curious, small, green area called Ferry Park, with a small cement boat ramp. The ramp is not able to accommodate motorboat trailers, which usually leaves it open and free to car-top boaters. Thus begins this paddling adventure.

Paddle west of Ferry Park past a private yacht club with a fine sandy beach that they do not want to share. Next to it is a respectable bed-and-breakfast and a tiny public shoreline beach. The coastline waterway, with heavy riprap rock erosion control, continues parallel to the town until Oxford Park. A small opening in the water

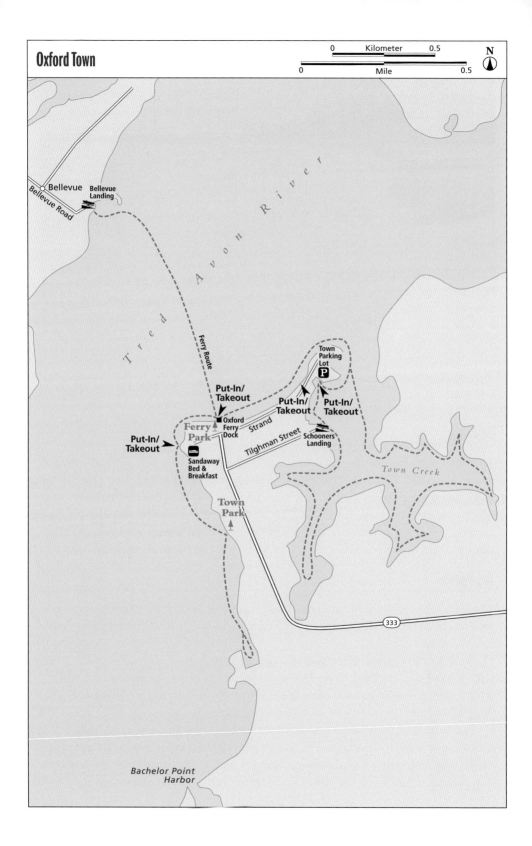

Oxford Town

0   Kilometer   0.5
0   Mile   0.5

N

Bellevue

Bellevue Road

Bellevue Landing

Tred Avon River

Ferry Route

Town Parking Lot

P

Put-In/ Takeout

Put-In/ Takeout

Put-In/ Takeout

Oxford Ferry Dock

Strand

Put-In/ Takeout

Ferry Park

Sandaway Bed & Breakfast

Tilghman Street

Schooners Landing

Town Creek

Town Park

333

Bachelor Point Harbor

break looks like it "might" accommodate a kayak, but also looks too sharp and rough to recommend. The coastline continues to the Bachelor Point Harbor marina (no ramp or pullout advertised). Turn around here for safety. The waterway continues to the confluence of the Choptank River and the Tred Avon River.

To the east of Ferry Park past the Oxford Ferry Pier is the town's community beach. Internet photos show the townsfolk enjoying all kinds of fun activities held here year-round, and a few folks actually sunbathing and swimming on the beach. Free public parking is offered at the end of the beach. The Town Parking Lot has shoreline access to Town Creek if you want to avoid the Tred Avon River altogether. Paddle around the point and the marina situated there to where the mouth of Town Creek or Oxford's harbor opens up. Here is pleasant, calm water for paddleboarding or slow recreational kayakers who love to peek and poke. My map shows at least three marinas, and I found a waterfront ice cream shop, the Schooners Restaurant, and a few coves. Who knows what else you will find exploring Oxford.

The folks on the shoreline on the other side of the ferry route say they also have a public boat ramp at Bellevue Park and two longer protected creeks to explore: Tar Creek and Plain Dealing Creek. But that's another day and another paddle.

39 St. Michaels Town

Easton, a few minutes away, is the largest city/town within an hour's drive, but St. Michaels is the gateway for kayakers in Talbot County. A small, residential, historical town where half the stores close for the season after Christmas, it seems the residents carry summer in their hearts year-round.

County: Talbot County
Suggested launch sites:
  East Chew Public Boat Ramp
  West Chew Shoreline Launch Park
Suggested takeout sites:
  Tunis Mill Bridge
  Oak Creek Landing Waterfront Park
Length and float time: 1.5 miles per hour (medium paddle)
  East Chew Ramp to Leeds Creek—1.5 miles across Miles River to Leeds Creek mouth, and 2 more miles to Tunis Mill Bridge landing
  East Chew Ramp to Oak Creek landing—3 miles one-way along Miles River; Oak Creek is 1-mile round-trip paddle in protected creek.
  St. Michaels round-trip on San Domingo Creek from West Chew shoreline launch

park—5 miles round-trip in a protected creek to islands and back
Difficulty: Easy on San Domingo Creek; rough and choppy on Miles Creek
Current: None in San Domingo Creek; the Miles River is deep and wide
Fishing: Anglers may find in St. Michaels area Catfish, Spot & White Perch
Season: Year-round
Fees or permits: None for car-top boats
Nearest city/town: St. Michaels
Boats used: Recreational boats; paddleboards only on San Domingo Creek
Organizations: None
Contact: Talbot County Parks and Recreation
Rest areas: None posted on maps
Restaurant pullouts: Three in St. Michaels' downtown harbor

Put-In/Takeout Information

Shore Pedal and Paddle (bike, kayak, and paddleboard sales and rentals), 500 S. Talbot St. (shop), 125 Mulberry St. (dock), St Michaels, MD; (410) 745-2320

East Chew Public Boat Ramp, Corner East Chew and West Harbor Road, St. Michaels, MD; GPS N38 47.043' / W076 13.134'

West Chew Shoreline Launch Park, 305 West Chew Ave., St. Michaels, MD; GPS N38 46.843' W076 13.577'

Oak Creek Landing (public boat ramp, also known as Newcomb), 26000 St. Michael's Rd. (Route 33/Oak Creek Bridge), Newcomb, MD; GPS N38 45.202' / W076 10.527'

Tunis Mill Bridge (public boat ramp), Tunis Mills Road Bridge, Easton, MD; GPS N38 49.294' / W076 10.049'

St. Michaels is a tourist town proud of its maritime history and it shows 365 days a year.

Overview

St. Michaels Town is a thriving waterfront tourist town. There are no shopping malls, 7-11s, or franchise stores, only 5 blocks of converted colonial homes and tiny storefront buildings filled with artist renderings of colorful knickknacks, fun-loving T-shirts, kayak sun hats in every other store, and ten or more neighborhood-type grills and sandwich shops. Everything is water oriented and upscale. I bought the last two kayak Christmas ornaments at the year-round Christmas store. The owner laughed and said the kayak ornaments were among the most popular and first to go when the new shipments came in.

St. Michaels is very kayak friendly with water access on both sides of the town. San Domingo Creek is a well-protected waterway that seems perfect for paddle-boards but does empty into a larger body of water called Broad Creek, which is better suited for sea kayaks and bolder recreational boats. The downtown harbor has calm water, three seasonal waterfront restaurants, a hotel, two bed-and-breakfast inns, and a first-class marine museum with inside and outside historical displays. For any paddle routes from the downtown harbor public ramps, travel is along the Miles River, which is wide and deep with prevailing weather making the difference of which route to paddle outside the mouth of the town harbor.

CAPTAIN JOHN SMITH'S SHALLOP

In 1607 Captain John Smith took members from the Jamestown colony and explored the Virginia and Maryland coastlines. His notes and maps are celebrated today as one of the first detailed explorations of land, coasts, and native peoples of those regions. The boat he sailed on is called a shallop. The ship that brought the colonists to a new land was tight for space, and only things of great import were sent whole. For example, the metal for shovels and picks was shipped but not the wooden handles. However, the shallop, designed and built in England, was sent to America cut and freighted in two pieces in the ship the *Susan Constant*, and reassembled later, which gives a sense of the boat's importance. Two engineered copies of the original shallop were built. One of those boats is at the Maritime Museum in St. Michaels. To celebrate Jamestown's 400th anniversary, in 2007 the second boat, staffed with a crew of twelve, undertook to repeat the voyages of Captain Smith.

A shallop refers to an open wooden boat that is small enough to row but also has one or two masts for sails. Engineers and designers calculate the Jamestown shallop design was about 30 feet long and 8 feet wide and designed to draw less than 2 feet of water, an important feature for navigating inland in uncharted waters. Historians say Smith's shallop was built of oak planks fastened together with wooden pegs. Like most boats of that time, it would have had at least one pole/mast and one or two sails made of hemp canvas. A shallop could carry heavy cargoes much like a barge of today. In his journals Captain Smith described his shallop as an "open barge near three tuns burthen," which meant it could carry up to three tons of cargo. Captain Smith crewed his first voyage with fifteen men. Smith's crew included a doctor, a carpenter, a tailor to mend sails, a fisherman, soldiers, and other colonists. Rowing teams of six to eight men would row when winds were not favorable for sailing; the other crew members rested until their turn at the oars.

The Paddle

Leeds Creek

There are two cement public ramps in the St Michaels downtown harbor, one for car-top boats and the other specifically for motorboats. The ramps are in the same marina area, but signs keep the two boating groups apart. Parking is free throughout the township, and everything is clean and well laid out. The town's harbor has low-level piers throughout, but the town's shoreline is actually very short. The two easier paddle routes include traveling along the Miles River. Weather plays a major factor in

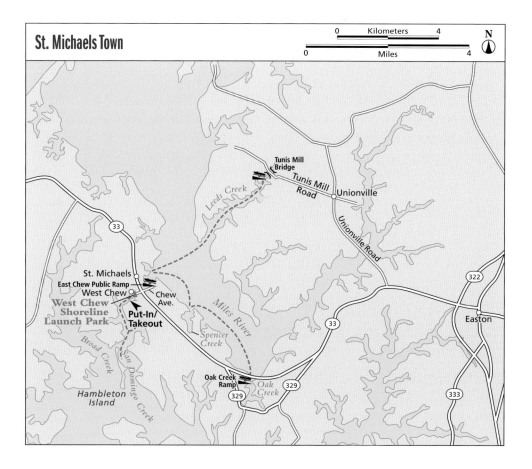

the journey as the river is wide and deep. It is only 1.5 miles across to the mouth of Leeds Creek, which is a protected waterway, and 4 miles round-trip to the Tunis Mill Bridge public boat ramp and back to the mouth. This is a long day of traveling for slow recreational paddlers, and we recommend a two-car system whether paddling from Tunis Mill Bridge to St. Michaels or the other direction.

Oak Creek Landing

The second adventure from the downtown harbor is to travel southeast and hug the shoreline while paddling the Miles River. There are several little coves and a small creek to explore while heading east. The rest area pullout target is Oak Creek Landing Waterfront Park. Located on Route 33-St. Michaels Road, this is a delightful neighborhood marina with dual cement ramps, year-round port-a-potties, grass, park benches, and lots of parking. It's a 3-mile one-way paddle to the park. This might be another good two-car system for a one-way adventure or just a good workout if you are a fast paddler. Oak Creek is small and well protected but only a 1-mile round-trip exploration.

San Domingo Creek

If you are looking for a quiet day on the water, try launching from West Chew Shoreline Launch Park. All the kayakers in the entire town of St. Michaels seem to store their boats here on wooden racks. The launch is a well-padded path with flat stones securing the walkway. There is a dock for a few motorboats. Early online photos show a swimming beach and a dog park of sorts. Thirty years later the area now consists of thick green grass and pussywillows. Calm water prevails, and there are good coves to explore. A minor boat portage is required from the street-parked cars. Talbot County Parks says it's a 3-mile round-trip paddle to the islands at the creek's mouth.

40 Tilghman Island

The entire island paddle route is strongly recommended for experienced boaters only, as the island has the Chesapeake Bay on one side and the Choptank River on the other, both wide, deep waters that are affected by winds and weather.

County: Talbot County

Suggested launch sites:
  Dogwood Harbor public ramp
  Tilghman Island Marina
  Knapps Narrows Marina

Suggested takeout sites: Same

Length and float time: 9.4-mile circumference / 1.5 miles per hour (medium paddle)
  Dogwood Harbor to Black Walnut Cove—4 miles one-way
  Black Walnut Cove to Knapps Narrows—4.5 miles one-way
  Knapps Narrows and Back Creek to Dogwood Harbor—1 mile one-way

Difficulty: Medium to rough

Current: The peninsula is surrounded by several bodies of deep water. The current is always strong around the peak of the island and milder near the narrows.

Fishing: Most fish are caught a few miles offshore, but on the western shore of the island are designated shoreline fishing spots. I have not found any blogs reporting kayak fishing results so far.

Season: Year-round

Fees or permits: None

Nearest city/town: Tilghman Island

Boats used: Sea kayaks and 12-foot-long recreational boats

Organization: Talbot County Parks and Recreation

Contacts: None

Rest areas: Several throughout route

Restaurant pullouts: None

Put-In/Takeout Information

Dogwood Harbor (public ramp), 21481 Dogwood Harbor Rd., Tilghman, MD; GPS N38 42.737' / W076 20.101'

Tilghman Island Marina (kayak rentals), 6140 Mariners Ct., Tilghman, MD; GPS N38 43.204' / W076 20.27'

Knapps Narrows Marina & Inn (kayak rentals), 617 Tilghman Island Rd., Tilghman, MD; GPS N38 43.237' / W076 20.041'

Overview

Tilghman Island is a relatively small tip of a long peninsula that caters to tourism. The island really is an island with a bridge connecting it to the larger peninsula, but the funny thing is, the whole peninsula wants to call itself Tilghman Island. Even the narrow two-lane roadway going to the island a few miles outside of St. Michaels Town calls itself the Tilghman Island Road till it passes over the only bridge, where the narrow road becomes skinnier and is called Black Walnut Road.

Knapps Narrows is the focus area for tourists whether paddling or fishing!

The Paddle

I found an old paddling route guide published years ago by the Maryland Department of Natural Resources (DNR) and Talbot County. I tracked down their suggested sites and explored a few more areas myself. Most old guide maps use the tip of the peninsula, the actual "Tilghman Island" as the baseline map, then suggest smaller, safer routes based on only part of, rather than the whole, island circumference.

There are lots of places to put in, depending on how adventurous and experienced you are. Route 33, Tilghman Island Road, starts outside St. Michaels Town. There are several county landings and private marinas along the way. The two long peninsulas, Bozman-Neavitt and Tilghman Island, are both subject to strong winds and currents from the Choptank River mouth and the open waters of the Chesapeake Bay. The entire Tilghman Island Route is exposed to both, so caution is advised, as the route can be a real adrenaline ride.

The actual Tilghman Island starts about two-thirds of the way down the peninsula. The dividing waterway is called Knapps Narrows; it's wide enough for two large yachts to pass each other but not much else. There is a community park just before the bridge with a nice playground, a wooden waterfront viewing area, and twenty steps down to a grassy waterfront with a portage length that will kill the joy of the freebie, so it's not recommended. There is an excellent parking lot in front of the park for meeting others if needed, before crossing over. Knapps Narrows Marina is next to

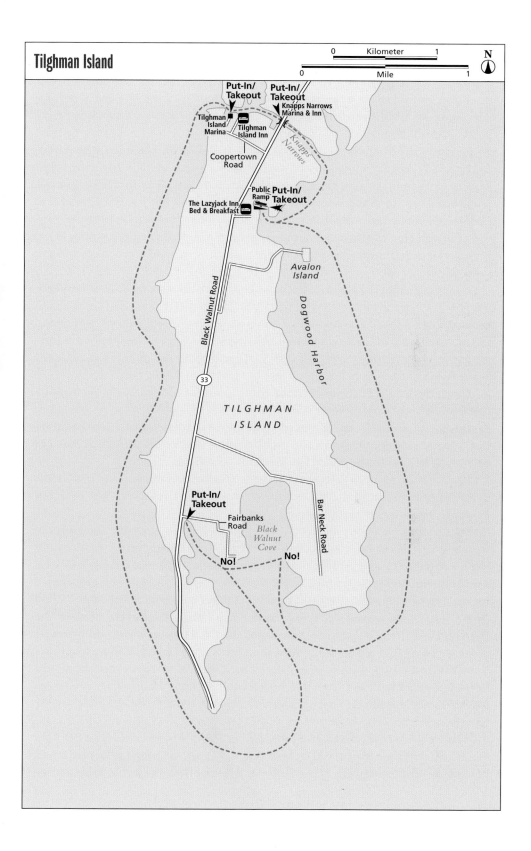

Tilghman Island

Put-In/
Takeout

Put-In/
Takeout
Knapps Narrows
Marina & Inn

Tilghman
Island
Marina

Tilghman
Island Inn

Knapps Narrows

Coopertown
Road

Public
Ramp

Put-In/
Takeout

The Lazyjack Inn
Bed & Breakfast

Avalon
Island

Dogwood Harbor

Black Walnut Road

33

TILGHMAN
ISLAND

Put-In/
Takeout

Fairbanks
Road

*Black
Walnut
Cove*

Bar Neck Road

No!

No!

N

0   Kilometer   1

0   Mile   1

the park and is the mover and shaker year-round. The marina has a nice little inn with rooms to let, a substation for the Marine Police (DNR) and the local sheriff if you need help, and a seasonal waterfront restaurant. Around back is a long metal floating ramp and paved picnic area with lots of tables. The marina is kayak friendly and rents boats to launch from here.

Just across the Narrows on the island side is the Tilghman Island Inn with rooms, a restaurant (closes for winter season), and kayaks for guests, and the Tilghman Island Marina, which rents an assortment of motorboats and kayaks. The Bridge Restaurant, immediately on the island waterfront, is open year-round but has no water access. Older maps and guides suggest other access points along the island side of the Narrows, but development has eased out the other dirt road freebie launch points. There is a colorful general store next to the bridge that sells long- and short-sleeve T-shirts, sodas, and ice cream.

A mile or so into the island on the left is Harrison's Country Inn. The atmosphere is unmistakably family oriented with a 1950s feel. Photos and newspaper clippings are laminated and displayed on the walls. The restaurant has large windows overlooking Harris Creek, its own pier with commercial yachts looking to take groups on fishing and hunting charters, a seasonal crab house, and bedrooms to let. I found a small beach from which to launch kayaks if you brought them during your stay.

Down the road is Dogwood Harbor with a cement public ramp. In the harbor I found a bed-and-breakfast home called the Lazyjack Inn, which has its own skipjack to take guests out for a ride. In the same area is the Tilghman Island General Store that caters to anglers and locals and provides good sandwiches and lunch makings year-round at non-tourist prices. Fun knickknacks abound.

For a short trip launch your kayak at the Dogwood Harbor ramp and head north to the Narrows to check out a protected little creek called Back Creek for a short but enjoyable 3 mile round-trip adventure.

For the circumference paddle head out of the harbor and turn south, hugging the shoreline, and proceed to the Black Walnut Cove basin. Mostly protected, the basin offers two public boating pullout areas. Bar Neck is a floating metal dinghy dock with a walkway and very little parking offered. Fairbanks Pier on the basin's other shoreline has no accessible shoreline for sit-in kayaks and offers only boat ladders. But I found an eye-opener just around the corner in the basin (bring the camera!). Follow the basin waterway to the west, where year-round there is a large family of white swans. I counted twenty in the wintertime. Also, the waterway will take you to the Fairbanks Road bridge with a good pullout shoreline. This is the 3.5- to 4-mile turnaround area for recreational kayaks and canoes. Travel back to Dogwood Harbor for a good 5- to 6-hour paddle. But if you have not been challenged enough and are ready for the "expert run," check the water and weather before reading on to the next paragraph.

The west side of the island is not for tourists. This is 4 miles of rough water from around Black Walnut Point NRMA to Knapps Narrows without a recognized pullout area or beach resting place. The point has a special B&B house, but it has a fence with a lock to keep out uninvited guests. There is a naval research facility not shown on the maps located here on the point, and a parking lot for anglers who want deep-sea fishing from the shoreline. Big riprap boulders line the shoreline as far as the eye can see. In the winter season on a calm day there are mini whitecaps. On a calm day in the summer a shore angler might claim you for a prize.

Maryland DNR says the circumference is only 9.4 miles for a 4-hour paddle. My estimates are much longer: 1.5 miles per hour in quiet water, and more like 1 mile per hour in rougher water. This expert run is going to be an estimated additional 4 hours long. From Knapps Narrows to Dogwood Harbor is only 1 mile. Good luck and fair weather.

41 Harris Creek

Often used as an extension of the Tilghman Island paddle routes, this location is much more protected from the deep open waters of the Chesapeake and is a pleasant paddle north or south.

County: Talbot County
Suggested launch sites:
    Cummings Creek Ramp
    Sherwood Pier
Suggested takeout sites: Same
Length and float time: 1.5 miles per hour (medium paddle)
    Cummings Creek Ramp to Sherwood Pier—3 miles one-way with limited cove exploration
    Cummings Creek Ramp north into the mouth of Northwest and Northeast Branches of Harris Creek—about 3 miles one-way

Difficulty: Mild
Current: Mild to medium
Season: Year-round (creeks may freeze with ice in winter)
Fees or permits: None
Nearest city/town: St. Michaels
Boats used: Recreational boats; paddleboards in calm weather
Organization: Talbot County Parks and Recreation
Contacts: None
Rest areas: Multiple shoreline possibilities
Restaurant pullouts: None

Put-In/Takeout Information

Cummings Creek Ramp, Howeth Road, Wittman, MD; GPS N38 47.414' / W076 17.872'

Sherwood Pier, Sherwood Landing Road, Sherwood, MD; GPS N38 45.727' / W076 19.029'

Overview

Perhaps not as well known, but more favored by locals, is the "Other Tilghman Island Route." Rather than face deep, open waterways and unpredictable weather, this route is in the northern Harris Creek area between the two peninsulas of the northern Tilghman area and Bozman-Neavitt. Cummings Creek is a two-pronged basin about 1.5 miles long. The ramp used to be named "Pot Pie Landing" after the Pot Pie Road access from Route 33.

The Paddle

Traveling south from Cummings Creek Ramp, Harris Creek offers three coves to explore before reaching Sherwood Pier off Waterhole Cove. The ramp is in good working order, although an adjoining waterfront wharf building used for commercial

Harris Creek

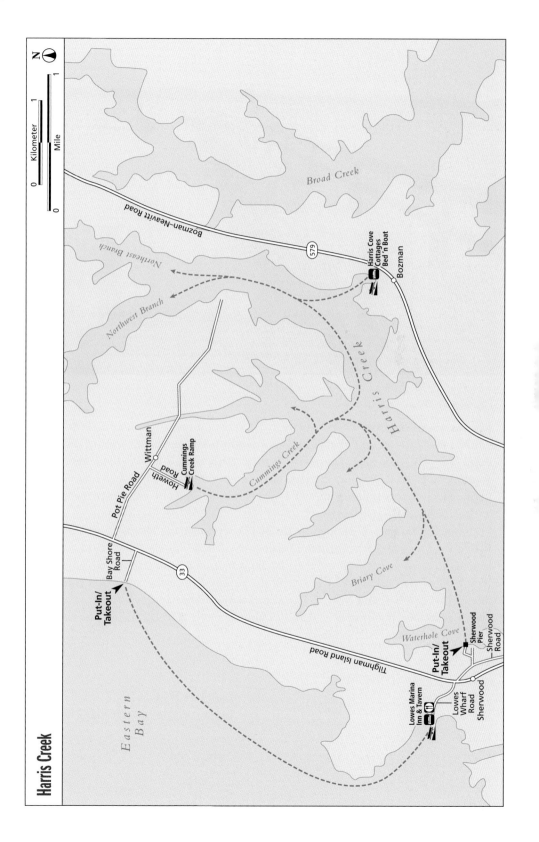

Eastern Bay

Broad Creek

Bozman–Neavitt Road

579

Harris Cove
Cottages
Bed 'n Boat

Bozman

Northeast Branch

Northwest Branch

Harris Creek

Wittman

Pot Pie Road

Howeth Road

Cummings
Creek Ramp

Cummings Creek

Bay Shore
Road

33

**Put-In/
Takeout**

Briary Cove

Waterhole Cove

Tilghman Island Road

Sherwood
Pier

Sherwood
Road

**Put-In/
Takeout**

Lowes Marina
Inn & Tavern

Lowes
Wharf
Road

Sherwood

N

Kilometer

0   1

0   1

Mile

This is a Tilghman Island secret—just for paddlers.

services was in disrepair when I last visited. Sherwood Pier is also in excellent condition, but is located on a skinny neighborhood road; boaters may want to drop off boats and park elsewhere. The pier is a small affair with a low-level dinghy dock attachment. From Cummings Creek Ramp, another option is to travel 3 miles north to find Harris Creek splitting into the Northeast Branch and Northwest Branch, each with an estimated 1-mile length.

If you're thinking of staying a night or two, consider the Harris Cove Cottages Bed 'n Boat off Harris Creek on the Bozman-Neavitt peninsula. They have a cement launch ramp for guests who use their kayaks. Or, if it's a summer evening, go across Route 33 to the Chesapeake Bay side of the peninsula near the Sherwood community, to Lowes Wharf and Marina. This seasonal operation has rooms to let, a bar and grill, a party beach atmosphere with swimming, and a graveled incline for car-top boats and even trailered motorboats.

42 Windy Hill and Miles Creek

This is a 4-mile ramp-to-headwaters paddle. Calculate your location and watch for an appropriate turnaround time. Move fast on the Choptank River and keep track of your time on the creek waterway, as it is very relaxing. The afternoon breeze kicks in around 2 to 4 p.m.

County: Talbot County
Suggested launch sites: Windy Hill Public Landing
    Bruceville Bridge (***Caution:*** posted No Parking on private land)
Suggested takeout sites: Same
Length and float time: 4 miles one-way; 1 mile per hour (slow paddle)
Difficulty: Easy

Current: Some mild to medium in the Choptank River
Season: Year-round
Fees or permits: None
Nearest city/town: Trappe
Boats used: Recreational kayaks
Organizations: None
Contact: Talbot County Parks and Recreation
Rest areas: Bruceville Road Bridge
Restaurant pullouts: None

Put-In/Takeout Information

Windy Hill Public Landing, 4950 Windy Hill Rd., Trappe, MD; GPS N38 41.032' / W075 58.476'

Bruceville Bridge is a "Drop and Park" location, with limited spots near bridge recently cleared for public use.

Windy Hill is a good access to the Choptank River.

"LLOYDS LANDING IS CLOSED"!?

While doing research for this area in Maryland, I found years of records for a public boat launch area at Lloyds Landing. Then suddenly the location was removed from the lists without explanation. I called some friendly people at Talbot County Parks and Recreation, but they didn't know Lloyds and could not give an answer—"Sorry about that." I called the US Army Corp of Engineers because they always seem to have records of public waterways—"Nope, not in the files." Maryland's Department of Natural Resources changed its name back in the 1960s and hired some new folks to update their lists of public launch sites from each county and to eventually put that information on a website (which we are grateful to have available today). No luck from those knowledgeable professionals either. The Pratt Library in Baltimore City has a whole floor designated just to Maryland history; that's where I originally found the records but could not find any more leads. I went to the Maryland Archives in Annapolis, checked into a research booth, and asked for help—"Nada" again.

While I was driving the back roads in Talbot, I looked up the location and found a farmer shooing away kayakers who demanded to be let in so they could launch from the county property! He shook his head and kept the chain locked across the dirt road. I put on my best smile, parked the car, and took out my camera. The farmer did not have a chance. We talked for a while and then he showed me the riverfront location: a grassy knoll with some beat-up aluminum skiffs flipped over and some very shallow water around the shoreline. I promised to tell the family's story. It took six months and a cup of tea to get a simple answer.

Many times counties do not actually purchase the lands they want to use. They lease the waterfront right of way for public access. The county then invests money to create a boat landing and also spends money yearly on maintenance that includes cutting up driftwood that washes up, fixing or building piers, and sometimes dredging the sand and silt away from a site when the currents from the river or creek build it up. Usually these leases are for many years. Such was the case at Lloyds Landing. When the lease ran out, so too did the enthusiasm for repeatedly fixing an outlying launch area for vast sums from a lean budget. Windy Hill was chosen as an alternative site, and Lloyds Landing was taken off the list.

Boaters should remember that access to water is a privilege, not a right. Counties spend huge amounts of money for maintenance, and car-top boat folks usually get a "free lunch." We need to learn to say thank you more often and willingly pay the small launch fees at marinas, state parks, and township ramps. The counties and private property owners need to know we appreciate the service. Ask with a smile and a thanks, and remember the boater coming behind you.

"The property was never owned by the county, but after so many years, it is still hard for locals and outsiders to get the idea that Lloyds is closed to the public. Thanks for asking."

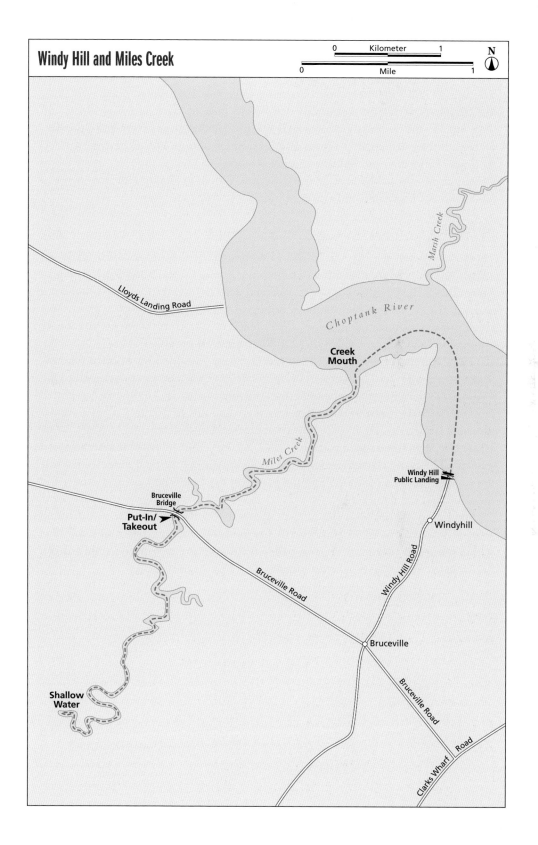

Windy Hill and Miles Creek

0   Kilometer   1

0   Mile   1

N

Lloyds Landing Road

Marsh Creek

Choptank River

Creek Mouth

Miles Creek

Windy Hill Public Landing

Bruceville Bridge

Put-In/ Takeout

○ Windyhill

Bruceville Road

Windy Hill Road

Shallow Water

◉ Bruceville

Bruceville Road

Clarks Wharf Road

Overview

The Windy Hill Public Landing boat ramp once was a scheduled dock stop along the Choptank River for steamships that would pick up agricultural products and drop supplies for the folks in that area. It was just another stop a couple of miles farther south than its neighbor Lloyds Landing, which also provided the same service. As times changed, so too did the farming business—as well as the river itself. Talbot County moved its public boat launch area from Lloyds to Windy Hill years ago and built a modest boat ramp and a strip of beach.

The Paddle

The county paved the street at Windy Hill enough for five or six cars to park and maintains the location. The Windy Hill ramp is about 1.5 miles from the mouth of Miles Creek. The Choptank River is wide and deep in this area, and the wind plays a major factor in whether the waterway is rough and choppy or smooth as glass. Miles Creek itself is a protected area and is excellent for paddleboarding—it's just the 45 minutes on the Choptank that raises caution flags for boarders.

The 2.5 miles on Miles Creek are full of curves and one low, wooden roadway bridge about midway. The wooden bridge at Bruceville Road has a deer path to the water and is all right for an emergency pullout, but the private landowner has posted signs asking boaters not to park their cars there and not to use his land as a regular shoreline launch site. High tide is always appreciated in tidal creeks, but Miles is fine at low tide, with the mindful paddler keeping to the center and watching for exposed mudflats. The water changes about 12 to 18 inches during the tidal shift. At high tide the paddler can go an extra 15 minutes to where the headwaters get real skinny and the fauna and wildlife change.

Hunting is seasonal, but shooting shotguns at seagulls seems to be a year-round sport. If you hear repeated gunshots, they're probably coming from some old boys with a snoot full after football games. Blow your emergency whistle or horn if you find yourself in that kind of environment.

43 Skipton Creek

The Wye Conference Center and Wye Island have a bit of national notoriety. Skipton Creek is a small confluence off one of the nearby rivers. The launch is near the head of the creek; a second, larger launch ramp is a paddling goal for a nice round-trip and full day of quiet paddling.

County: Talbot County
Suggested launch sites:
    Skipton Creek Landing
    Wye Mills Landing
Suggested takeout sites: Same
Length and float time: 2 miles one-way; 1 mile per hour (slow paddle)
    Skipton Creek Landing to headwaters—0.5 mile one-way
    Skipton Creek Landing to Mill Creek—0.5 mile one-way
    Skipton Creek Landing to mouth of creek—1.5 miles one-way

Skipton Creek Landing to Wye Mills Landing—2 miles one-way
Difficulty: Easy
Current: Mild
Season: Year-round
Fees or permits: None
Nearest city/town: Cordova
Boats used: Recreational boats and paddleboards
Organizations: None
Contacts: None
Rest areas: Multiple along shoreline
Restaurant pullouts: None

Put-In/Takeout Information

Skipton Creek Public Landing, 28900 Skipton Landing Rd., Cordova, MD; GPS N38 53.464' / W076 04.297'

Wye Mills Public Landing, 12500 Wye Landing Rd., Wye Mills, MD; GPS N38 53.529' / W076 06.179'

Overview

This is a wonderful, protected creek area. The tidal drop is about 24 inches, but only the headwater areas of Skipton and Mill Creeks are affected with less ability to travel the extra 5 to 10 minutes, now with mudflats. It is 2 miles from landing to landing, with good swimming in the deeper coves. For speed demons, the Wye River goes north for a long day's added adventure.

The Paddle

Skipton Landing would not be on any motorboat ramp guide's lists as a recommended launch site. But for car-top boats it's ideal. The ramp is less than a mile off Route 50 on a narrow, gravelly homestead road. It's not until you are absolutely sure that you've gotten the directions wrong and are almost turning into the neighbor's

Loons gather in groups or live alone. We'd never seen a group on a tree branch before!

driveway that the pavement takes a sharp left turn and goes down the hill to a perfect, well-maintained, shorty boat ramp and pier with parking for about three cars. The ramp pavement is more than an incline, but way less than a regular paved boat ramp.

The headwaters are to the left. At high tide a boater can get within a stone's throw of the shoreline where there is a boat store. I met the owner working on his shoreline bulkhead, and we had an interesting conversation; seems most boaters have not been adventurous enough to make it that far for years. At one time the water must have been deep enough for some boating, but now there is just too much silt.

To the right Skipton Creek heads west. In about half a mile Mill Creek conjoins. At high tide the paddle up Mill Creek might take you a full mile before becoming too shallow. Skipton continues to a larger bay area and then into the Wye River and Wye Island. We found a small cove with a duck blind just before the Skipton mouth basin with a nice shoreline to pull up on for lunch. The water is clear and deep—a good swimming hole. There is a sailing boat that is well anchored in the creek, but

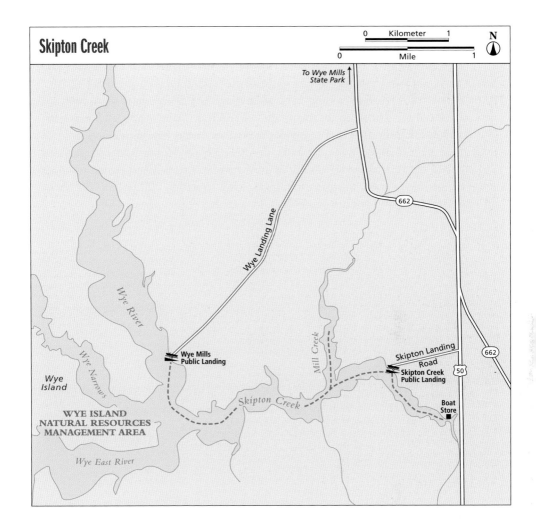

To Wye Mills
State Park

662

Wye Landing Lane

Wye River

Wye Mills
Public Landing

Skipton Landing
Road

662

Skipton Creek
Public Landing

50

Wye Narrows

Mill Creek

Wye
Island

Skipton Creek

Boat
Store

WYE ISLAND
NATURAL RESOURCES
MANAGEMENT AREA

Wye East River

the spot the owner chose for mooring on the creek was poorly chosen. For the second year at low tide we've seen the sailboat tipped over and listing badly with its keel stuck in the mud.

Paddle out of the basin and bear right; Wye Mills Landing with its multiple cement ramps looms ahead. A whole troop of port-a-potties is available here. We launched from here once in the fall, and met a wounded Canada goose who had been adopted as a pet by the locals. The goose followed us around while we prepared our boats and posed for some fun photo shots. The goose even followed us for a while, swimming as we paddled north up the Wye River. (Look for the pet and bring some bread.) Turn around here for a quiet 4-hour round-trip paddle. Are you a demon paddler and want some more? Go north!

The northern-bound Wye River is a 4-mile paddle from the ramp to the headwaters (a natural fallen tree barricade). This is a wonderful "long day adventure";

keep in mind that the return paddle might be against a wind tunnel. But that's part of kayaking too.

The Skipton Creek ramp is truly a "shorty," as it only goes about 12 feet (the size of my kayak) and then disappears with a 2- to 3-inch drop to the mud/ground. Launching is a breeze, but coming back at low tide is a challenge. It's too high for ramming speed for a nose up on the pavement and too shallow for a side dismount. You could paddle into the muck and pull the boat up on the side shoreline, but I had on good sneakers that day. Instead, I had a tie-up line handy, connected it to the boat, and climbed up a metal ladder on the end of the pier. I towed and pulled my boat along the pier and up the shorty without too many scratches. Pulling my wife's boat up was simple and we kept dry. Good luck to you also!

Wicomico County

Wicomico County, in southeast Maryland, is a good example of a county govern-
ment working to support the environment. Wicomico County's Department of Public
Works–Roads Division's donation in 2014 of nearly forty used street sign poles to the
Maryland Water Fowlers Association (MDWFA) and Maryland Wood Duck Initiative
(MWDI) will be used to install wood duck nesting boxes. Wood duck boxes simu-
late a natural nesting structure—a tree knothole—found in the wild. Since late 2004,
MWDI's scope has grown to more than 1,700 boxes on eighty-five public project sites.
MWDI's mission is to enhance Maryland's wood duck population and to generate a
greater appreciation of the wetland habitats in which they live. Wicomico's river and
creeks are flat and easy to paddle and to observe wildlife. Be sure to bring a camera.

*Wicomico's easy-to-paddle creeks, like Wetipquin Creek also off Nanticoke River, are enjoyable
year-round.*

44 Mardela Springs to Vienna

Both ends of the adventure have good boat ramps and parking. The Vienna ramp sits on the wide Nanticoke River, and the Mardela Springs ramp is directly on narrow, winding Barren Creek. Choose your starting point based on a turnaround time, the weather, and boating traffic.

County: Wicomico and Dorchester Counties
Suggested launch sites:
    Mardela Springs Ramp
    Vienna Municipal Marina & Ramp
Suggested takeout sites: Same
Length and float time: Estimated 14 miles round-trip; 1.5 miles per hour (medium paddle)
    From Mardela Springs Ramp to the confluence with the Nanticoke River—about 6 miles on Barren Creek
    From mouth of Barren Creek to Vienna Municipal Ramp—1 mile
Difficulty: Easy on Barren Creek; mild to medium on Nanticoke River

Current: Mild in creek; the river can have a strong pull
Season: Year-round
Fees or permits: None
Nearest city/towns: Mardela and Vienna
Boats used: Paddleboards fine on Barren Creek. Sea kayaks might have the advantage on the Nanticoke River, but whether smooth or choppy the river is fine for recreational boating.
Organizations: None
Contacts: None
Rest areas: Delmarva Sporting Clays & Shooting Facility, 23501 Marsh Rd., Mardela Springs, MD 21837; (410) 742-2023 or (800) 310-2023; www.dscfff.com
Restaurant pullouts: None

Put-In/Takeout Information

Mardela Springs Boat Ramp, 500 Bridge St., Mardela Springs, MD; GPS N38 27.237' / W075 45.363'

Vienna Municipal Marina & Ramp, Town of Vienna, MD; GPS N38 29.013' / W075 49.385'

Overview

In 1893 the village of Barren Creek Springs changed its name to Mardela Springs. The change was mostly economically motivated. The railroad had arrived in town in 1890, and several businessmen saw the chance to expand the market for the town's bottled mineral water. The "Medicine Water" used so much by American Indians flows from the earth, pregnant with iron, sulfur, and magnesium. Fearing city consumers would shy away from "creek water," they suggested changing the town's name to a new combination of Maryland and Delaware—Mardela Springs. Many residents objected but were outvoted, and the town has been Mardela Springs ever since.

Lush green plants and a narrow deep protective creek

The Paddle

We chose to first visit the town of Vienna, a small village of older residential homes. The shoreline bulkhead, piers, and waterfront park, however, felt new and clean. Posters advertised upcoming events near the cement boat ramp. From the waterfront a visiting guest would certainly be taken with the town and want to explore. Parking cars is done a bit farther back on a main street about a block away This is a drop-and-park ramp.

Back on the highway, we looked down on the Nanticoke River and were impressed, but not intimidated, by this big, wide body of water. Although the shorelines have little or no real development, the waterway surface appears calm and smooth rather than having the wind tunnel effect we have experienced in the past with other flat, eastern shorelines.

Mardela Springs is also a small town; no big signs point to the boat ramp, just little road signs that we missed driving by the first time. The Mardela Springs ramp is well maintained, and when we visited the area, it was quiet and peaceful. The swamp flowers were in full bloom, and the air was intoxicating, like a flower shop. Everything was green.

The creek waterway is gentle and the sea grass fairly tall. The width of the creek stays fairly narrow but is workable and so too is the depth of the creek. What scared us to death was the sound of gunfire very close by. We shouted, "Kayaks coming through,

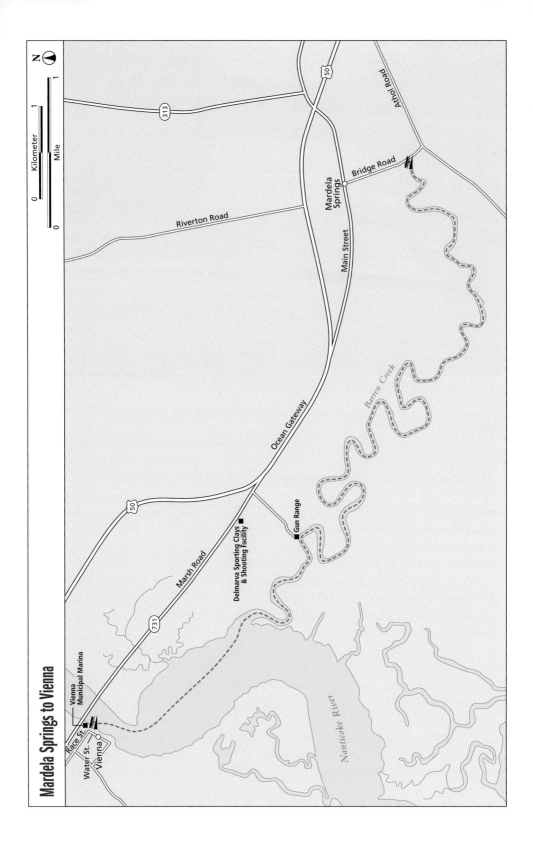

Mardela Springs to Vienna

don't shoot!" But nobody seemed to hear us. Every so often we blew whistles and honked bike horns—but no response, and the shots were getting louder. About midway we seriously thought about turning around and getting out while we were still in one piece. But you know, curiosity got the better of us. We soon found ourselves on the shoreline of a firing range. The groundskeeper smiled and waved at us. We pulled up and displayed a bit too much of the city folk out in the country, I guess—lots of smiles and handshakes. They offered us the use of some picnic tables and, even more important, the use of the port-a-potties. We also noticed a cute little multicolored beach house with rocking chairs; it would be a good landmark to look for to know where you are.

It had been a long day, so we turned around and headed back to Mardela Springs. The firing range is about half a mile from the mouth of the Nanticoke River; it would be another hour of paddling to Vienna. We promised ourselves to do the whole adventure another day.

Worcester County

Worcester County is known for its big-name destinations like Ocean City, Assateaque Island, and the Pocomoke River State Parks. Described here are two excellent adventures that touch the rich back bays away from the hustle and bustle of tourists. These are long day paddles from top to bottom, so look at what portions seem interesting and doable for you. Either route will meet the needs of sea kayakers as well as recreational boaters and paddleboarders. The routes will take you to the front door of Maryland's summer fun town. As they say in Baltimore, "Welcome to the Ocean-Hon!"

Bahia Marina and Restaurant is full of color and fun. A kayak-friendly place.

45 Bishopville to Isle of Wight

This can be a 2.5-mile straight paddle or a delightful out-and-back adventure with lots of distractions to explore, from little islands to short prongs to the unique boating canal waterways that run through the community of Ocean Pines.

County: Worcester County

Suggested launch sites:
   Bishopville Crossroads Launch
   Shell Mill Public Ramp
   Isle of Wight Nature Park

Suggested takeout sites: Same

Length and float time: 1.5 miles per hour (medium paddle)
   Bishopville Launch to Shell Mill Public Ramp—1.5 miles
   Shell Mill Public Ramp to White Horse RV Park—2 miles
   White Horse RV Park to Isle of Wight Nature Park—2.5 miles

Difficulty: Mild to medium depending on weather and boat traffic

Current: Mild to medium

Season: Year-round

Fees or permits: None

Nearest city/town: Ocean City

Boats used: Sea kayaks and recreational boats; paddleboards maybe for the prong

Organization: Worcester County Recreation and Parks

Contacts: None

Rest areas: White Horse RV Park and Ocean Pines ramps are private (rest stop and emergencies only)

Restaurant pullouts: None

Put-In/Takeout Information

Bishopville Crossroads Launch, Bishopville Road and St. Martin's Neck Road, Bishopville, MD; GPS N38 26.526' / W075 11.610'

Shell Mill Public Ramp, Shell Mill Road, Bishopville, MD; GPS N38 25.448' / W075 11.261'

Isle of Wight Nature Park, Corner of Route 90 and St. Martins Neck Road before crossing bridge; GPS N38 23.325' / W075 06.519'

The Paddle House (canoe, kayak, and paddleboard rentals), 11930 Ocean Gateway, Ocean City, MD; (443) 664-2528

Overview

I found Bishopville through sheer luck by following the rivers and streams to their headwaters. The tide levels will make the difference in the beginning, but even the state engineer I spoke with, who silently cursed the creek, said it was beautiful. I found four community launch areas not for public use along the St. Martin River shoreline. I recommend this adventure as a one-way paddle with a two-car system no matter where you start or end.

The Shell Mill Public Ramp is not affected by tidal changes and is available year-round.

The Paddle

The Bishopville Crossroads shoreline launch area looks like a winner just from driving over the bridge—a small town park, benches, a short portage across green grass, a sandy shoreline, other small boats turned over and stored against trees. The problem is the ebb and flow of the tide. I was following a map and found the crossroads bridge and shoreline just by chance. When I started taking pictures of the location, an irritated county engineer came over to say hello. After a handshake, he started to smile and told me the problems he was having repairing that little town bridge. The heavy-duty scaffolding had to be built elsewhere and floated up the creek to the bridge. He growled and said half his budget went just to paddle and pole the barge up the Bishopville Prong. He laughed and said that the water deserved its name and that kayakers might just have a good ride after he fixed the bridge and water holding the run-over gate.

It's about 1.5 miles down the waterway to the Shell Mill public ramp, and the water is deep there even at low tide. A few retired folks pier-fish from the quiet reflecting water year-round. The waterway here is called a "prong" rather than a creek. A mile farther is another prong about a mile long and wider. From the mouth the waterway becomes the St. Martin River. A curious rest area is about another paddler's mile; an old ADC map shows a public ramp symbol in this area. There is a year-round RV campground named White Horse on one side of the road and an excellent boat ramp and dirt kayak pull-up "owned" by Ocean Pines on the other.

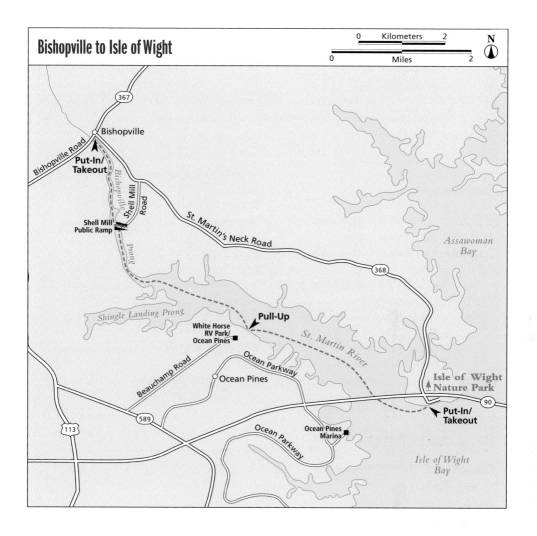

Bishopville to Isle of Wight

After making inquiries I was shooed away as a troublemaker. The site had port-a-potties and a good gravel driveway. The Ocean Pines community has strong support for its privacy. In my research I found that a few old Maryland public ramps sites were "given" to communities when the cost of maintenance overrode their availability for general public use. I suspect the land was taken at blueprint conception and given back when the county budget got too tight.

It is about a 2.5-mile paddle to Isle of Wight Nature Park. There is a soft shoreline launch area with signs designating it just for kayaks, with good parking and restrooms.

46 Gum Point Ramp to Bahia Marina

The intercoastal waterways of Ocean City are divided into four bay areas. Northernmost are Assawoman Bay and Isle of Wight Bay, protected by the Ocean City Peninsula; southernmost are Sinepuxent Bay and Chincoteaque Bay, protected by the Assateaque Island.

County: Worcester County
Suggested launch sites:
  Gum Point Public Ramp
  Bahia Marina, Restaurant & Marine Store
Suggested takeout sites: Same
Length and float time: 1.5 miles per hour (medium paddle)
  Gum Point Public Ramp to mouth of Turville Creek—1.5 miles
  Mouth of Turville Creek to Keyser Point Island—1.5 miles
  Keyser Point Island to Swordfish Basin and Bahia Marina—2 miles straight
Difficulty: Mild to medium depending on boat traffic and weather

Current: Most of route in protected water and close to shoreline
Season: Year-round
Fees or permits: None at public ramps; fee for use at Bahia Marina
Nearest city/town: Ocean City
Boats used: Sea kayaks and recreational boats; too much boat traffic for paddleboards
Organization: Worcester County Recreation and Parks
Contacts: None
Rest areas: Multiple possibilities throughout route
Restaurant pullouts: Family-oriented seafood restaurant at Bahia Marina

Put-In/Takeout Information

Gum Point Public Ramp, Gum Point Road, Berlin, MD; GPS N38 21379' / W075 09.644'

Bahia Marina, Restaurant & Marine Store (boat ramp and kayak rentals), 2107 Herring Way, Ocean City, MD; (410) 289-7438; GPS N38 21.069' / W075 04.730'

The Paddle House (canoe, kayak, and paddleboard rentals), 11930 Ocean Gateway, Ocean City, MD; (443) 664-2528

Overview

This route is off the beaten path, and most tourists don't know about it. Hug the shorelines and explore the coves. On seasonal weekends the big boys might cause a ruckus with boat wakes near the "island"; nonetheless, this route should be an outdoor adventure worth repeating.

Gum Point Ramp to Bahia Marina

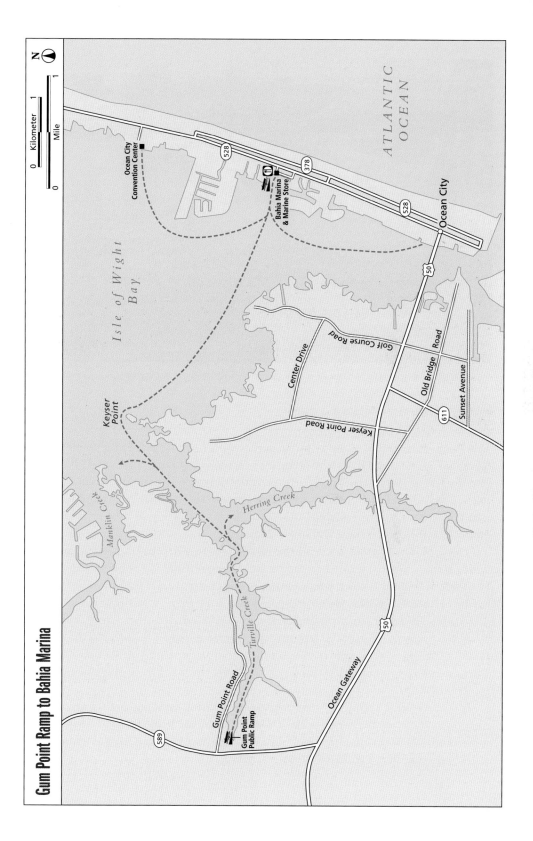

N

0   Kilometer   1
0   Mile   1

ATLANTIC
OCEAN

Isle of Wight
Bay

Ocean City Convention Center

Bahia Marina & Marine Store

Ocean City

528

378

528

50

Center Drive

Golf Course Road

Old Bridge Road

Sunset Avenue

611

Keyser Point Road

Keyser Point

Manklin Creek

Herring Creek

Turville Creek

Gum Point Road

Gum Point Public Ramp

589

Ocean Gateway

50

Colorful rental kayaks, boat store, ramp, and family restaurant await your arrival.

The Paddle

The Gum Point public ramp is found just south of the Ocean Pines community between Route 90 and Route 50 going into Ocean City. Of the three creeks flowing into the Isle of Wight Bay, Turville Creek is the only one with a public ramp. From this southern waterway location, boaters can paddle for 1.5 miles, protected in Turville Creek, then hug a residential shoreline almost all the way to where yachts and motorboats stir up the water with their traffic.

The 5-plus-mile route is a 3.5-hour paddle one-way to a kayak-friendly marina with a family-oriented seafood restaurant and a cement ramp (fee for use). The Bahia Marina is so brightly colored that even a morning grouch would have to smile before having his morning coffee. Sit-on-top ocean kayaks are for rent year-round. The large parking lot and ample street parking area would serve well for a two-car system.

If you want more water to explore, the marina is only 1.5 miles north of the Route 50 bridge or less than a mile south of the Ocean City Convention Center. There are no recommended rest stop pullouts along the way. Plenty of restaurants are on Route 50.

If the bay water seems too stirred up and rough for kayaking due to either the motorboat traffic or the weather, try a route from Gum Point that just keeps to a more protected area adjoining creeks like Manklin and Herring. Each is about 1.5 miles long and offers a good day of quiet kayaking.

Washington, DC

Located downtown on the National Mall is the Washington Monument. It is an obelisk, which is a tall, four-sided, narrow-tapering pillar that ends in a pyramid shape at its top. The Washington Monument was built to celebrate George Washington as the country's commander in chief and the first American president. The monument is the tallest stone structure in the district and is the world's tallest obelisk. It was damaged in an earthquake in 2011; structural cracks were repaired and the monument reopened May 12, 2014.

Your DC paddling adventure will pass by this and other icons on the Potomac River, the C&O Canal, the Anacostia River, and the DC Channel.

Prime shot of the Lincoln Memorial and the Washington Monument taken from a kayak (paddle 48).

47 Anacostia River–North and South

The Anacostia River has lots of sights to see, places to explore, quiet protected waterways, and no fast motorboats competing for water space. There are shorelines that can be accessed for lunch, but limited access to restrooms is available for 6.5 miles. Anacostia Park is a safe, family-oriented site, despite the downtown location. Bladensburg Waterfront Park might confuse your GPS as to where to turn into the park grounds, but the atmosphere is safe, too, and the rental boats inexpensive and clean.

County: Washington, DC, and Prince George's County

Suggested launch sites:
Anacostia Park
Bladensburg Waterfront Park
River Terrace Park

Suggested takeout sites: Same

Length and float time: 1.5 miles per hour (medium paddle); returning south with current, 2 miles per hour
Anacostia Park to Anacostia Island Bridges—1 mile
Anacostia Island Bridges to Golf Course Bridge—1 mile
Golf Course Bridge passing National Arboretum to Kenilworth Aquatic Gardens—1 mile

Kenilworth Aquatic Gardens to Bladensburg Waterfront Park—1.5 miles
Going south from Bladensburg to the Anacostia Park ramps is about 6.5 miles.

Difficulty: Easy

Current: Mild

Season: Year-round

Fees or permits: None

Nearest city/town: Washington, DC

Boats used: Recreational kayaks, canoes, and paddleboards

Organizations: None

Contacts: None

Rest areas: RFK Stadium, National Arboretum, and Kenilworth Aquatic Gardens

Restaurant pullouts: None

Put-In/Takeout Information

Anacostia River Recreation Park, Fairlawn Avenue SE, Washington, DC; GPS N38 52.783' / W076 58.219'

River Terrace Park, Anacostia Avenue NE, Washington, DC; GPS N38 53.804' / W076 57.662'

Bladensburg Waterfront Park (boat ramp and canoe and kayak rentals), 4601 Annapolis Rd., Bladensburg, MD; (301) 779-0371; GPS N38 56.019' / W076 56.301'

Buzzard Point Marina, 22158 Half St. NW, Washington, DC; (202) 448-8400; GPS N38 51.835' / W077 00.698'

Overview

The Anacostia River flows from Prince George's County in Maryland into Washington, DC, where it empties into the Potomac River. It is approximately 8.7 miles

The northern Anacostia River and Park islands are calm quiet places to paddle.

long including the muddy flatlands above Bladensburg Waterfront Park. The name "Anacostia" derives from the settlement of Necostan or Anacostan Native Americans on the banks of the Anacostia River. There are several long islands in the center of the river that make for a dual passageway. Today heavy pollution in the Anacostia has led it to become what many call "DC's forgotten river." Advisories are posted to not touch the water or eat the fish caught in the river. The river is divided by a permanent, low-level train track bridge that allows for only small motorboats, crew rowing shells, kayaks, canoes, and paddleboarders sitting down to pass under it. Anacostia Park is adjacent to the bridge.

The Paddle

Anacostia River North

Turn right from the Anacostia Park ramps, pass under the low entrance of the railroad track bridge, and head north. The river flows on both sides of the islands. At the old cement bridge foundation, veer left into a narrow and quieter river, called the Kingsman Marsh access point. The water trail takes you past the RFK Stadium and a cleared area that would be good for a rest. Security is vigilant, so put-ins and takeouts are not possible at this site, but I did find seasonal restrooms within walking distance. The US Army Corps of Engineers created the two islands found here: the smaller Heritage and the elongated Kingsman. Farther up is a tidal area of protected greenery and rare wildlife. The island water trail ends at an abutting golf course bridge at the Langston

A SHOCKING TALE OF FISH

Ever see a scientist or biologist do a fish survey/census in a stream? Recently a team from the Metropolitan Washington Council of Governments went to several branches off the Anacostia River to examine and survey the fish populations, their health, and the types of fish species currently in the area. This team was looking particularly at shad and their reproduction rates. Shad are anadromous fish, which means they are born in freshwater, head to the ocean to live their lives, and return to freshwater for breeding. The samples found were normal and promising. The biologists travel in teams with what looks like a "Ghostbuster" backpack, which sends out a mild electric shock through a pole with a loop on the end. The pole is swished back and forth in a 10-foot arc. The stunned fish float to the surface, are collected in a net, and put into a bucket for the biologists to conduct their survey of the health, types, and numbers of fish. The fish revive and are released unharmed.

The Anacostia River has received a lot of attention over the last few years due to the high pollution content from factories, the Navy Yard, and fertilized soil runoff. Many of the fish caught by locals for home consumption have internal and external cancerous lesions and tumors. There are posted warnings not to eat the fish or even touch or drink the river water.

By the end of the day the team found hickory shad, gizzard shad, alewifes, pumpkinseed sunfish, redbreasts, bluegills, American eels, tasselled darters, a white sucker, a quillback sucker, spottail shiners, mummichogs, and some banded killfish.

Golf Course. Farther north you pass the Anacostia River back door entrance to the National Arboretum, open from 8:30 a.m. to 4:30 p.m. with restrooms only 6 minutes uphill through the gardens' Chinese section. Follow a tan cement pathway up to the main road, then turn right and look for a brick building in a parking lot. The rest area has an excellent dinghy dock and picnic tables but is not a put-in/takeout location.

Next is Kenilworth Aquatic Gardens (a wildlife and plant protected area) that specializes in lily pad ponds (very shallow marsh water into the park). A muddy shelf at the mouth of the park entrance is a "kayak rest area" —no put-in or takeout. It's a 0.5-mile walk on a trail to the ranger office for restrooms. Head north into Maryland; the water trail goes up to Prince George's County's Bladensburg Waterfront Park with a cement ramp and rental boats. This is a good turnaround. Coming back, stay to the left of the golf course. The current is mild but will carry boats south. *Caution:* Look out for crew and single rowing boats. These boats usually like to occupy the center of the waterway as their occupants cannot see what's ahead of them while facing to the rear. The boats with one or more rowers paddle fast! Look for rowing crew logos painted on the Route 50 bridge.

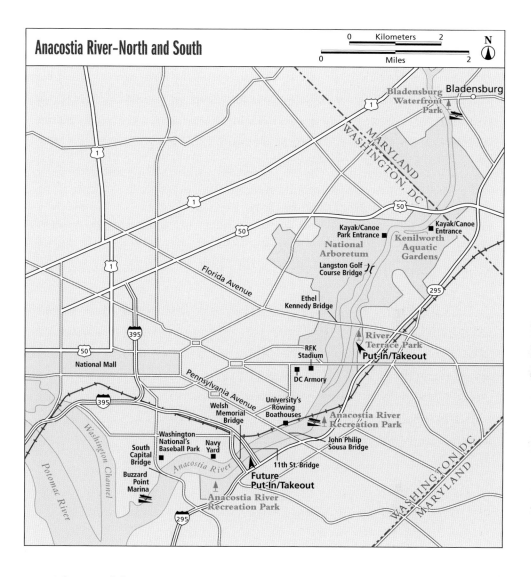

The next full crossing bridge is Ethel Kennedy Bridge on Benning Road, where boaters will find River Terrace Park with a bulkhead shoreline access point and a short portage to street parking. There's a DC rental bike rack here, too, but no public restroom, or one the nearby offices, gas station, or 7-11 will share. Anacostia Park is only a bit more than a mile away.

Anacostia River South

When launching from Anacostia Park headed south, keep in mind that the water is a bit rougher and there are fewer places to pull over to rest. The river becomes wider and deeper. Sweeping wind becomes a factor in the morning as well as the afternoon. Sea kayaks are recommended as the primary type of boat to use, but recreational kayaks with advanced paddlers who can navigate swells and yacht wakes will have a hearty adventure too.

Just before you reach the low-level railroad bridge that separates the river's northern and southern areas, you'll see white plastic huts that serve as university boat storage and clubhouses, part of the Anacostia Community Boathouse. In warmer months crew racing takes up most of the upper river, and other boats are asked to refrain from entering the area while competitions are taking place. The southern water trail continues past the Navy Yard and Washington Nationals stadium. Somewhere between the yard and the stadium is the Captain John Smith marker showing how far he traveled up the river. Something new for the Anacostia Park in 2016 will be a metal floating launch pier under the 11th Street Bridge for canoes and kayaks. The Matthew Henson Earth Conservation Center also has a floating dock and welcomes visitors to its educational facilities during business hours. Buzzard Point Marina can be a good waterfront destination and turnaround area for resting.

48 Washington, DC, and Potomac River

The Potomac River travels the southern border of Washington, DC, where boaters can view national memorials and even Japanese cherry blossoms in season. During the 4th of July, fireworks explode all around the Washington Monument—a rare treat, especially from the waterfront! The Potomac River route takes the paddler from Columbia Island Marina to the historical Fletcher's Boathouse.

County: Washington, DC
Suggested launch sites:
Columbia Island Marina
Harry T Thompson Boat Center
Key Bridge Boathouse
Fletcher's Boathouse (Potomac and C&O Canal)
Suggested takeout sites: Same
Length and float time: 1.5 miles per hour (medium paddle)
Columbia Island Marina to Arlington Memorial Bridge—1 mile
Arlington Memorial Bridge to Thompson Boat Center—1 mile
Thompson Boat Center to Key Bridge Boathouse—0.5 mile
Key Bridge Boathouse to Fletcher's Boathouse—2 miles
Fletcher's Boathouse to Roosevelt Island paddle around and return—3 miles
Difficulty: Mild to medium depending on weather and motorboat traffic
Current: Medium
Season: Year-round
Fees or permits: None
Nearest city/town: Washington, DC
Boats used: Recreational boats and paddleboards
Organizations: None
Contacts: None
Rest areas: None
Restaurant pullouts: None

Put-In/Takeout Information

Columbia Island Marina (boat ramp and snack shop), George Washington Memorial Pkwy., Arlington, VA; (202) 347-0173; GPS N38 52.516' / W077 02.980'
Harry T Thompson Boat Center (rents kayaks, canoes, and bikes), 2900 Virginia Ave. NW, Washington DC; (202) 333-9543; GPS N38 54.014' / W077 03.510'
Key Bridge Boathouse (rents kayaks, canoes, and paddleboards), 3500 Water St. NW, Washington, DC; (202) 337-9642; GPS N38 54.240' / W077 04.180'
Fletcher's Boathouse (Potomac and C&O Canal) (rents kayaks, canoes, rowboats and has snack shop), 4940 Canal Rd. NW, Washington, DC; (202) 244-0461; GPS N38 55.044' / W077 06.086'

Overview

This is a 4.5-mile one-way paddle from Columbia Island Marina to Fletcher's Boathouse. Using the medium paddle measure of 1.5 miles per hour, this is a 3 hours up and 3 hours back paddle in calm water and weather. Trouble is there is so much to

This route is full of eye-catching icons like Georgetown University.

see and do and so many pictures to take, you might just run out of time. But you will have a great adventure no matter where you start or finish.

The Paddle

Columbia Island Marina will give your GPS unit heartburn as the roads twist and turn as you drive in the infamous Washington circles, but have patience; you will finally get there. This is a National Park Service (NPS) site contracted and run by Guest Services Inc. (GSI). The marina is clean, well-kept, and a nice family place to enjoy. I met a GSI manager who showed me a map of the Potomac River and where GSI provides contracting services. While you are in Washington walking the National Mall or a museum, renting a boat, or just using the boat ramps, there's a good chance you bought an ice cream or sandwich from these professional folks. The marina snack shop is just what a car-top paddler needs to start the day, and finish it. The dual cement ramp launches boats into what used to be called the "Pentagon Lagoon." If you have ever seen a full frontal picture of the Pentagon, it was probably taken from this dockage. Bring a camera!

Your first selfie shot should be with the Pentagon and the American flag. The second shot may be the Merchant Marine Memorial statue of flying seagulls in Lady Bird Johnson Park and the garden of tulips and other flowers outside the mouth of the marina. Across the river is the Thomas Jefferson Memorial overlooking the

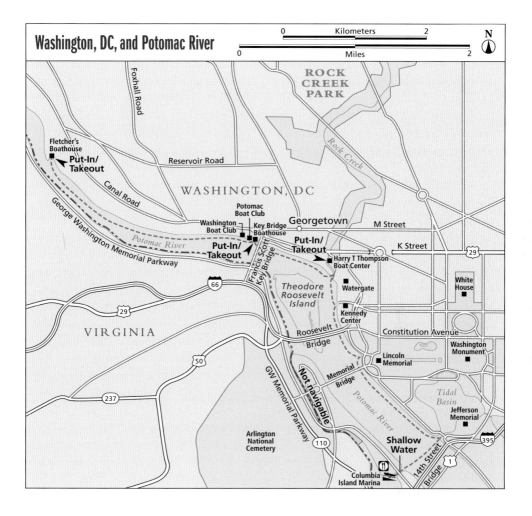

Tidal Basin. Catch the Cherry Blossom Festival in April for breathtaking photos up and down the shoreline in this area. The Washington Monument is always good for a photo. Traverse Arlington Bridge, and you can get another selfie with the Lincoln Memorial on the waterfront. Turn to the side, and the Kennedy Center's outside raised terrace always has visitors who will wave back. Paddle on the east side of Theodore Roosevelt Island and you'll find the Thompson Boat Center with public rental boats; it specializes in storing and launching crew rowing boats from its metal dinghy dock. To the side of the boathouse is the mouth of Rock Creek, one of those with currents that flow only downhill. Go for a quick 30-minute round-trip paddle at low or high tide and see massive office buildings just feet from the creek shorelines. There is also the last lock built that was designated number 1 as the official start of the C&O Canal.

The boater can only go a few minutes past Lock Park before encountering the first of many Class I rapids.

As you paddle back to the river, look to the left—you might spot the Watergate Hotel. The Georgetown waterfront park is fun to see but is not a pullout area. The park steps where people sit to rest and check out the waterfront are not wide enough to support a boat. The west side of the Roosevelt Island parking lot does not have a "recognized" access area to the Potomac River, but I saw city kayakers carrying their boats down the large riprap boulders from the Virginia side of the river with lots of smiles. Columbia Island Marina has a channel that most maps also show as an exit or entrance in this area. Unfortunately, too much silt has closed the mouth except in the highest of tides.

Adjacent to Key Bridge are three other boathouses: the new Key Bridge Boathouse, the Potomac Boat Club, and the Washington Canoe Club. The renovated Key Bridge Boathouse (formerly "Jacks," a Washington landmark for thirty years) is the only public facility and is chock-full of canoes, kayaks, and paddleboards for rent. This is a party place; if you bring your own boat, you can launch from here for a small fee.

Farther up the river the water depth gets shallow year-round. Motorboats anchor here singly or in groups for a weekend of swimming and socializing. In warmer months the waterway reminds one of a college campus where laughter is prevalent and almost anything goes (in a family-friendly manner). A bit of nature and wildlife can be seen for a mile, then Fletcher's Boathouse is on the right. Fletcher's is also managed by the GSI. Fletcher's Boathouse has been at this same location since the 1850s and is renowned as a fishing and recreational area. After 145 years in business, the fourth generation of the Fletcher family retired in 2004. The area surrounding the boathouse was then officially named Fletcher's Cove by the NPS, though most people still call it Fletcher's Boathouse in keeping with tradition, and since the row of other facilities on the Potomac River are called "boathouses." There are picnic areas, fishing rowboats and kayaks to rent, and a small snack shop. The pier access is at a very low water level, and during low or high tide the area is mudville. The nearby Abner Cloud House is the oldest building on the canal, dating back to 1802.

On our last visit in March 2014, the whole shoreline had been inundated with a forest of dead tree trunks and branches from earlier northern Potomac River floodwaters. The NPS rangers we spoke to earlier in the year were concerned with the ultra-slim budget they had for general maintenance and floodwater cleanup services for park lands under their jurisdiction. Fletcher's will take several years to completely restore, but the landing can and does provide adequate launch facilities both at the pier and in the picnic area. Kayakers and organized clubs launch from the picnic grounds on a gravel road leading directly to the water's edge. During heavy traffic weekends and holidays, some folks find it inconvenient or aggravating to move out of the way of boaters' cars and trucks. In those instances be prepared to count to ten, then portage a short way from the parking lot to the water and just step over intoxicated folk or those just plain stubborn families. The landing is safe for families, but there are lots of children and folks who are looking around for fun, so bring a cable and lock to chain up your boat to a tree while buying an ice cream or using the facilities.

49 Fletcher's to Georgetown-C&O Canal

This is a wonderful family adventure. This weather-protected waterway is only 3 miles long, and you can't get lost. Wildlife and green trees are evident. Call Fletcher's Cove/Boathouse during the season to make sure the canal is "watered," or call the National Park Service for off-season inquires. Occasionally the canal water is drained to kill sea grass.

County: Washington, DC
Suggested launch site: Fletcher's Boathouse
Suggested takeout site: Midway and 34th Street
Length and float time: 3 miles round-trip; 1 mile per hour (slow paddle)
Difficulty: Easy
Current: Mild
Season: Summer

Fees or permits: None
Nearest city/town: Washington, DC
Boats used: Recreational boats and paddleboards
Organization: National Park Service
Contacts: None
Rest areas: Midway to Georgetown
Restaurant pullouts: Possible at 34th Street

Put-In/Takeout Information

Fletcher's Boathouse (Potomac and C&O Canal) (rents kayaks, canoes, rowboats and has snack shop), 4940 Canal Rd. NW, Washington, DC; (202) 244-0461; GPS N38 55.044' / W077 06.086'

Overview

George Washington's house in Virginia, called "Mount Vernon," is directly on the Potomac River. The fortunes and strength he received from the river gave him the courage to start the Potowmack Company in 1785. This investment company strove to make navigation engineering improvements to the Potomac River. The five skirting canals around the major falls are today considered the first steps in the story of the C&O Canal. Unfortunately, they were not commercially or financially successful.

In 1825 President Monroe signed a bill chartering the construction of the canal. The Chesapeake and Ohio Canal, abbreviated as C&O Canal, came from the plan to connect a waterway from an eastern section of Washington, DC, to Cumberland, and a second section going west over the Allegheny Mountains to the Ohio River. An interesting footnote: The canal was to have a 2-mile-per-hour water current downstream that would not only keep the canals watered, but also help the mules pull the barges. The Potomac River has a natural current flowing downstream; it was the uphill and upriver transportation of goods and cargo that was the key.

This is a camera-worthy paddle route, with canal bridges everywhere!

Today the pathways along the canal are remnants of that mule towpath. Unfortunately, the eastern section, as we know it today, was the only part of the canal to be completed. A couple of rejected names for the canal included the "Potomac Canal" and "Union Canal." In November 1830 the Chesapeake and Ohio Canal opened from Little Falls to Seneca. It was a year later, in 1831, that the C&O section of Georgetown was opened. The canal initially connected to the Potomac River on the east side of Georgetown by joining Rock Creek at Lock 1, also called the Tidewater Lock. These canal locks still exist within a 15-minute paddle from the Potomac River.

The Paddle

The trip begins at Fletcher's Boathouse. The C&O Canal is watered at this location, and launching is done from a non-specific grassy and root-bound hillside area beside the parking lot. No portage is needed. Fletcher's Boathouse is run by Guest Services Inc. (GSI), a National Park Service concessionaire, and they rent kayaks for canal paddling during the season. Paddleboarding is also good, as the water is very calm. *Caution:* Heavy sea grass growth, stagnant water, and odd smells are usual for this sad waterway. But after several days of heavy rainfall, the water level rises 2 to 3 inches and paddling becomes possible and pleasant again. The top to bottom adventure is about 3 hours long without rest. The canal comes to a stop in the center of Georgetown at 34th Street. Here paddlers find a waterway blockage and an old deteriorated

Fletchers to Georgetown—C&O Canal

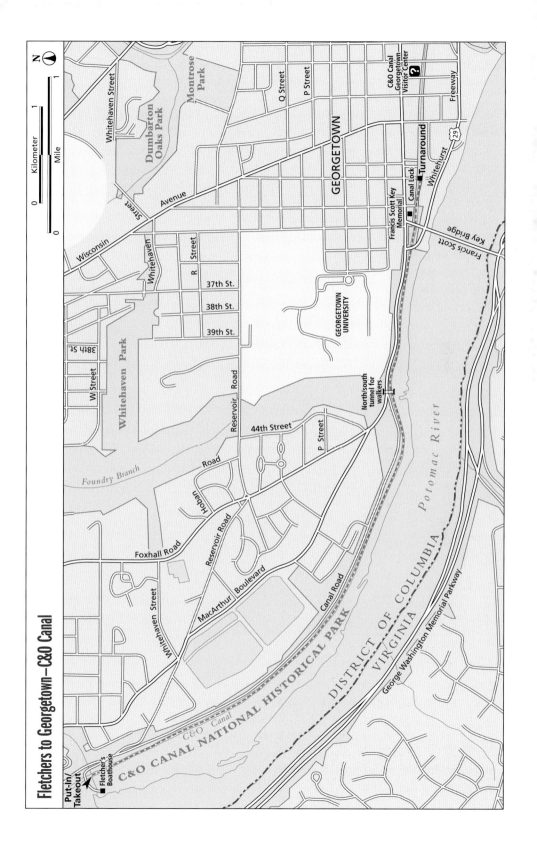

Put-in/Takeout

Fletcher's Boathouse

Foundry Branch

Whitehaven Park

38th St.

W Street

Reservoir Road

Road

Foxhall Road

Reservoir Road

MacArthur Boulevard

Canal Road

44th Street

P Street

Hobart Road

North/south tunnel for walkers

C&O Canal

C&O CANAL NATIONAL HISTORICAL PARK

DISTRICT OF COLUMBIA

VIRGINIA

George Washington Memorial Parkway

Potomac River

Francis Scott Key Bridge

Canal Lock

Francis Scott Key Memorial

Turnaround

Whitehurst

29

C&O Canal Georgetown Visitor Center

GEORGETOWN

GEORGETOWN UNIVERSITY

39th St.

38th St.

37th St.

R Street

R Street

Whitehaven Street

Whitehaven Street

Wisconsin Avenue

Dumbarton Oaks Park

Montrose Park

Whitehaven Street

Q Street

P Street

P Street

Freeway

N

0   Kilometer   1

0   Mile   1

barge that used to ferry tourists up and down the canal in better days. Pulling out and securing boats here is possible for a safe walk around Georgetown.

While paddling boaters will see lots of impressive vistas and sights missed by tourists and locals alike. By passing under bridges and tourist walkways, kayakers will find Washington's old-town flavor and architecture alive and vivid. Halfway along the waterway we found an unusual pullout on the canal pathway across from the merging of Foxhall Road and MacArthur Boulevard. A low-level resting place for boats was purposefully created by the caretakers and designers of the C&O pathway; it's a great place for a picnic. Curiosity led us to do a little exploring, and we found some other unique things about this resting area. A set of steps nearby leads down to a dirt pathway, running parallel to the canal pathway. The dirt pathway leads to a damp tunnel that provides passage to and from the road across the way, undoubtedly an access for Georgetown University students to safely cross over to the canal pathway. The dirt path also takes a turn down to the Potomac River where students occasionally go swimming in the warm, shallow water. The watered canal extends for a small distance beyond the boathouse landing.

50 Washington, DC, Channel

The Washington Channel's eastern shoreline is populated with restaurants and three marinas: Washington Marina, Gangplank Marina, and Capital Yacht Club. The Main Avenue Fish Market is situated at the north end of the channel as are several Potomac River touring ships. The *Titanic* Memorial, Fort McNair, the National War College, and the Coast Guard Administration Building are found on the southern side of the channel near the channel's mouth. On the western side is East Potomac Park.

County: Washington, DC
Suggested launch sites:
  Buzzard Point Marina
  Gravelly Point Park
  Columbia Island Marina
Suggested takeout sites: Same
Length and float time: 1.5 miles per hour
  Channel Mouth to Tidal Basin Lock—4
    miles round-trip
  Buzzard Point Marina to Channel Mouth—1
    mile round-trip
  Gravelly Point Park to Channel Mouth—2.5
    miles round-trip
  Columbia Island Marina to Channel
    Mouth—4 miles round-trip

Difficulty: Easy in channel; moderate to choppy on Potomac River
Current: Mild in channel; moderate to rough in Potomac River in afternoon
Season: Year-round
Fees or permits: None
Nearest city/town: Washington, DC
Boats used: Recreational boats
Organizations: None
Contacts: None
Rest areas: No "recognized" areas; East Potomac Park has many low bulkheads along the shoreline
Restaurant pullouts: None

Put-In/Takeout Information

Buzzard Point Marina, 22158 Half St. NW, Washington, DC; (202) 448-8400; GPS N38 51.835' / W077 00.698'

Columbia Island Marina (boat ramp and snack shop), George Washington Memorial Pkwy., Arlington, VA; (202) 347-0173; GPS N38 52.516' / W077 02.980'

Gravelly Point Park, George Washington Memorial Pkwy., Arlington, VA; GPS N38 51.837' / W077 02.471'

Overview

This is a journey for advanced paddlers, since the Potomac River can change from mirror flat to rough and choppy within hours due to weather as well as swells and wakes from motorboats and touring ferryboats. The route has the most exclusive view of cherry tree blossoms without the crowds during the April festival, but its most tantalizing draw and the end game for the Washington, DC, Channel paddle is a back-door peak at the tidal pool next to the Jefferson Memorial.

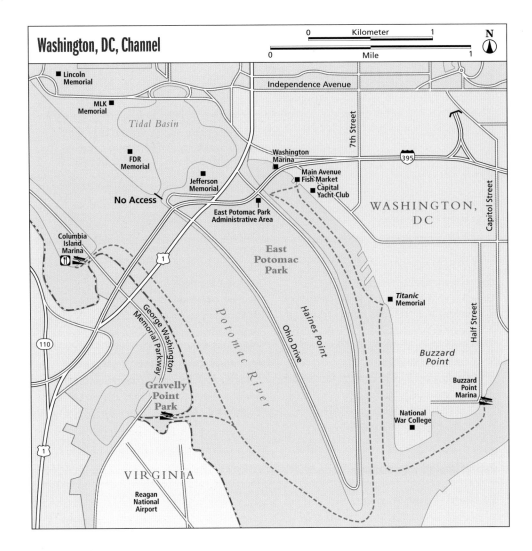

Washington, DC, Channel

0   Kilometer   1
0   Mile   1

N

Lincoln Memorial

Independence Avenue

MLK Memorial

Tidal Basin

7th Street

Washington Marina

395

FDR Memorial

Main Avenue Fish Market

Capital Yacht Club

Jefferson Memorial

No Access

East Potomac Park Administrative Area

WASHINGTON, DC

Capitol Street

Columbia Island Marina

1

East Potomac Park

Titanic Memorial

Half Street

George Washington Memorial Parkway

Potomac River

Haines Point

Ohio Drive

Buzzard Point

110

Gravelly Point Park

Buzzard Point Marina

National War College

1

VIRGINIA

Reagan National Airport

The Paddle

The Washington Channel has calm water except when ferryboats travel and create large wakes. The channel is also the back door for seafood vendors on boats docked at the Washington Fish and Seafood Market at Water Street. There are multiple possible areas along the fenced area to tie up and explore East Potomac Park. It's a 2-hour paddle from the mouth of the channel to the tidal lock.

Buzzard Point Marina (DC) is run by a private contractor for the National Park Service. The marina, though located in a convenient site, is not very congenial to visitors or responsive to inquiries. The rough cement ramp is 12 feet wide and has an elevated incline. There is a small parking lot, permanent restroom building, picnic tables, and low-level floating dock.

The Channel is a short comfortable paddle; crossing the Potomac is the challenge!

Gravelly Point Park (Virginia) is famous for its location adjacent to Ronald Reagan National Airport and the closeness of the airplanes that fly directly over this large park, which has several grassy fields for various sports and other recreational activities. The memorial bike path travels through the park and runs along the protected shoreline from Mount Vernon to Rosslyn. Year-round restrooms and dual cement ramps for motorboats and car-tops are available as are picnic tables and a large parking lot for cars and trailers. The park is highly frequented and busy with marine traffic from morning to late evening.

Columbia Island Marina (DC) is another NPS location and is kayak friendly. This is a long day paddle with much of the journey hugging East Potomac Park on the Potomac River side and then hugging the park again once inside the channel; it's recommended for advanced paddlers and sea kayaks.

Appendix A: Waterfront Restaurants with Kayak Docking

ANNE ARUNDEL COUNTY

Cantler's Riverside Inn
Waterfront restaurant with low-level piers; owner happy to serve "all" boaters; small beach at low tide at front of dock area, shallow at high tide with steps to front of dock; kayaks can tie up or pull up on dockage; Mill Creek–Annapolis

Chesapeake Harbour/Sam's Restaurant
Waterfront restaurant; planned residential community; marina; long beachfront area for resting, kayak storage, pool area for residents; low-riding dingy dock for visitors and outside bar at Sam's; no ramp; Chesapeake Bay open waters

Deep Creek Marina & Restaurant
Waterfront restaurant; ramp is in disrepair; deep mud; pier; Magothy River

Ferry Point Marina & The Point Restaurant
Waterfront restaurant, crab house, and grill; marina; fee for boat ramp; Middle Magothy River

Herrington Harbour North at Calypso Bay Restaurant
Waterfront restaurant; marina; Herring Bay, Rockhold Creek, and Tracy's Creek; party beach at Calypso Bay Restaurant

Mutiny Pirate Bar & Island Grill
Not a waterfront restaurant but adjacent to Captains Cove Marina; arrangements must be made prior to possible launch and arrival for lunch/dinner by boat

Nabbs Creek Dock Bar & Grill
Waterfront restaurant, bar, and grill; part of Maurgale Marina; access from Nabbs Creek and Stoney Creek; no boat ramp but lots of pile-driven docking; kayaks think twice, ok for canoes and paddleboards

Pier 7 Marina & Coconut Joe's Restaurant
Waterfront restaurant; marina; hard and soft boat ramps; ramp fee; South River

Point Pleasant Beach Tavern
Waterfront restaurant, bar, and grill; private beach and boat ramp; Furnace Branch Creek and Marley Creek; owner allows kayaks

Reckless Ric's Bar & Grill
Waterfront restaurant with pier and beach; Furnace Creek; not a family-oriented destination; thin layer of riprap rock between wide beach area and dining area

Severn Inn Restaurant

Waterfront restaurant; rear parking lot access to sandy beach launch area; Severn River; across from Naval Academy

Skipper's Pier

Waterfront restaurant and dock with bar; tie-up areas for visiting boats; shares parking lot with Paradise Marina (no ramp); possible shoreline for flat boats across the street

Stoney Creek Inn Restaurant

Waterfront (close) seafood restaurant; beach area on property next door; recommended as part of kayaking day trip

Thursday's Steak & Crabhouse

Waterfront restaurant; docking; parking lot has shoreline put-in; West River

Yellow Fin Steak & Fish House

Waterfront restaurant; boat ramp; Jet Ski shop area; South River

BALTIMORE CITY

Bo Brooks Restaurant and Catering

Waterfront restaurant and crab house with upscale atmosphere and prices; low floating dock with walk-up ramp; picnic area on rocks; parking lot nearby but not a put-in opportunity

Captain James Crab House

Waterfront restaurant; large parking lot for restaurant and sister restaurant across the street; mixed surface of rough cement on mini boat ramp

Nick's Fish House

Waterfront restaurant specializing in seafood served in a casual atmosphere; low-floating piers; kayak friendly; Canton Kayak Club launch site

BALTIMORE COUNTY

Hard Yacht Café Restaurant

Waterfront restaurant; crab house; part of Anchor Bay Marina with boat ramp; special events

Malibu Restaurant & Bar

Waterfront restaurant; no boat ramp, but a small shoreline for kayaks

River Watch Restaurant & Marina & Nightclub

Waterfront restaurant; boat ramp between two restaurants with no public parking; marina; Middle River and Hopkins Creek

Stouten's Bear Creek Marina

Waterfront ice cream store and snowball stand; marina and boat ramp

Sunset Cove Coffee and Wine House

Waterfront restaurant adjacent to or part of a marina; pier with kayak low deck for launching and pullouts; party beach on bulkhead with low pier for docking; seasonal entertainment

The Seasoned Mariner Restaurant

Waterfront restaurant with beach and low piers

CALVERT COUNTY

Zahniser's Yachting Center and Dry Dock Restaurant

Waterfront restaurant and marina; no ramp; docks specifically for smaller boats in rear of marina near swimming pool

CECIL COUNTY

Chesapeake Inn & Marina

Waterfront restaurant and marina; Chesapeake & Delaware Canal; no boat ramp; dinghy docks and low-floating pier

Granary Marina & Restaurant

Waterfront restaurant and Sassafras Bar & Grill; marina on Sassafras River; no ramp; dinghy dock signs say for water taxi use, with walk-up steps and dock pilings to tie dinghy boats

Perryville—Rodgers Tavern & Mule School

Waterfront restaurant and historical tavern; destination for family adventures; access by long pier

Schaefer's Canal House Restaurant

Waterfront restaurant with refurbished shoreline, docks, and building; destination point but possible launch area from parking lot to water by bridge

Susky River Grille at Tomes Landing

Waterfront restaurant; Susquehanna River; low-level guest pier; not a put-in but destination point; live entertainment

CHARLES COUNTY

Captain Billy's Crab House
Waterfront restaurant; high and low piers for docking; no boat ramp

Captain John's Crab House & Marina
Waterfront restaurant; marina, boat ramp; adjacent to Shymanskys Marina

Gilligan's' Pier Restaurant
Waterfront restaurant; seasonal live music; beach and pier

Port Tobacco Marina & Crabby Dick's Restaurant & Bar
Waterfront restaurant; live band seasonally; marina, boat ramp; Port Tobacco River

DORCHESTER COUNTY

Hoopersville Public Launch at Rippons Harbor & Crabhouse
Waterfront restaurant adjacent to Rippons Harbor & Crab House; seasonal restroom; Honga River and mid- and lower Chesapeake Bay; boat ramp; large parking lot

Hyatt Regency at River Marsh Marina
Beach areas primarily for hotel guests; outside bar and grill; no boat ramp; kayak rentals

Old Salty's Restaurant
Waterfront restaurant beach put-in off Fishing Creek; rumors of ghost in restaurant

Slaughter Creek Marina & Palm Beach Willies Restaurant
Waterfront restaurant and marina; no boat ramp; soft launch beaches at both ends of marina

Suicide Bridge Restaurant & Marina
Waterfront restaurant with family seafood; no boat ramp; small beach for soft launch; Cabin Creek and Choptank River

KENT COUNTY

Fish Whistle Restaurant
Waterfront, full-service family restaurant in Chestertown's public dock area

Georgetown Yacht Basin Inc.
Waterfront restaurant, ice cream store, marina and store; Sassafras River; kayak rentals; soft launch beach

Harbor Shack Bar & Grill

Waterfront restaurant; more adult than family oriented; easy access from boating area; own parking

Haven Harbor Marina LLC

Waterfront restaurant, bar, and grill; marina, dinghy piers, docks; kayak and dinghy boat racks; swimming pool with bar and grill; full marina store; sand tot lot; Haven and Swan and Chesapeake waters

Kitty Knight House

Historical waterfront restaurant and full-service inn; panoramic views of Georgetown Harbor and Kent and Cecil County landscapes

Mears Great Oak Landing Resort & Marina

Waterfront restaurant, beach bar, and grill; marina; soft launch areas

Waterman's Crab House

Waterfront seafood restaurant; low-level piers; seasonal live entertainment

MONTGOMERY COUNTY

C&O Canal at Old Anglers Restaurant

Historic inn and restaurant adjacent to park—historic and fun landmark; soft launch beach; seasonal restrooms; long portage

PRINCE GEORGE'S COUNTY

Fort Washington Marina & Proud Mary Restaurant

Waterfront family restaurant; Captain John Smith Water Trail; access to Piscataway Creek; rental kayaks available; boat ramp or pier launching

National Harbor—Fosters Restaurant

Waterfront restaurant under a tent (National Harbor is a jumble of restaurants, condos, and hotel services on the waterfront); no boat ramp but easy tie-up for fun destination spot

National Harbor—McCormick & Schmick's

Waterfront restaurant for fancy seafood and atmosphere (National Harbor is a jumble of restaurants, condos, and hotel services on the waterfront); world-famous "man in the ground" statue on shoreline

QUEEN ANNE'S COUNTY

Hemingway Restaurant & Bar
Waterfront restaurant; dinghy docks; walking distance to sandy beach launch area

Kentmorr Marina & Restaurant
Waterfront family-style restaurant/bar owned by chef; great desserts; private-property beach for restaurant customers

SAINT MARY'S COUNTY

Sandgates Inn Restaurant
Waterfront restaurant at soft launch beach on Patuxent River

Seabreeze Restaurant & Crab House
Waterfront restaurant at soft launch beach on Patuxent River

TALBOT COUNTY

The Crab Claw Restaurant
Waterfront family restaurant adjacent to town's dinghy dock; seasonal

Oxford Town Scottish Highland Creamery
Waterfront sweet shop, 600 ice cream flavors; short-term docking; seasonal April–October

Schooners Restaurant at Oxford Town
Waterfront Restaurant adjacent to public boat ramp at Town Creek and Tred Avon River; seasonal restrooms

WICOMICO COUNTY

Brew River Restaurant
Waterfront restaurant and winery; weddings and events off Wicomico Creek; pier and shoreline

WORCESTER COUNTY

Bahia Marina and Fish Tales Restaurant & Bar
Waterfront restaurant, marina, and marine store; boat ramp fee; kayak rentals

Appendix B: Kayak-Friendly Waterfront Hotels, Bed & Breakfasts, and Inns

Anne Arundel County

Herrington Harbor South Marina & Inn

Rents kayaks and canoes, two large private beaches; Chesapeake Bay

Calvert County

Back Creek Inn B&B

Waterfront location bed & breakfast with seven rooms; private sandy beach

Holiday Inn Select

Hotel on Back Creek quiet waters; shoreline soft launch area; rentals; weekend live music; park and drop area

Dorchester County

Hyatt Regency at River Marsh Marina

No boat ramp; kayak rentals on beach areas; primarily for hotel guests; outdoor bar and grill

North Fork Bed and Breakfast

Established in 1994; excellent access to Nanticoke River as it becomes manageable creek width

Kent County

Moonlight Bay Inn & Marina

Waterfront inn and marina for guests; Swan Creek, Tavern Creek, Chesapeake Bay; private beach for soft launch

Osprey Point Inn & Restaurant

Marina Bed & Breakfast Inn Swimming Pool; Swan Creek rental kayaks; soft launch area

Queen Anne's County

Kent Manor Inn & Restaurant

Waterfront historical hotel with pier; Thompson Creek local rental shop will deliver kayaks to hotel

Rolph's Wharf Marina–River Inn Bed & Breakfast

Chester River; open-water marina with boat ramp and soft launch beach; bed & breakfast

Somerset County

Inn of Silent Music

Surrounded on three sides by water; stunning views, charming rooms, and wonderful food; birding, canoeing, charters available

Talbot County

Black Walnut Point Inn

Bed & breakfast inn; kayak launch

Harrison's Chesapeake House

Country inn with dining; chart fishing, crabbing, skipjack sailing, hunting

Oxford Town Sandaway Bed & Breakfast

1875 adults-only Victorian mansion; waterfront rooms with porches and private beach; small public beachhead next door for kayak launches

St. Michaels Habour Inn

Waterfront restaurant and hotel; immediately adjacent to town public boat ramps

Tilghman Island

The Lazyjack Inn

Waterfront B&B; Dogwood Harbor sailing on owner's yacht; boat ramp; historic 160-year-old inn

The Mansion House Bed & Breakfast

Waterfront establishment with private pier next to old public landing ramp, which is now a new public fishing pier with new cement ramp and soft launch beach area 1 block away

Tilghman Island Inn

Waterfront hotel adjacent to Tilghman Marina waterfront dockage

Appendix C: Local Kayak and Canoe Clubs

American Canoe Association
www.americancanoe.org

Canton Kayak Club
www.cantonkayakclub.com

Chesapeake Paddlers Association, Inc. (CPA)
PO Box 341
Greenbelt, MD 20768
www.cpakayaker.com

Coastal Canoeists
www.coastals.org

Delmarva Paddlers
www.groups.yahoo.com/group/delmarvapaddlers

Greater Baltimore Canoe Club
www.baltimorecanoeclub.org

Monocacy Canoe Club
PO Box 1083
Frederick, MD 21702
www.monocacycanoe.org

Washington Canoe Club
3700 Water St. NW
Washington, DC 20007
www.wcanoe.org

Appendix D: Reference and Collaboration

Text Sources

ADC The Map People (Kappa Map Group). All counties in Maryland published various years (except Allegany and Somerset Counties, which were never published).

John Smith's Chesapeake Voyages 1607–1609 by Rountree, Clark, and Mountford, 2007

Maryland and Delaware Canoe Trails by Edward Gertler, 2002

Patuxent River & Trails Guide by the Patuxent Riverkeepers (two-sided map and information)

Washington Post newspaper

Internet Sources

Maryland Department of Natural Resources
www.dnr.state.md.us

MarinaLife
www.marinalife.com

Marinas.com
www.marinas.com

Potomac River Guide
www.riverexplorer.com

Sourced Departments of Recreation and Parks

Anne Arundel County
Anne Arundel County Recreation & Parks
1 Harry S. Truman Pkwy.
Annapolis, MD 21401
(410) 222-7300 (8:00 a.m.–4:30 p.m.)

City of Annapolis
1 Dock St.

Annapolis, MD 21401
(410) 263-7973; fax (410) 295-9018
www.annapolis.gov/government/city-departments/harbormaster

Baltimore City
Baltimore City Recreation and Parks
Bureau of Parks Administration Building
2600 Madison Ave.
Baltimore, MD 21217
(410) 396-7931

Baltimore County
Baltimore County Recreation and Parks
9831 Van Buren Ln.
Cockeysville, MD 21030
(410) 887-3871

Calvert County
Calvert County Parks and Recreation
Courthouse Square
205 Main St., First Floor
Prince Frederick, MD, 20678
175 Main St.
Prince Frederick, MD 20678
(410) 535-1600 ext. 2225

Cecil County
Cecil County Department of Parks & Recreation
Cecil County Administration Building
200 Chesapeake Blvd., Ste. 1200
Elkton, MD 21921
(410) 996-8101

Charles County
Charles County Parks & Outdoor Sports
Department of Public Works
1001 Radio Station Rd.
La Plata, MD 20646
(301) 932-3470 or (301) 870-2778

Dorchester County
Dorchester County Recreation and Parks

446 Willis St.
Cambridge MD 21613
(410) 228-5578

Frederick County
Frederick County Department of Parks & Recreation
118 N. Market St.
Frederick, MD 21701
(301) 600-1646

Harford County
Harford County Department of Parks and Recreation
702 N. Tollgate Rd.
Bel Air, MD 21014
(410) 638-3570, (410) 638-3571, or (410) 879-5082
www.harfordcountymd.gov

Howard County
Howard County Recreation and Parks Headquarters
7120 Oakland Mills Rd.
Columbia, MD 21046
(410) 313-4700

Kent County
Kent County Department of Parks & Recreation
11041 Worton Rd.
PO Box 67
Worton, MD 21678
 (410) 778-1948; fax (410) 778-4602 or (410) 778-1948
http://kentparksandrec.org

Montgomery County
Montgomery County Department of Parks
9500 Brunett Ave.
Silver Spring, MD 20901
(301) 495-2595, (301) 495-2500; Fax: (301) 495-9340
http://montgomeryparks.org

Ocean City Tourism/Convention Center
4001 Coastal Hwy.
Ocean City, MD 21842
(410) 723-8617 or (800) 626-2326; fax (410) 289-0058
www.ococean.com

Prince George's County
Prince George's Parks & Recreation Department
6600 Kenilworth Ave.
Riverdale, MD 20737
(301) 699-2255

Queen Anne's County
QAC Department of Parks & Public Landings
1945 4-H Park Rd.
Centreville, MD 21617
(410) 758-0835; fax (410) 758-0566

St. Mary's County
St Mary's County Department of Recreation and Parks
St. Mary's County Government
P. O. Box 653, 41770 Baldridge St.
Leonardtown, MD 20650
(301) 475-4200 ext. 1800; fax (301) 475-4108
www.stmarysmd.com

Talbot County
Talbot County Department of Parks and Recreation
10028 Ocean Gateway
Easton, MD 21601
(410) 770-8050; Fax (410) 822-7107
www.talbotparksandrec.com

Wicomico County
Wicomico County Recreation, Parks & Tourism
500 Glen Ave.
Salisbury, Maryland 21804
(410) 548-4900; fax (410) 546-0490

Worcester County
Worcester County Department of Recreation and Parks
6030 Public Landing Rd.
Snow Hill, MD 21863
(410) 632-2144; fax (410) 632-1585

Paddle Index

About the Author

Jeff Lowman was born in Washington, DC, and has kayaked extensively throughout the region. He earned a bachelor's of science from Pennsylvania State University and a master's degree in education from Loyola College in Baltimore. He currently lives in Annapolis, Maryland, with his kayak-companion wife.